9/09

A
MORE
UNBENDING
BATTLE

A
MORE
UNBENDING
BATTLE

The **HARLEM HELLFIGHTERS'**
STRUGGLE *for* **FREEDOM** *in* **WWI**
and **EQUALITY** *at* **HOME**

PETER N. NELSON

BASIC
CIVITAS
BOOKS

BASICCIVITAS
A Member of the Perseus Books Group
New York

Books published by Basic *Civitas* Books are available at special discounts
for bulk purchases in the United States by corporations, institutions, and
other organizations. For more information, please contact the Special Mar-
kets Department at the Perseus Books Group, 2300 Chestnut Street, Suite
200, Philadelphia, PA 19103, or call (800) 810-4145, ext. 5000, or e-mail
special.markets@perseusbooks.com.

Designed by Pauline Brown
Typeset in 10.5 point Janson

Library of Congress Cataloging-in-Publication Data

Nelson, Peter N.
 A more unbending battle : the Harlem Hellfighters' struggle for freedom
in WWI and equality at home / Peter N. Nelson.
   p. cm.
 Includes bibliographical references and index.
 ISBN 978-0-465-00317-4 (alk. paper)
 1. United States. Army. Infantry Regiment, 369th. 2. World War,
1914–1918—Regimental histories—United States. 3. World War,
1914–1918—Participation, African American. 4. United States. Army—
African American troops—History—20th century. 5. France. Armée—
African American troops—History—20th century. 6. African
Americans—Social conditions—To 1964. I. Title.

 D570.33369th .N456 2009
 940.54'1273—dc22

                                                               2008053113

10 9 8 7 6 5 4 3 2 1

*I did not care what or where I were at. I ask God to help me
and he did so, and that is how I came through that
terrible and hell place for the whole entire battle field were hell.
So it were no place for any human being to be.*

—HORACE PIPPIN

Contents

Preface

The last French veteran of World War I, Lazare Ponticelli, was born December 7, 1897, in Bettola, a town in northern Italy, and died on March 12, 2008, at the age of 111. The last German veteran, Erich Kaestner, died on New Year's Day 2008 at the age of 107. Three British veterans are still alive at the time of this writing, though they may not be by the time this volume is published: a 107-year-old named William Stone, a 109-year-old named Harry Patch, and a 111-year-old named Henry Allingham. In the United States, one veteran, Frank Woodruff Buckles, 107 now but only 15 years old when he joined the U.S. Army, is still alive. Of the remaining veterans, Harry Patch did not speak of the war until he was 100 years old, when a flash of light beyond his bedroom window brought the memories back, and he began to discuss his wartime experiences, the feelings of being paralyzed by fear, eaten alive by lice, surrounded by death, and sick of it all. Soon, no one will be left to give a first-person accounting of what happened during the war, and only then will the war truly be over.

The irony of the First World War, dubbed the "War to End All Wars," is not that it failed to end all wars, if anybody believed that P. T. Barnum–ism in the first place, but that something terrible enough to generate such hyperbole has fallen so far from the collective American consciousness. For baby boomers, World War I ended thirty to thirty-five years before we were born and seemed part of ancient history, though events thirty years ago today don't seem very distant at all. We may have seen a few souvenirs or photographs in our grandfathers' dens, watched old men marching in Fourth of July, Memorial Day, or Armistice Day parades, or perhaps accompanied our parents on visits to nursing home ice cream socials where veterans of the First World War sat on benches eating spumoni and drinking lemonade from paper cups. We might think we know about the First World War, but how many of us can say what it was about, or who the Central powers were, or how it reshaped the world we live in as arguably the most transformative event of the twentieth century?

One can't say it went undocumented. Much has been written about the war, not just by historians but also by poets like Siegfried Sassoon, Wilfred Owen, Rupert Brooke, David Jones, and others; it is depicted in the prose of Robert Graves, Edmund Blunden, and Ernest Hemingway, as well as in that of German writers like Georg Trakl or Erich Maria Remarque. It might be that the war has faded from memory partly because so much has been written about it that we think the record is complete; we can file it all away, look it up if we need to, and move ahead if we want. This book tells the story of a group of men who fought in World War I but could not be forgotten because they were never fully known. Part of the reason was that although they were Americans, they were loaned to, and fought as part of, the French army. The rest of the reason is that they were African Americans, whose history went largely untold (or untaught) until the second half of the twentieth century. They were men primarily from New York and the upper East Coast who volunteered for duty at a time when a large portion of the country did not want to get involved in a war so brutal and so far from home. They formed in 1916 and were, at first, simply the Fifteenth New York National Guard, a title they preferred even after they became the 369th U.S. Infantry Regiment to the War Department, the 369th RIUS to the French, and eventually the "Harlem Hellfighters" to the Germans.

In a war where the vast majority of the black soldiers served in the Service of Supply, unloading ships and building roads and railroads, the men of the 369th trained and fought side by side with the French at the front and ultimately spent more days in the trenches, 191, than any other American unit. They also went to war (and many paid the ultimate price) in defense of a country that did not defend them, a country at the time widely afflicted by segregation, Jim Crow laws, lynchings, and racial violence—yet a country they managed to believe in all the same.

The men of the 369th altered history's course, but too often, histories make soldiers seem like active players in a larger sociopolitical drama. The men who became known as the Harlem Hellfighters were just ordinary men in extraordinary circumstances, men with families, with wives and children, and with plans for after the war. If they had a sense of the part they were playing in the larger sociopolitical scheme, it was on the level of faith rather than anything they knew for certain. They rarely knew what was happening in the war itself, beyond their small section of the line. They lived in a very proscribed and finite world. To tell their story is to name the things they would have seen and heard and smelled and felt and to show how it changed them. More than that, however, it is to remind the reader that by standing up for what they believed in, what they thought was right, they created a narrative about good men who did something brave and noble when they had every reason to turn their backs on a country that had too often turned its back on them—it's a story about pride and honor and a struggle on two fronts, one in France and one at home. Of the first front, only a handful of very, very old men remain who can tell of it. Of the other struggle, the story is still alive and ongoing.

one

Parades

Over in France there's a game that's played
By all the soldier boys in each brigade
It's called Hunting the Hun
This is how it is done!
First you go get a gun
Then you look for a Hun
Then you start on the run for the son of a gun
You can capture them with ease
All you need is just a little Limburger cheese
Give 'em one little smell
They come out with a yell
Then your work is done
When they start to advance
Shoot 'em in the pants
That's the game called Hunting the Hun!
—ARCHIE GOTTLER AND HOWARD E. ROGERS,
"HUNTING THE HUN," 1918

In the summer of 1916, it was not uncommon to see military parades assembling outside the Lafayette Theater on Seventh Avenue between 131st and 132nd streets in the heart of Harlem's club and theater district. War was in all the papers. It was in the air. It was not our fight, but how could we avoid it? Americans of all races needed to be ready, although it was a war no one could adequately prepare for.

The first parades were relatively motley affairs and served a dual purpose. One was to turn citizens into soldiers. Teaching discipline, obedience, and unit cohesion, the parades forced the men to practice and memorize military behaviors until they became instinctive, following a martial tradition where soldiers fought in formation, on battlefields where organized troops conquered and dispatched disorganized opponents. The war they were preparing for in France was changing all the old rules, but order was still preferable to chaos.

The second purpose was to advertise the regiment, the newly authorized all-black Fifteenth New York National Guard, and to attract recruits to the cause. Marchers assembled outside regimental headquarters, a place often referred to simply as "The Corner." They were men of color, some still teenagers, others in their forties, waiting beneath the theater's broad marquee or standing out front in the shade of an elm tree dubbed the "Tree of Hope" and thought to be lucky. Some of the marchers wore suits, while others patched together makeshift uniforms. Some were used to wearing the uniforms of doormen, porters, waiters, redcaps, theater ushers, and elevator operators. The Lafayette Theater served as their armory. The recruiting office was in the back of a cigar store on the corner of Seventh and 132nd. Some of the men carried broomsticks instead of rifles. The men with broomsticks were told to march in the middle of the formation, where their lack of proper equipment would be less conspicuous.

The war had begun in 1914 when Gavrilo Princip, one of a group of Sarajevan radicals, assassinated Archduke Franz Ferdinand, heir apparent to the Austrian throne, and his wife. A month later, Austria-Hungary declared war on Serbia; Russia came to Serbia's defense; Germany came to Austria's defense and declared war on Russia; Germany entered France, Luxemburg, and Belgium; England came to Belgium's defense; Italy allied itself with Germany; and something that would have seemed impossible twenty years before, an entire continent at war with itself, came to pass. Some were saying that the conflict had started before 1914, when ancient enemies began rattling sabers, manufacturing weapons and ammunition, increasing defense allocations, mobilizing and growing their armies and navies, implementing drafts and mandatory military service, and building railroad lines that could move troops more quickly and in larger numbers over greater distances than ever before. Adversaries watched each other warily for years, calculating the time it would take for a rival to launch an attack. Militarists and worried politicians advocated for greater preparedness, as well as better defensive and offensive capabilities, and governments and countries wheeled in slow motion toward war, forming alliances and signing agreements promising to come to each other's assistance. Treaties meant to deter war by guaranteeing retaliation bound nations to irreversible courses of action once shots were fired, shortening the time between the opening salvo and the point of no return.

The marchers were aware of what people were saying. According to some, the world would not be safe for democracy until the Central powers—Germany, Austria-Hungary, Turkey, and Bulgaria—had been vanquished. Politically savvy enlistees could have surmised by the summer of 1916 that the world was not safe for monarchies, colonial empires, dynasties, theocracies, or dictatorships either, but democracies and monarchies were abstractions to the men assembled in front of the Lafayette Theater. They had their own personal safety to consider. Transatlantic telegraph cables stretching across the ocean floor from London to Newfoundland carried newspaper reports of the staggering numbers of men killed or wounded in the war.

"Preparedness" was the national cry. Early enlistees (Republican governor Charles Whitman signed the order to form the regiment on June 16, 1916) would have mustered in, despite many Americans' belief that the Great War was not our war. President Woodrow Wilson ran for reelection in 1916 under the banner "he kept us out of war," a war "with which we have nothing to do." Although the sinking of the *Lusitania* by German submarines on May 7, 1915—with over one thousand Americans on board and twelve hundred passengers lost, including nonparticipating civilians, women, and children (one way the old rules of war had changed)—had galvanized anti-German sentiment, many during the summer of 1916 still saw the war itself as costly and far off and as someone else's problem, one that might be resolved soon.

To prepare, the enlistees marched from the shade of the Tree of Hope south on Seventh, then right on 131st, past the Libya Café (*"The place to dine well. When visiting New York City, make it your first stop—we will make it your best. The gateway to refinement."*), then north on Lenox, past the Schaeffer Furniture Company.

They were teachers, craftsmen, and postmen. They were factory workers, night watchmen, churchgoers, fathers, gamblers, artists, criminals, and musicians. Many of the men marching were recent transplants from the South who had moved north to look for work in the industries ramping up to manufacture and supply war materials to U.S. allies in this "world" war. Some of the men who'd relocated from Louisiana spoke French, which they hoped would serve them if they ever got to France.

About sixty thousand Negroes lived in Manhattan in 1916, with about fifty thousand of them residing in Harlem and the rest primarily in the San Juan Hill area, north of Hell's Kitchen. Americans of African origin comprised about 12.5 percent of the U.S. population. The "world war" was an Old World war, a dispute primarily among countries Americans had fled in ships a long time before— or not so long before. About one-third of all Americans had been born abroad or were one generation removed. The men of Harlem did not have roots in the Old World—at least, not in that one. Their blood connections tied them to another continent entirely, to Africa, though to what part of that continent, to which region or country, few could say, the particulars of their individual affiliations having been long ago lost or stolen. They had not been born abroad, and most were more than one generation removed. They had what W. E. B. DuBois called a "sense of two-ness." They knew themselves as Americans and as Negroes, a duality that cried for reconciliation. Their reasons for marching derived in part from that dichotomy, that imperative, and were uniquely their own.

The city's colored community had hoped to raise its own militia since before the Civil War. In 1911, a group of Harlem's civic leaders calling itself the Equity Congress appointed Charles Fillmore, a middle-aged black attorney and Treasury Department official, as a provisional colonel with the mandate to establish a regiment. Fillmore had military experience, having served in the Spanish-American War, and was well liked by the Republican Party. The Equity Congress persuaded a white New York assemblyman to sponsor legislation to authorize a regiment, but Gov. John Adams Dix, fearful of losing votes among his white constituency, thwarted their efforts. The state legislature had approved the establishment of a black guard unit as early as 1908, which was also vetoed. Governor Whitman had agreed to let William Hayward, his former campaign manager, form a regiment on the condition that the officers be white.

William Hayward was an ambitious, forty-year-old, white Republican lawyer. A handsome, rock-jawed, transplanted Nebraskan (and son of a U.S. senator from Nebraska), Hayward had risen to the rank of colonel in the Nebraska National Guard and moved his law practice to New York in 1910. The white officers Hayward appointed were of a similarly privileged and politically connected caste, men of social prominence who gave the regiment credibility. This made practical, if not purely military, sense since Hayward's job initially entailed raising funds from private sources, making speeches at banquets and benefits, and petitioning his personal acquaintances for contributions to pay for the regiment's uniforms and equipment. For his second in command, he chose a lieutenant colonel named Woodell Pickering. He appointed Maj. Lorillard Spencer Jr. as his adjutant. Spencer was a wealthy, white, portly New Yorker who, with his round wire-rimmed glasses and moustache, bore a striking resemblance to Teddy Roosevelt. Spencer's mother was a ball-attending socialite, while his father was a rich magazine publisher and clubman with a brownstone on East Eighty-sixth Street and a mansion in Newport. Hayward also enlisted a senior captain named Arthur W. Little, publisher and editor of *Pearson's Magazine*, where British author H. G. Wells's science fiction story *War of the Worlds* first appeared in America.

More socially credentialed and politically connected than all of them was a strapping all-American footballer from Harvard named Hamilton Stuyvesant Fish III. The son of a congressman and grandson of a former New York governor, Fish was a founding member of the Military Training Camp Association, a social club whose membership included ex-president Theodore Roosevelt, former army chief of staff Maj. Gen. Leonard Wood, Secretary of War Elihu Root, Assistant Secretary of the Navy Franklin Delano Roosevelt, and other members of New York's social elite. At the club's facilities in Plattsburgh, New York, young men from "the best families" could play war, fire machine guns and mortars, and partake of military training, learning self-discipline, military tactics, combat strategies, marksmanship, hygiene, virility, and (temporarily) the virtues of celibacy and self-restraint—all the particulars ascribed to the Rooseveltian Rough Rider ideal of manliness. The Military Training Camp Association was, in effect, an extension of the Boy Scouts movement started ten years earlier in England by Lt. Gen. Robert Baden-Powell (Lorillard Spencer Jr. was a disciple of Baden-Powell and one of the founders of Boy Scouting in America), which similarly emphasized preparedness, fraternity, and esprit de corps—though the camp had a deadlier purpose.

Fish was aware that if he hoped to follow in the family tradition and pursue political office after the war, he would need a military record to campaign on. To an extent, all the white officers who signed on with the Fifteenth New York National Guard acted out of self-interest, cognizant of the stature and respect that would accrue to them from military service, apart from any personal commitment to the causes of nationalism, democracy, or racial equality. At the same time, ambitious white men hoping to climb the ranks or gain status through military service would also have been aware that joining a colored regiment was not the fast track or path of least resistance to self-advancement; in fact, serving with the Fifteenth could negatively impact one's standing within the white military establishment. Fish acknowledged in a letter that his situation was "not ideal." Yet, idealism of another sort played a part in his decision: "I am quite proud of my company," he wrote his father. "It is a privilege to fight for America and I'm glad of the opportunities."

Hayward offered to form a colored regiment on the condition that he be appointed colonel, but he also understood that he would not succeed without support from the black community. Thus, contrary to Governor Whitman's mandate, he promised the leadership in Harlem, the politicians, clergymen, and men of prominence who'd advocated for their own regiment, that he would appoint colored men as field officers and keep the command officers who'd enlisted so far: George C. Lacy, formerly of the all-black Eighth Illinois; Col. Charles Fillmore, now demoted to captain, Company B; and forty-one-year-old attorney Napoleon Bonaparte Marshall.

As formidable a personality as his name suggested, Marshall was a welcomed addition to Hayward's officers' cadre. He was a graduate of Howard University and Harvard Law, as well as a friend of Lorillard Spencer. Marshall had been a track star at Harvard, practiced law first in Massachusetts and then on Wall Street, and married into a family prominent in Harlem society. Before the war, he had spoken out against the Booker T. Washington school of acquiescent self-effacement and inveighed against Jim Crow laws and other forms of white hegemony. More usefully to Hayward's purposes, however, he'd advocated in military courts on behalf of black soldiers and could, if called upon, serve as a bridge between white officers and aggrieved black personnel. He was a Democrat who favored Wilson over Roosevelt, but he believed blacks could demonstrate their value as citizens through military service and had, in fact, suggested forming a colored regiment before Hayward took command.

Reactions to those early parades of 1916 were mixed. For many in Harlem, a white-led regiment was better than no regiment at all. Some whites would have preferred no regiment to one led by either whites or blacks. For a portion of black men of Harlem, the idea of doing nothing was preferable to joining a fight of catastrophic proportions between white men an ocean away. African American journalist James Weldon Johnson reported a conversation overheard in a Harlem barbershop: One man asked another if he intended to join the war effort. "The Germans ain't done nothing to me," the second man shrugged in reply. "And if they have, I forgive 'em."

As a recruiting tool, the parades were meant to demonstrate the Fifteenth's viability, attract the curious, and persuade the intrigued. Hayward needed to enlist two thousand volunteers to reach combat strength. Some of the volunteers were celebrities recognizable to young men watching from the sidewalk. One celebrity was Spottswood "Spots" Poles, born December 9, 1887, and dubbed "The Black Ty Cobb." Though bowlegged and small of stature, standing only five foot seven and weighing 165 pounds, he was one of the fastest men in the Negro leagues and in 1911 stole forty-one bases in the sixty games he played with the New York Lincoln Giants. In 1914, he batted .487, and in exhibition games against white major league teams, his batting average was .610.

Another celebrity was George "Kid" Cotton, perhaps less recognizable but hard to miss. A giant who smoked cigars and wore his bowler hat cocked at a jaunty angle, Kid Cotton was a professional boxer originally from Pittsburgh, who for a time served as exiled heavyweight champion Jack Johnson's sparring partner. Cotton's record was only so-so, but the fact that he fought Jack Johnson would have given him considerable prestige.

The early parades met with only limited success. The hope was that young men watching from the sidewalk would see a procession, ask a few questions, and perhaps even follow it back to the Lafayette Theater and the recruiting office. Before television or radio, parades were a way to get the word out, but a parade alone, particularly a ragtag and haphazard one, was not enough to make the residents of Harlem run to their windows to see what the commotion was all about. For that, Hayward needed music loud enough to carry down the city streets. He needed a marching band to lead the parades. The first band he managed to slap together was as unimpressive as his soldiers carrying broomsticks, a honk-and-bleat assemblage that did little to build the regiment's reputation. That all changed when Hayward convinced a man named James Reese Europe to form and lead a new band, one that would perform at benefits and represent the Fifteenth as a regiment to be proud of.

Jim Europe was a big man in every sense of the word. Of imposing physical stature (at least when he wasn't standing next to George Cotton), he was also one of the most celebrated and respected figures in Harlem. Born in 1880 in Mobile, Alabama, he was raised in Washington, D.C., by a musical family, his father an Episcopal minister and postal worker, his mother a piano teacher, and his siblings both musicians. John Philip Sousa, "The March King," lived nearby. It was an era before recorded music and radio, when every town had a brass band that served as the main public entertainment, playing parades, fairs, and picnics.

After his father died, James Europe followed his older brother John to Harlem, seeking musical opportunities as a way to support his mother and sister. He watched his brother play in piano carving contests at Barron Wilkin's Little Savoy on West Thirty-fifth Street with Eubie Blake, Willie "The Lion" Smith, and others, and he spent time at the Marshall Hotel on West Fifty-third, where all the prominent black musicians hung out. It was there that in 1903 he met a man looking to hire black musicians to play at a birthday party for Rodman Wanamaker, son of Philadelphia department store millionaire John Wanamaker. Jim Europe put together a quartet, played the party, and found he had a genius for booking society gigs (Europe coined the term *gig*, according to Eubie Blake), organizing small ensembles, and finding wealthy patrons looking to spice up their private dances with black musicians and their exotic syncopations. He played the kind of music his white employers wanted to hear—minstrel and burnt-cork music, plantation songs (*"Oh, the good old days are pass'd and gone,/I sigh for them in vain;/I want to see the cotton fields,/And the dear old home again"*), and "coon songs"—at one point forming a minstrel group with a Marshall Hotel musician named Ernest Hogan, who wrote "All Coons Look Alike to Me" (*"And now ma honey gal is gwine to quit me/Yes she's gone and drove this coon away"*).

Jim Europe began his musical career as a classically trained violinist. His ambition was to discover and create authentic African American music, and he knew plantation and coon songs were not it. His personal tastes drew him to rag, to what would come to be called the blues, to the energy of cutting contests, the cabaret scene, and popular song.

In 1910, when 125 musicians at the Marshall Hotel wanted to form a union of their own (they were excluded from the white unions), they elected Jim Europe president and called themselves the Clef Club. Europe's reputation as a leader of musicians got a boost when he organized a concert at Carnegie Hall in May 1912 to benefit a music school for African American children. The sold-out, standing-room-only performance included twelve upright pianists playing ragtime on back-to-back pianos and garnered standing ovations and rave reviews.

Society gigs soon became more numerous and more lucrative. The Clef Club orchestras played Philadelphia, Baltimore, Richmond, and Washington, D.C. In 1913, Jim married Willie Angrom Starke, a woman prominent in Harlem's high society, but he continued to see a chorus girl named Bessie Simms on the side. That year he also became the band leader for Vernon and Irene Castle, an internationally acclaimed white dance team popular for adapting and cleaning up "vulgar" black dances, the fox-trot, the Grizzly Bear, the Texas Tommy, and even the tango, a dance deemed so decadent that it was banned from the 1914 Yale junior prom. With the Castles (who hired him on the spot after hearing his music at a private party), Europe played in better and better venues—the Palace Theater, Hammerstein's Victoria Theater in Times Square, Fifth Avenue hotel ballrooms, Boston's Copley Hall, Washington, D.C.'s Willard Hotel for President Woodrow Wilson's daughter Eleanor—as well as at tea dances, society dances in Newport, and private functions in Saratoga or the Hamptons for some of the wealthiest people in America with last names everybody knew, like Vanderbilt, Astor, Gould, and Stuyvesant Fish.

As a band leader, Jim Europe made sure his musicians were disciplined, dressed in tuxedos, and remained on their best behavior, though they still had to enter through the back door, eat in the kitchen, and occasionally use an upright piano when a Steinway grand was available but covered with a tablecloth, topped with flowers in a vase. Jim Europe knew mistreatment and suffered indignities, but he took the high road, refusing to let himself be reduced or diminished. When a member of the staff at one society gig served him soup that tasted like dishwater, Europe swallowed in silence.

On some Sunday afternoons, Jim Europe would take a train to the Castles' country estate in Manhasset to play parlor music with his employers. A genuine friendship developed—as did a mutual respect. On April 8, 1914, the famous Castles agreed to appear before a benefit Jim Europe organized at the Manhattan Casino, where Vernon and Irene would perform sanitized versions of black dances for an audience of twenty-five hundred black people, many of whom knew the unsanitized versions. The Castles had a palpable charisma, a star quality. An idealized, modern (white) male, Vernon started a fashion trend by wearing a wristwatch instead of carrying a pocket watch, while Irene, rail thin, graceful, and metropolitan, embodied the New Woman. Vernon once fined a white member of the Castles' dance company $50 for using the word "nigger." When in October 1914 the Castles went into production on Broadway in a new Irving Berlin musical, *Watch Your Step*, they took Jim Europe, although he was later cut from the show (as was a young comedian named W. C. Fields) for missing a rehearsal after, according to one report, "hearing the siren call of a woman in Chicago." His reputation was nevertheless secure, and his was a name to be spoken along with the likes of Scott Joplin or Paul Robeson.

Jim Europe's decision to volunteer for the Fifteenth National Guard was in part informed by his friend Vernon Castle's decision to join the war effort after the sinking of the *Lusitania* in May 1915. A British citizen and a celebrity, Castle could have done his bit simply by entertaining the troops, but he wanted to do more than dance while others fought and died. Walking away from the successful run of *Watch Your Step*, Castle paid his own way to Newport News, Virginia, to learn how to fly, even though aviators in the air over France had a life expectancy of about a month. The dancing Castles gave a farewell performance on December 15, 1915, at the Hippodrome in front of five thousand people, after which Vernon Castle enlisted in the Royal Flying Corps for service in France.

Jim Europe's decision to enlist was also informed by a belief that Harlem needed a strong institution for the training of young men. Europe was something of a social activist, helping in 1908 to form a group called "The Frogs" with the intention of uniting black actors, artists, writers, and scientists to a common purpose. Later, in 1912, Europe wrote a march called "The Strength of a Nation" for the proposed guard unit, long before William Hayward's involvement carried the idea to fruition. Yet, he was first and foremost a musician, laboring for equal treatment and equal pay for black performers and composers, saying, "I have done my best to put an end to this discrimination, but I found that it was no use. The music world is controlled by a trust, and the Negro must submit to its demands or fail to have his compositions produced. I am not bitter about it. It is, after all, but a small portion of the price my race must pay in its at times almost hopeless fight for a place in the sun. Some day it will be different and justice will prevail."

In the summer of 1916, there were nights when Europe had fifteen bands playing at the same time, and he had to rush from club to hall to club to conduct a tune or two at each. A man of ambition, he had big plans and big dreams: he hoped to establish a national Negro orchestra, to write and produce Broadway musicals with all-black casts.

On September 19, at age thirty-five, he put those dreams on hold and joined the regiment. Using his formidable powers of organization and persuasion to recruit other members of the band, he brought in experienced bandmaster Eugene Mikell as his assistant and pulled in ringers: Ila White on bugle and Frank Debroit from Chicago on cornet. Europe traveled to Puerto Rico to round up men to supplement his horn section, bringing in thirteen members of Manuel Tizol's band, the Jolly Boys, recording artists on the Victor label. From Charleston, South Carolina's famous Jenkins Orphanage (where Mikell had formerly given musical training to its homeless "black lambs" as young as age seven), he enlisted Amos Gilliard on trombone and a pair of unrelated young drummers named Steven and Herbert Wright, who nevertheless became known as the "Percussion Twins." Europe intended to create a military band the likes of which the world had never known, a venture that Colonel Hayward wholeheartedly supported, even securing private funding to help Europe equip his band members. Marching would have reminded Jim Europe of the cadet drill teams he marched with in high school and the Sousa-led U.S. Marine Corps Marching Band he had heard in Washington, D.C. He would have felt at home with this music, but with the jazzola man's sensibility, where home is just the place you start from, before you take it outside and see where the music can lead you.

There was a market as well for songs about the war. The national mood was changing, with George M. Cohen's "Over There" challenging Al Bryan and Al Piantadosi's "I Didn't Raise My Boy to Be a Soldier" for its position as the most popular song in America. Everybody was writing war songs, including Archie Gottler, who'd written "Hunting the Hun," as well as other popular novelty songs like "'Oogie Oogie Wa Wa' Means 'I Wanna Mama' to an Eskimo," "Would You Rather Be a Colonel with an Eagle on Your Shoulder or a Private with a Chicken on Your Knee?" and "Mammy's Chocolate Soldier" (*"Come lay your kinky head on Mammy's shoulder/ Don't you cry, you're Mammy's chocolate soldier!"*).

With Jim Europe on the roster, others soon followed. Among the first was Europe's friend and fellow musician Noble Sissle. Born in Indiana, the slender and bespectacled son of a Methodist minister was a singer with a beautiful baritone voice and something of a refined sensibility compared to Eubie Blake, their friend and business partner, who had played piano in brothels and clubs where Sissle would have felt out of place. The same age as Jim Europe, Blake deemed himself too old to join the regiment and agreed to stay behind and run the business while Jim and Noble were away. Europe joined as a private in a machine gun company but soon became a sergeant, then a lieutenant, appointing Sissle his drum major.

⤙❧ ❧⤚

By July 15, Hayward had the two thousand men he needed, men from all walks of life, men of all ages. Some had already served under arms and were perhaps past their fighting prime, including forty-two-year-old Pvt. Jasper Dorsey, a thirteen-year veteran, forty-nine-year-old Pvt. Robert Miller, and forty-five-year-old Sgt. James H.

McCoy, all from the Twenty-fourth Infantry; Pvt. Henry Raymond and Pvt. John Thomas, both forty years of age, from the Tenth Cavalry; forty-two-year-old Pvt. Frank Johnson from the Twenty-fifth; and forty-one-year-old Pvt. John Shaw from the Eighth Illinois. Kids joined too, many signing up after the Selective Service Act passed on May 18, 1917—better to volunteer to serve with men from your own hometown than to get drafted and serve with strangers. Fresh-faced eighteen-year-olds like Harry Powell, Walter Williams, Ivan Hudson, and James Jackson were probably awestruck to serve in the same machine gun company as Big Jim Europe. A boy named Hannibal Davis joined on September 20, 1916, claiming to be eighteen when he was in fact only fifteen. Arthur Little described other men as giants (and chose them as his personal bodyguards for that reason): a Sergeant Giles; a Sergeant Gaillard, who had already crossed the Atlantic twice and been sunk twice by German warships; and a Sergeant Bayard, who, according to Little, had been acquitted on murder charges on three separate occasions, each time on grounds of self-defense. Said to have his own private police unit tasked to follow him around and nip any violence in the bud, Bayard was nonetheless a "wonderful soldier, leader of men, quiet . . . gentlemanly in manner of speech, and well-educated."

There was Pvt. G. J. Williams of Company A, a Brooklynite from 461 Carlton Avenue; Pvt. Herbert White from 2 West 137th Street in Harlem; and Pvt. John Graham, who worked as a shipping clerk at 1667 Broadway. Pvt. James Turpin, who believed democracy was something worth fighting for, and Pvt. John A. Jamieson, who wrote poems. Peter Sands, a gambler of much skill. Thirty-three-year-old Pvt. Lionel Rogers, Company L; Pvt. William Jackson, eager to kill Huns; and Pvt. James Henry Jackson from Huntington, Long Island, whose father had worked on whaling ships.

There was Needham Roberts of 249 Church Street, Trenton, New Jersey, a graduate of Lincoln Elementary, then a high school dropout who worked as a hotel bellhop and a clerk in a drugstore. His father ministered at the African Methodist Episcopal Zion

Church in Mt. Holly. Roberts, like Hannibal Davis, was turned down the first time he tried in 1916 to join while underage, so he stole some money from his father, took a train to New York, lied about his age again, and successfully enlisted.

There was Horace Pippin, a shy, pious country boy born in West Chester, Pennsylvania, but raised in Goshen, New York, by his mother, Harriet. As a child, Pippin would rather draw than do his schoolwork. The pair moved when Horace was ten to Middletown, New York, where at fourteen Pippin hired on with a farmer, who offered to send him to art school. Pippin had to support his mother and rejected the offer, working instead in a coal yard, then in a feed store and as a porter at a hotel. When his mother died in 1911, Pippin moved to Paterson, New Jersey, took a job packing furniture for shipping at the Fidelity Storage House, then found work as a molder for a company that made steel brake shoes. In March 1917, he took a ferry from Hoboken and signed his name to the muster roll, bringing with him notebooks, pencils, and crayons.

There was Elmer McCowan, a New Yorker from 669 Lenox Avenue, and there was William Butler, an elevator operator from Salisbury, Maryland. There was Henry Johnson, a baggage handler and porter at the train station in Albany, born in Winston-Salem in 1889, small of stature but tough, not inclined to back down from a fight. One story said that Henry Johnson was playing craps with his fellow redcaps on a blanket at the train depot and vowed that he was going to jump on a train, go down to Harlem, and enlist if he made his number.

Some men joked, "If it wasn't for that damn band, I wouldn't be in this army." But for many, the words Frederick Douglass spoke in 1863 still resonated:

> Let the black man get upon his person the brass letters U.S.;
> let him get an eagle on his buttons and a musket on his shoulder, and bullets in his pocket, and there is no power on earth
> which can deny that he has earned his right to citizenship.

two

The Argument

Sometimes the reason to go to war is clear. More often, a number of falsehoods must be sold to a populace before one nation can enter into combat with another. Proponents of war may claim that the conflict will be over quickly, that victory will come easily and at a meager cost, that the enemy is less than human, that he deserves everything he gets, that he has it coming to him. Among the remarkable lies that made the Great War possible was one promising that the war would be fun; it is surprising as well how long that lie was perpetuated, in song and story, long after the actual news and numbers from the front revealed the truth of the matter.

In 1916, African Americans had cause to question whether the promise of citizenship was just another lie, a false assurance from a race hardly cognizant of its own duplicity. Part of the propaganda campaign meant to prepare America for war involved demonizing the enemy. The papers and popular magazines were full of true accounts of pillaged Belgian villages, French children gutted with bayonets, girls gang-raped, churches burned to the ground. Germans were commonly referred to as "the Hun" and depicted on posters and in political cartoons as hulking, subhuman savages. The caricatured Hun resembled a massive, drooling, slope-browed ape with black skin, bearing virtually no resemblance to real Germans, who

17

were pale in complexion. One black writer, Kelly Miller, a dean at Howard University, described the enemy as "the German, ungainly, acrimonious and obdurate, part Saxon, part Hun, part Vandal and part Visigoth, a creature of blood and iron." The Hun was a brute, a barbarian, a savage. And in the cartoons, he was black.

It was a characterization many Americans, black and white, believed. It was a portrait of evil incarnate, something that had to be stopped.

Yet, many white Americans would have declined to characterize, or failed to recognize, as "Hunish" the treatment given to Jesse Washington, a seventeen-year-old boy in Waco, Texas, accused on May 8, 1916, of killing Lucy Fryer, the fifty-three-year-old wife of a white farmer for whom he'd been working. Jesse Washington had been seen nearby, prior to the time the crime was committed, working in a field. Still working in the same field when the police arrived after the murder was discovered, he made no effort to flee. Reports described him as "feeble-minded."

Jesse Washington confessed to the crime of murder and rape, although the medical examiner offered no evidence of rape and, according to one account, members of the sheriff's office had coerced his confession by telling him if he did so, he wouldn't be lynched. After he was tried and, following a mere four minutes of deliberation, convicted by a white jury, in front of a white judge and a white prosecutor, a white mob was allowed to drag Jesse Washington from the courtroom. He was taken to the City Hall lawn. On the way, he was beaten by members of the mob, which was growing in size and frenzy. He was struck by shovels, bricks, and clubs. He was stabbed and cut until he was red with blood. According to the *Waco Times Herald*,

> Life was not extinct within the Negro's body, although nearly so, when another chain was placed around his neck and thrown over the limb of a tree on the lawn, everybody

trying to get to the Negro and have some part in his death. The infuriated mob then leaned the Negro, who was half alive and half dead, against the tree, he having just enough strength within his limbs to support him. As rapidly as possible the Negro was then jerked into the air at which a shout from thousands of throats went up in the morning air and dry goods boxes, excelsior, wood and every other article that would burn was then in evidence, appearing as if by magic. A huge dry goods box was then produced and filled to the top with all the material that had been secured. The Negro's body was swaying in the air, and all of the time a noise of thousands was heard and the Negro's body was lowered into the box. No sooner had his body touched the box than people pressed forward, each eager to be the first to light the fire, matches were touched to the inflammable material and as smoke rapidly rose in the air, such a demonstration as of people gone mad was never heard before. Everybody pressed closer to get souvenirs of the affair. When they had finished with the Negro his body was mutilated.

People took fingers, toes, and ears as keepsakes. The crowd, estimated at ten thousand, included women and children. Jesse Washington was one of fifty-one colored men known to have been lynched in 1916, "as if by magic." "There are crimes," a Texas paper said of lynching, "which make sane and sober men mad; there are crimes which set aflame the minds." A Texas congressman defended such behavior as "the call of blood," an instinct white men had received from God himself, "a call to the preservation of the race." Defending the white race was a noble vocation, heroic, according to the depiction of the Ku Klux Klan in D. W. Griffith's 1915 movie *Birth of a Nation*.

The atrocity in Waco gained national attention. It outraged members of the National Association for the Advancement of

Colored People, founded in Harlem in 1909 by magazine editor
W. E. B. DuBois, suffragette Ida Wells, and attorney Archibald
Grimke, among others. The "Waco horror" was notorious for its
extreme nature, but for most black Americans, there were other,
smaller incidents as well, indignities too numerous to track or count,
brutalities too small to make the local papers. There were beatings,
humiliations, insults, and slights, with no end in sight. Jesse Washington, in Waco, had been taken from a government courthouse and
murdered by ten thousand people in front of City Hall. The city police had done nothing to stop the lynching. And this was precisely
the government, the country, the democracy that the men on the
muster rolls were signing up to defend.

"Men of darker hue have no rights which white men are bound
to respect," argued Archibald Grimke's brother Francis, a minister
at Fifteenth Street Presbyterian Church in Washington, D.C. "And
it is this narrow, contracted, contemptible undemocratic idea of
democracy that we have been fighting to make the world safe for, if
we have been fighting to make it safe for democracy at all."

Yet, W. E. B. DuBois, editor of *Crisis* magazine, saw it as a simple syllogism. "If this is our country," he reasoned (a substantial "if"
to some), "then this is our war." In the July 1918 issue of *Crisis*, he
wrote, "We of the colored race have no ordinary interest in the outcome. That which the German power represents today spells death
to the aspirations of Negroes and all darker races for equality, freedom and democracy. Let us not hesitate. Let us, while this war lasts,
forget our special grievances and close our ranks, shoulder to shoulder with our white fellow-citizens and the allied nations that are
fighting for democracy. We make no ordinary sacrifice, but we make
it gladly and willingly with our eyes lifted to the hills. We urge this
despite our deep sympathy with the reasonable and deep seated feeling of revolt among Negroes at the present insult and discrimination
to which they are subject even when they do their patriotic duty."

For the men of Harlem, the conversation was ongoing, a discussion held in the saloons and barbershops, on soapboxes and

stepladders at the corner of 135th and Lenox, and from the pulpits of the churches. Some saw military service as an opportunity.

"The future historian," preached Rev. F. M. Hyden of St. James Presbyterian Church, "when he comes to set down the facts in connection with the world war, should have before him the fact that coloured men went to war not as an endorsement of the President, but as a measure of national defense . . . volunteered service in such a time as this constitutes . . . the strongest argument and the noblest appeal for political and economic rights which colored men could present to the nation after the war is over."

On the same day, Rev. Adam Clayton Powell at the Abyssinian Baptist Church told his congregation, "This is the proper time for us to make a special request for our constitutional rights as American citizens. The ten million colored people in this country were never so badly needed as now. . . . As a race we ought to let our government know that if it wants us to fight foreign powers, we must be given some assurance first of better treatment at home. . . . Why should not the colored Americans make a bloodless demand at this time for the rights we have been making futile efforts to secure [from a] government that has persistently stood by with folded arms while we were oppressed and murdered."

Others saw it as a trick, or perhaps a false hope. "Since when," asked A. Philip Randolph in the *Messenger*, "has the subject race come out of a war with its rights and privileges accorded for such a participation. . . . Did not the Negro fight in the Revolutionary War, with Crispus Attucks dying first . . . and come out to be a miserable chattel slave in this country for nearly one hundred years?"

⁓⁓

Colonel Hayward needed two thousand men to qualify for federal service. Some qualified men in Harlem understood that service in the National Guard unit offered little hope of advancement and was no place for a colored man with career ambitions. The men who believed in the regiment did what they could to bring in recruits.

Napoleon Marshall took the stage at the Lafayette Theater between acts to speak on behalf of the regiment—only to find himself booed.

"What has that uniform ever got you?" a voice in the crowd called out.

"Any man who was not willing to fight for his country was not worthy to be one of its citizens," Marshall replied.

There was considerable resistance in white society as well as within the military to the idea of arming large numbers of colored American men, training them, and giving them permission to kill Huns, who, despite the cartoons in the magazines, were white people. The image of a race war had lodged in the American imagination since before Nat Turner's 1831 rebellion and even before the 1791 slave revolt in Haiti. Colored men had served in the armed forces since the Revolutionary War, the War of 1812, the Civil War, and the Spanish-American War, but since the Civil War, they'd primarily fought against nonwhite enemies: Native Americans in the American West or Insurectos in the Philippines when the United States took command of Spanish colonies following the Spanish-American War. William Hayward commanded black troops in Cuba. More recently, black troops of the Tenth Cavalry had distinguished themselves fighting with Gen. John Pershing against Pancho Villa at Carrizal. The War Department felt its job was to prepare to win a war, not to solve the nation's race problem. As such, its approach was to circumvent the problem of race by establishing separated and segregated regiments and divisions, or regiments in which white officers commanded black soldiers.

Secretary of the Navy Josephus Daniels claimed that the navy did not practice discrimination, then added, "however, to avoid friction between the races, it has been customary to enlist colored men in the various ratings of the messmen; that is cooks, stewards and mess attendants."

Other commanders refused to let white and colored units serve together, calling such a policy "impracticable." The selective service statutes stated explicitly, "White and colored enlisted or enrolled men shall not be organized in or assigned to the same company, battalion or regiment."

Pershing asserted repeatedly that American troops were neither ready nor prepared to fight the war in Europe. Yet, rather than send to France the Twenty-fourth and Twenty-fifth infantries and the Ninth and Tenth cavalries, the colored units he already had, he deployed them to Mexico, the Philippines, and Hawaii. For the war in Europe, black soldiers were recommended only as stevedores, laborers, or support troops. The army chief of engineers suggested, "The class of white men who would seek service . . . in these battalions could not be very desirable and more time would be required to train them than would be necessary with the intelligent colored man."

The army chief of engineers cited one problem: "There will be vacancies in the non-commissioned grades which must be filled from time to time and unless white men are taken from other ranks and transferred to these battalions there results a permanent vacancy or the promotion of a colored man. The promotion of the colored man is then impossible as it gives a mixed class of non-commissioned officers."

The War Department found the prospect of racial conflict difficult to set aside. Racial violence within army ranks had occurred before.

It occurred first on August 13, 1906, when a black battalion, the First Battalion of the Twenty-fifth Infantry, upon being stationed at Fort Brown on the Mexican border in Brownsville, Texas, found Jim Crow laws enforcing racial segregation firmly in place and signs in the town park reading, "No niggers and no dogs allowed." Uniformed men were occasionally knocked to the ground for what the local whites deemed disrespectful behavior. After a fight between a black soldier and a Brownsville storekeeper, the city tried to bar colored soldiers from entering town. On the night of August 13, sixteen to twenty unidentified colored soldiers allegedly walked into town and shot up the buildings, wounding a police officer and killing a bartender. The white commanders at Fort Brown testified that the men were in their barracks at the time in question. Only spent shell casings from army rifles could be produced as hard evidence, and the defense argued that these could easily have been planted. When the soldiers refused to cooperate with official inquiries, either by confessing or giving evidence against those responsible—which one government investigator termed a "conspiracy of silence"—the army, with President Theodore Roosevelt's consent and by his order, dishonorably discharged all of the men in Companies B, C, and D. In total, 167 soldiers, including men with over twenty years of service and approaching retirement, were released without receiving the back pay due them. They were denied all benefits and pensions and excluded from any further government service. The chief attorney for the defendants was a thirty-year-old lawyer named Napoleon B. Marshall, who developed evidence that later (but not in his lifetime) persuaded the government to grant the men honorable discharges.

The director of the War Plans Division, Brig. Gen. Lytle Brown, wrote of the problem: "The fighting value of colored men has been much discussed and while there is considerable doubt as to their value for furnishing officer material, it seems to be pretty generally agreed that under white officers or largely officered by white men, their capacity and work as noncommissioned officers and privates, even on the firing line . . . has been considerable."

Brown addressed the inherent problem of men serving without hope of promotion:

> It is, moreover, considered a very unsafe policy to utilize colored men in a way to accentuate the race discrimination against them. This is not a time to stir up race-feeling which is, under the best condition, a very serious problem with us. If they are to be used in such a way that only subordinate positions are open to them and if they are made to feel that

faithful and satisfactory service cannot bring them the reward of advancement to higher grades in the unit in which
they are serving, it can hardly be supposed that they can give
their best efforts or that a proper pride and morale can exist
in such units. The colored drafted men will include the best
of that race, and it is to be expected that some excellent non-
commissioned officer material will be found which should
be recognized and utilized.

Brown had a lower opinion of the black men entering the army
through the draft:

A large proportion of these colored men are ignorant, illiterate, day labor classes. A great many of them are of inferior
physical stamina and would not hold up under the conditions of strenuous field service and could not withstand the
rigors of the damp cold winter in France. The percentage
of sickness among them has been very high, particularly of
venereal disease.

At the time, however, the French had seventy-three thousand
colonial soldiers from West Africa already serving in that same damp,
cold climate. The U.S. government already used colored troops from
the First Separate Battalion (Colored) of Washington, D.C., to protect the White House, the Capitol, and other federal buildings and
charged them with preventing white German spies from infiltrating
and passing as guards. Nevertheless, the army's leadership did not
trust colored soldiers to serve in combat. Many of the draftees Lytle
Brown cited as illiterate, ignorant, or disease-ridden came from the
South, where they lived in poverty, had inadequate schools, and
lacked access to health care.

Some in the military resorted to the pseudosciences of the day
to justify their biases. One officer cited a "well known fact to anthro-
pologists," who had used head measurements of members of the

black race to indicate limited cranial capacities, inferring a correlation between intelligence and hat size. Others in the military cited the poor performance of draftees on intelligence tests, which asked questions like "What is a mimeograph?" "Where are Overland Railroad cars manufactured?" "In which does the character of Scrooge appear: *Vanity Fair*; *A Christmas Carol*; *Romola*; or *Henry IV*?" or "Who is Christy Matthewson?" He was a well-known baseball player, granted, but such a question was hardly useful in measuring native intelligence. In fact, the test scores of draftees of all races taking the army intelligence test indicated that just about everyone was "subnormal," though how the average score of an entire population could be less than "normal" remained unaddressed.

Six days after the first American troops stepped ashore in France, racial violence erupted in the United States. On Sunday, July 1, 1917, in East St. Louis, white workers went on strike at a local plant, which then recruited black strikebreakers. About one hundred thousand people lived in East St. Louis, but the white labor pool had not grown since the war put an end to European immigration, while the black population was swollen with recent migrants from the South. Conflict between white and black workers was aggravated when speakers at a rally at City Hall urged white citizens to take action against colored laborers. A car drove into a black neighborhood, firing bullets into black homes. When another car filled with white policemen followed, armed blacks retaliated by shooting at the car as it drove away, killing two of the policemen. The ensuing riot lasted for three days. Blacks were beaten, stabbed, kicked, stoned, hanged, or shot while trying to escape their burning homes. The police looked on, doing nothing. Some members of the Illinois state militia who had been sent in to assist the police joined them in their inaction. One soldier even invited a white man to "kill all the Negroes he could, that he did not like them either," according to the *St. Louis Post-Dispatch*. By the end of the riots, thirty-nine African Americans were dead, and hundreds of black homes had been reduced to ashes.

A month later, at a Carnegie Hall reception for a delegation representing the new government of Russian premier Alexander Kerensky, Samuel Gompers, head of the American Federation of Labor (AFL), in a room full of AFL supporters, excoriated the strikebreakers in East St. Louis and said they got what they deserved. Ex-president Theodore Roosevelt was on the podium. When Gompers applauded the riots in East St. Louis, Roosevelt leapt from his seat and crossed the stage to shake his finger in Gompers's face, saying, "Murder is murder, whether white or black. I will never stand on any platform and remain silent and listen to anyone condoning the savage and brutal treatment of Negro strike breakers." A near-riot ensued, and Roosevelt needed a police escort from the hall. Leaving with him was one of the event's organizers, a Capt. Hamilton Fish of the New York Fifteenth National Guard.

Sunday, July 28, 1917, saw another parade in Manhattan, prompted by what had happened in Waco and East St. Louis and by racial strife in Memphis, but no marching bands accompanied this one. The papers that day spoke only of the war and of mundane things, like the Yankees losing to the Indians and the price of bacon being up six cents a pound since the war started. From Harlem, perhaps as many as fifteen thousand black citizens—little girls in white church dresses with ribbons in their hair, little boys in jackets and ties, men and women in their Sunday finery—marched silently down Fifth Avenue, holding signs.

> We march because by the grace of God and the force of truth the dangerous, hampering walls of prejudice and inhuman sacrifices must fall.
>
> We march because we want to make impossible a repetition of Waco, Memphis, and East St. Louis, by arousing the conscience of the country, and to bring the murders of our brothers and sisters, and innocent children to justice.

We march because we deem it a crime to be silent in the face of such barbaric acts.

We march because we are thoroughly opposed to Jim Crow laws, segregation, discrimination, disenfranchisement, lynching and the host of evils that are forced upon us.

It is time that the spirit of Christ should be manifested in the making and execution of laws.

We march because we want our children to live in a better land and enjoy fairer conditions than have fallen to our lot.

The silent march ended peacefully and inspired no reciprocal racial hostilities, as it might have had it occurred in St. Louis, or Memphis, or Waco. The men of the Fifteenth would have only read about it in the paper, for they were already elsewhere. Having met the goal of mustering two thousand men, the regiment was sent, on July 15, to Camp Whitman near Poughkeepsie, New York, for training. The order came at 8:00 A.M. A mad scramble ensued to find everybody and get them to the railroad station in time.

They went to prepare for violence. They did know that they would meet with violence before their training was finished.

three

A Resented Presence

Camp Whitman was located about fifteen miles east of Pough-keepsie, New York. There, they slept in pyramidal tents and learned to set up latrines and field kitchens. They practiced military courtesy, how to address and speak to superior officers, how to salute in a style the men made all their own, an exaggerated dip and snap that simultaneously showed respect and mocked it. They learned how to stay down and out of sight during an attack, how to stand guard, and how to march in formation. Col. William Hayward commanded a group of men to dam up a nearby stream, where the men could take their clothes off and swim or bathe. The men read from Moss's *Privates Manual* and from the *Non-Commissioned Officers Manual*. They learned how to delouse their clothes with gasoline and how to sterilize a tent. When Charles Fillmore brought the problem of lice to Capt. Arthur Little's attention, saying, "I insist that something be done," Little reprimanded him for using admonitory language when addressing a superior officer.

Following two weeks at Camp Whitman, the unit went on active duty. The First Battalion, under Maj. Lorillard Spencer, was asked to guard railroad lines and terminals in New York and New

Jersey. The Second Battalion, under Maj. Munson Morris, pulled construction and guard duty at Camp Upton in Yaphank, Long Island.

Sgt. G. J. Williams, a Brooklynite in Company A, found serving at Camp Upton an unpleasant experience: "When we arrived at Camp Upton, we found that the camp was not as yet built up, the roads still being uncut in many places and the so-called Main Street knee deep with mud. In addition to this, there were millions of mosquitoes and it was necessary for us to wear mosquito net masks while doing guard duty. There were times when you could take your hands and wipe them across your mask and get a handful of mosquitoes. All this was very uncomfortable, but then it was part of the soldier's life. While at Upton we had to contend with all sorts of disturbances, such as riots, fights; and forest fires were not an uncommon occurrence."

The Third Battalion was assigned to Camp Dix in Wrightstown, New Jersey, while the machine gun company guarded two thousand German spies at Ellis Island. In all battalions, black noncommissioned officers led their men. A few men were hurt on the job or during fights among themselves, but in general everything ran smoothly, and there were no complaints about the quality of the work they were doing.

If any questions lingered about the capabilities of black troops in the minds of America's military leaders, the French colonial troops from the Sudan and Senegal, the Bataillons d'Afrique, were performing well and proving themselves on the battlefield, according to official assessments: "They are particularly apt for attack and counter-attack . . . [and] are excellent grenadiers, but they are less prepared in the use of the machine gun and the automatic rifle. . . . These troops are not only devoted to their officers, but they are equally devoted to France, whom they serve most loyally. . . . It is because these soldiers are just as brave and just as devoted as white soldiers that they receive exactly the same treatment, every man being equal before death, which all soldiers face."

Yet, the men of the Fifteenth, serving as guards, could only watch when the famous Twenty-seventh "Rainbow" Division received a farewell parade down Fifth Avenue before entraining for the town of Spartanburg, South Carolina, for final preparation prior to being sent to France. Colonel Hayward pleaded to be included in the "Rainbow" Division, so-called because it comprised guard units from twenty-seven states and not for its ethnic diversity. Hayward was coldly informed that black was not one of the colors of the rainbow.

Hayward returned to headquarters, raised his hand, and swore an oath to his men: "Even if they won't let us parade with them in going away, that we will have a parade when we come home that will be the greatest parade . . . that New York has ever seen, and I swear to you that we won't let any division have us attached to them for that parade."

He made his men stand and swear with him "that whichever may be in survival as commanding officer of this regiment when we get back to New York, that we see to it that the glory and the honor of the Negro race in America may be served by having our welcome home parade celebrated."

"And to that pledge and prophecy," Arthur Little would later recall, "all present clasped hands—and said:—'Amen!'"

⚜ ⚜

Colonel Hayward wanted combat training for his men more than he wanted parades. The difficulty was determining where colored troops could be most effectively instructed.

While the men of the Fifteenth guarded railroad tracks and prisoners, the army's attempt to station black troops in racially intolerant communities backfired a second time with tragic consequences. In Houston, on August 23, 1917, the War Department assigned guard duty at Camp Logan, still under construction, to the all-colored Third Battalion of the Twenty-fourth Infantry, with the First Battalion in Waco and the Second in Denning. Black soldiers in Houston were unwilling to display what whites deemed proper subservience, refusing to sit in segregated black sections in theaters or on streetcars. Called insolent by the locals, they met with racial abuse, slurs, arrests, and public beatings for refusing to obey Houston's Jim Crow laws. A newspaper ad on August 20 urged Houstonians to "Remember Brownsville," warning that the army intended to station three thousand Negro troops in the city.

On August 23, a black private named Edwards tried to stop white police officers from beating a black woman. Edwards was in turn beaten and arrested, as was a Cpl. Charles Baltimore, an MP who witnessed and questioned Edwards's mistreatment. To their commanding officer, the men complained that they were being treated like dogs, but he could do nothing about it. The men of the Twenty-fourth Infantry had finally had enough of police brutality, particularly that of Houston's mounted police. "To hell with going to France, get to work right here," one soldier said. Approximately one hundred soldiers armed themselves, marched into town, and were met by police and armed white civilians. When the shooting ended, four soldiers were dead, as were four policemen and a dozen other whites.

The newspaper headlines proclaimed and denounced the "Blood Lusts of Negro Soldiers." After the riot, the army arrested 164 soldiers from the Third Battalion and sent them to prison at Fort Bliss outside El Paso. At their court-martials, nineteen received the death penalty, and fifty were sentenced to life in prison. Those sentenced to death were hanged in what was bitterly referred to as a "military lynching" to appease and avenge racist white Houstonians and Southerners. While W. E. B. DuBois conceded, writing in *Crisis*, that black troops had committed crimes for which they could be punished, he decried "the shameful treatment which these men, and, which we, their brothers, receive all our lives, and which our fathers received, and our children await; and above all we raise our clenched hands against the hundreds of thousands of white murderers, rapists and scoundrels."

Maj. Gen. Charles Ballou, commander of the Ninety-second Division, later issued an announcement, Army Bulletin 35, following more racial trouble when a theater manager in Manhattan, Kansas, refused to sell a ticket to a black sergeant from Camp Funston:

1. It should be well known to all colored officers and men that no useful purpose is served by such acts as will cause the "color question" to be raised. . . .

2. To avoid such conflicts the Division Commander has repeatedly urged that all colored members of his command, and especially the officers and non-commissioned officers, should refrain from going where their presence will be resented. This sergeant entered a theater, as he undoubtedly had a legal right to do, and precipitated trouble by making it possible to allege race discrimination in the seat he was given. He is strictly within his legal rights in this matter, and the theater manager is legally wrong. Nevertheless the sergeant is guilty of the GREATER wrong in doing ANYTHING, NO MATTER HOW LEGALLY CORRECT, that will provoke race animosity.

3. The Division Commander repeats that the success of the Division with all that success implies, is dependent upon the good will of the public. That public is nine-tenths white. White men made the Division, and they can break it just as easily if it becomes a trouble maker.

4. All concerned are again enjoined to . . . avoid every situation that can give rise to racial ill-will. Attend quietly and faithfully to your duties, and don't go where your presence is not desired.

5. This will be read to all organizations of the 92d Division.

By command of Major-General Ballou:
(Signed) ALLEN J. GREER,
Lieutenant Colonel, General Staff, Chief of Staff

In 1917, any black man endeavoring to "refrain from going where his presence would be resented" would have sensibly refrained from going to Spartanburg, South Carolina. A mill town and transportation hub of about thirty thousand people, twenty-five miles northeast of Greenville and sixty-five miles southwest of Charlotte, North Carolina, Spartanburg was home to Wofford and Converse colleges, an opera house, and a shop-lined town square. Spartanburg was also the former home of Millie and Christine McCoy, a pair of conjoined African American twins born into slavery in 1851 and turned into a novelty singing act toured before the crowned heads of Europe. Prior to the Civil War, Spartanburg's slaves were held at the Walnut Grove, Thomas Price, and Mountain Shoals plantations, a lifestyle mourned in the local minstrel shows in songs like "I Want to See the Old Home" or "The Little Old Cabin in the Lane," in which the freed slave mourns, *"Dar was a happy time to me, / 'twas many years ago."* In Spartanburg on May 1, 1871, the Ku Klux Klan gunned down a black man named Wallace Fowler in front of his grandchildren as he ran from his house.

Black men would sensibly not go to Spartanburg, where, because of the town's deep-rooted Jim Crow laws and customs, the suppression and subjugation of the Negro population was seen as a fact of nature, normative and justified, part of the "Southern way of life." The idea of treating a colored man fairly was equated with the pejorative term "Northern." If the notion of treating African Americans with dignity or respect was (with exceptions but generally) inconceivable to the white population of Spartanburg, it was equally inconceivable and intolerable that Negroes be permitted to consider themselves with dignity or self-respect. Black men in Spartanburg were expected, when in white company, not only to submit meekly and subject themselves to racist insults, derision, and mockery without resistance but to play along, to act as if they liked it, to bow their heads, smile, defer, and never look a white man in the eye or cast anything but a brief sideways glance at any part of a white woman, in the certain knowledge that violations of the local code of racial conduct, any showing of impudence, "uppitiness," or pridefulness, could be met with swift and severe punishment.

When the regiment learned that it had been assigned to Spartanburg for training, Hamilton Fish saw trouble coming and tried to head it off, using his personal connections to reach as high up in the War Department as he could, in this case appealing to a friend of the family.

> [To] Franklin Roosevelt
> Navy Department Washington DC
>
> Understand that third battalion fifteenth New York Infantry colored is ordered to Spartanburg my brother officers believe with me that sending northern volunteer Negro troops south would cause recurrence of race troubles. This battalion could render immediate valuable service in France on line of communications where there is great present need to relieve French troops. Why not solve difficult southern problem by letting these northern Negro soldiers go where they can be of immediate use and train for firing line quicker than in the south?
>
> Captain Hamilton Fish Jr.

The men of the Fifteenth New York National Guard nevertheless went to Spartanburg's Camp Wadsworth on October 8, 1917, to receive actual combat training. Camp Wadsworth was a two thousand–acre facility, about 1.5 miles west of town center at the end of Main Street, where the army had constructed dugouts and rows of trenches to simulate, as much as possible, conditions in France. It was, to be fair, better than some camps designated for training Negroes: better than Camp Hill in Virginia, where troops slept on the ground with scarcely more than campfires for warmth and without bathing or mess facilities. The army had sent other New York guard units to Wadsworth, training soldiers from the Twenty-seventh "Rainbow" Division (the same group that had paraded down Fifth Avenue two months before), the Twenty-second Regiment Engineers, the Seventh Infantry, and the Seventy-first and Twelfth divisions. It made sense for the army to send the Fifteenth to Spartanburg with the other New York units, even though the army was aware of what had happened in Houston, as were Spartanburg's city fathers, who had campaigned to establish the training camp and welcomed the cash subsequently infused into the local economy by the thirty thousand men stationed at Wadsworth; still, they did not welcome the presence of two thousand Negro troops.

Lest anyone think otherwise, the mayor of Spartanburg took it upon himself to explain, apprising New Yorkers and the *New York Times*, in an article printed on August 31, of just where fabled "Southern hospitality" drew the line:

> I am sorry to learn that the Fifteenth Regiment has been ordered here, for, with their northern ideas about racial equality, they will probably expect to be treated like white men. I can say right here they will not be treated as anything except Negroes. We shall treat them exactly as we treat our resident Negroes. This thing is like waving a red flag in the face of a bull, something that can't be done without trouble. We have asked Congressman Nicholls to request the War Department not to send the soldiers here. You remember the trouble a couple of weeks ago at Houston.

An unnamed Chamber of Commerce official quoted in the *Times* article added,

> We asked for the camp for Spartanburg, but at that time understood that no colored troops were to be sent down. It is a great mistake to send Northern Negroes down here, for

they do not understand our attitude. We wouldn't mind it if the Government sent us a regiment of Southern Negroes, for we understand them and they understand us.

I can tell you for certain that if any of those colored soldiers go into any of our soda stores and the like and ask to be served they'll be knocked down. Somebody will throw a bottle. We don't allow Negroes to use the same glass that a white man may later have to drink out of. We have our customs down here, and we aren't going to alter them.

The Chamber of Commerce hoped the War Department would "explain to the Negro soldiers the difference between South Carolina and New York City," even though the men from New York already knew the difference—for many of them, it was precisely why they'd moved to Harlem. The War Department's position on the matter was nevertheless clear: "The Race segregation system will be carefully observed."

Hayward understood, as did his men, that a repeat of the events in Houston would destroy any chance they had of seeing action in France. His men understood that the simple act of standing at attention, chest out, shoulders back, chin up—a pose of strength, dignity, and pride—would likely offend the Southern Jim Crow mentality. They had already had trouble at Camp Dix, a week before leaving for Spartanburg, when a group of Southerners from the Twenty-sixth Engineers hung a sign saying "No Niggers Allowed" on a building. The sign was removed, but when the Southerners persisted, posting a second sign reading "Whites Only," two hundred armed men from the Third Battalion gathered to tear it down. The men, newly arrived in Spartanburg, knew that if such antagonisms could arise in the North, the odds of further conflict would only worsen in the South.

Hayward and Fish did what they could to appease the white establishment of Spartanburg, meeting with local political and law-enforcement officials to ask for forbearance and restraint and offering the same in return, vowing that their men would behave. Local businessmen assured Colonel Hayward that not everybody in Spartanburg agreed with Mayor Floyd, that they deplored the mayor's bigotry, and that he did not speak for them. A local country club even extended honorary memberships to the white officers of the Fifteenth, offering to hire the band to play at a country club social. Hayward asked Jim Europe and his band to perform at open-air concerts in the town square where Noble Sissle sang; a dozen of the regiment's white officers mixed in the crowd undercover, hiding their uniforms beneath their overcoats but remaining on the scene in case trouble arose.

Tolerant whites found the music pleasing. Intolerant whites considered the tolerant whites traitors to their race. Tolerance had been raising its ugly head in town lately. There had even been talk at the Friendship Baptist Church, near the camp, of letting colored people worship inside the chapel, rather than in the tent pitched on the lot adjacent that they'd been using. Intolerant whites understood that if you give civil rights to one person, pretty soon everybody is going to want them.

At camp, Colonel Hayward explained the situation to his regiment, calling both enlisted men and officers to a meeting in an open field, where Hayward stood on the roof of a bathhouse in order to be heard. He reminded his men of Houston and Mayor Floyd's words. He told them (as later retold by Arthur Little) that the "unfriendly attitude" of whites in Spartanburg came from ignorance and misunderstanding, that "Southern people did not appreciate the fact that the colored man of New York was a different man than the colored man of the South—different in education, different in social, business and community status, different in his bearing a sense of responsibility and obligation to civilization."

He told them they had an "opportunity to compel the South to recognize the differences which people of the North already appreciated, simply by accepting the Spartanburg situation as an opening for the educated colored man to prove his moral worth as a citizen, by refusing to meet the white citizens upon the undignified plane of prejudice and brutality." It was an opportunity "to win from the whole world respect for the colored race."

He told them they could expect abuse, regardless of how well they behaved, that they should withstand it with "fortitude and without retaliation," and that they should come to him with the particulars of any and all insults or abuses. "See to it that if violence occurs, if blows are struck, that all of the violence and all of the blows are on one side, and that that side is not our side. If by wrong, disorder is to occur, make sure, and doubly sure, that none of the wrong is on our side."

From the roof of the bathhouse, he asked the regiment to raise their right hands and promise to refrain from violence of any kind. They responded with a "sea of hands."

It didn't take long for the first incident to occur. When Capt. Napoleon Marshall was roughly ordered off a trolley, even though he had paid his fare, he accepted the indignity and got off the car.

In another incident, two local white goons threw a black soldier off the sidewalk and into the gutter for no reason other than that he was on the sidewalk. The soldier got to his feet and bent over to pick up his hat, but the gathering crowd wanted a fight.

"I promised my colonel I wouldn't strike back," the black soldier explained.

A white soldier from the Seventh Regiment interceded, saying, "Well I didn't promise my colonel I'd keep my hands off you bullies." He was joined by a second white soldier, and together they beat down the locals, throwing them into the gutter to reciprocate. White soldiers from New York had previously shown Yankee solidarity by boycotting the local stores that refused to serve blacks. They explained, "The colored soldiers are all right. They're fighting with us for our country. They're our buddies."

"The white boys who were billeted next to our camp were from the New York 12th regiment, located at 66th street and Broadway," wrote Noble Sissle. "They knew a lot of our boys from the 'San Juan Hill' section. Therefore they were always sympathizing with our boys and only awaited the opportunity to have an excuse to blow up the town."

Tension mounted. When two colored soldiers went missing one morning at roll call, the rumor spread that they'd been lynched by the police. Forty-four men armed themselves and marched into town, where they stood in formation and at attention outside of police headquarters while two of them entered the station to make inquiries. When Colonel Hayward got word, he drove into town at high speed to prevent another Houston and head off a race war. When he got to the police station, he was surprised and impressed by the discipline and good order his men were showing. The police told Hayward they knew nothing of the two missing men, who, it turned out, had gotten lost in the dark coming home from town the night before and fallen asleep in a field. Outside the police station, Hayward gave the order to fall in and marched the men back to camp.

"Those men never drilled better in their lives," he told Arthur Little. No one in the crowd that had gathered outside the police station knew how close they'd come to armed insurrection. "As they swung off, and snapped their pieces up to right shoulder," Hayward said, "that crowd of civilians applauded. . . . I almost had hysterics."

A few reporters got wind of what happened but agreed to keep the incident secret to avoid further racial conflict.

For a while, tensions eased. Tolerant white businessmen arranged entertainment for the enlisted men. The colored civilian population of Spartanburg invited the men from Harlem to their churches, had them over for Sunday dinner, invited them to parties. There was talk that the regiment might be spending the winter at Camp Wadsworth, and some prepared to settle in for the long haul.

Colonel Hayward knew it was only a matter of time before something went wrong, before somebody pushed his men too far. The army knew it too. Brigadier General Phillips, the camp commandant, acknowledged to Colonel Hayward that racial conflict in Spartanburg had been defeating the purpose of being at Camp Wadsworth, which was to train to fight Germans. "Of course," the general told Hayward, "that has not been your first task. . . . Your first task has been, is, and must continue to be, to guard against a clash with the townspeople." The general commended Hayward, saying that in his opinion Hayward's men had already demonstrated enough discipline to qualify for service abroad.

On October 18, Hayward traveled to Washington, D.C., upon General Phillips's recommendation and bearing his letter of introduction to lobby the secretary of war for immediate dispatch to France.

The trouble came three days later while he was gone. While passing down the sidewalk after attending an evening church service, Lt. Jim Europe asked a "local gentleman of color" where he could buy a New York newspaper. The man pointed to a hotel down the street and said there was a newsstand in the lobby. Europe double-checked, asking the man if colored men were allowed in the hotel. The man said several colored soldiers had already purchased papers there that day.

"Go on over, Siss," Europe told his friend, Noble Sissle, "and get every paper that has the words 'New York' on it. I never knew how sweet New York was."

Inside the hotel, Sissle bought the paper and was halfway to the door when the owner of the hotel grabbed him roughly by the collar and knocked his hat to the floor, saying, "Say, nigger, don't you know enough to take your hat off?"

Noticing that everybody else in the lobby was wearing a hat, Sissle made no attempt to retaliate but bent over to pick his up. As he did, the hotel owner kicked him in the seat of his pants, saying,

"Damn you and the government too—no nigger can come into my place without removing his hat!" As Sissle scrambled for the door, the owner followed, kicking him three more times and cursing. Sissle had visions of another Brownsville and tried to pretend nothing had happened, but a white soldier from New York ran outside, where about seventy-five men from the regiment were gathered at a food stand, and told them what happened.

Jim Europe took charge of the men on the street and ordered them to stay where they were, but the fifty white soldiers from New York in the hotel lobby were outraged. A cry went up to kill the owner, to "pull his hotel down about his ears." They rushed the proprietor, but just as they were about to kick his head in, Jim Europe stepped in to stop them.

"Attention!" he commanded, speaking firmly but in measured tones. "Get your hats and coats and leave this place, quietly, and walk out, separately or in twos, to Main Street."

The white soldiers obeyed Europe's command. When he asked the owner what the matter was, the proprietor explained his selective hat rule and threatened Europe with similar treatment if he didn't take his hat off too. Sissle expected a fight, but to his surprise, Europe doffed his hat politely, saying, "I'll take my hat off just to find out one thing—what did Sgt. Sissle do? Did he commit any offense?" The owner could only reiterate his previous position on haberdashery, then tried to order Europe off the premises.

Jim Europe, known in Harlem as "Big Jim," was strongly built and powerful in appearance, dark hued and broad featured, with a "majestry [sic] of command" in his demeanor. He possessed a stern gaze familiar to the men in his bands and orchestras who'd played wrong notes or complained about the soup. Europe's gaze was no doubt intensified, here in this small town in South Carolina, by a recent bout with hyperthyroidism, leaving him (apparent in photographs) with a condition known as "bilateral exophthalmos," causing his eyes to bulge slightly beyond their orbits. The whiteness of his eyeballs was offset by the darkness of his skin and magnified by the thickness of the lens in the eyeglasses he wore to correct his vision. Fearless and cool, Europe stared squarely into the eyes of the hotel proprietor, giving him a look that might have been described as witheringly "Northern," then quietly turned on a heel and exited.

As with the confrontation at the police station earlier, the hotel incident was kept out of the papers, due largely to Hayward, Little, and other white officers' importuning the local media, but the damage was done. Europe would later joke to Sissle that the hotel proprietor had kicked them all the way to France. Training in Spartanburg was no longer feasible. Four days later, the regiment received travel orders and departed for Camp Mills, near Garden City, Long Island. As they left Camp Wadsworth, the men of the Fifteenth New York National Guard saw white soldiers of the Twenty-seventh Division assembled to sing them off with a new tune growing in popularity:

> *Over there, over there,*
> *Send the word, send the word over there—*
> *That the Yanks are coming,*
> *The Yanks are coming,*
> *The drums rum-tumming*
> *Ev'rywhere.*
> *So prepare, say a pray'r,*
> *Send the word, send the word to beware.*
> *We'll be over, we're coming over,*
> *And we won't come back till it's over*
> *Over there*

At Camp Mills, just before Thanksgiving, the men of the Fifteenth found themselves billeted adjacent to men from the 167th Alabama National Guard. The Alabamans had already caused trouble on the Long Island Railroad, where they beat a black man so severely he became blind. The Alabamans had been abusing members of the

New York Sixty-ninth National Guard as well, and the men of the Fifteenth thought it their duty to stand up for their comrades.

When the Alabamans once again put up a sign on a camp building saying, "Whites Only," men from the Fifteenth were quick to tear it down. Shortly after that, Hamilton Fish heard word that the men of the 167th were planning to attack his men that evening. In defiance of Colonel Hayward's orders, Fish directed that his men be issued ammunition, telling them not to shoot first but to shoot back if fired upon. He was no longer inclined to back down from a fight, knowing his men were in the right.

According to the recollections of Sgt. John Jamieson, Hamilton Fish, accompanied by Napoleon Marshall and George "Kid" Cotton, faced the Alabamans down in their own camp. George Cotton, at six foot six and 260 pounds, was about a foot taller and 120 pounds heavier than the average white recruit. Fish, not nearly Cotton's size but a big man and former all-American footballer at Harvard, spoke, saying, "Of course, it is against regulations for an officer to engage in any battle or fight with an enlisted man, so I have brought with me a private who will fight any two members of your organization, and any officer who thinks he knows how to fight should come by and settle this argument with me, as I will be glad to have him." Cotton was already something of a hero within the regiment; Fish became one.

As a direct result of such repeated confrontations (not despite them), it could be argued that the men of the New York Fifteenth National Guard formed into a cohesive fighting unit where the officers respected their men and the men respected their officers. The men of Harlem knew for the most part that Hayward, Fish, Little, and the others—patricians and sons of privilege who engaged them with a sense of noblesse oblige and even patronized and condescended to them at times—were nevertheless willing to risk their careers and their physical well-being for the enlisted personnel under them. They respected Colonel Hayward, who did not simply order them to obey the local Jim Crow laws in Spartanburg but spoke to them directly. They respected Captain Fish, who was apparently tougher than he looked. Not despite but because of how they had joined together to confront racism, a bond was forged among the men of the Fifteenth, a fighting spirit they hoped would serve them well when they got to France.

Two weeks after leaving Camp Wadsworth, the Fifteenth received their orders to sail to France. Repeated shipboard mechanical failures delayed their departure, leaving some feeling jinxed and impatient. Between Poughkeepsie and Spartanburg, with only eight weeks of training, they had received less than half of what the army considered the minimum amount necessary.

On December 11, the army executed thirteen men who'd received the death penalty for their roles in the Houston riots, including Cpl. Charles Baltimore. The next day, the men of the Fifteenth New York set sail.

∾ ∾

The war they were eager to join looked as intractable as ever. It was a war of attrition where, contrary to the rumor going around Harlem that the French had been using their colored colonial troops as cannon fodder, "sitting duck" was something of a universal condition, and soldiers on both sides of no-man's-land felt very much like "cannon fodder."

What had seemed soluable at first proved to be anything but. When war broke out on August 4, 1914, journalists, politicians, and military men on both sides thought the conflict would be over in about six weeks. September 1914 saw the Battle of the Marne, where British and French troops turned aside the German advance on Paris. Armies then raced to outflank each other, expanding the front north to the Flemish town of Nieuport on the Belgian coast and south and east in an *L*-shaped line to the Swiss border. By year's end, both the Allies and the Central powers (Germany, Austria, Bulgaria, and what remained of the Ottoman Empire to the east) had dug themselves into fortified, entrenched positions along a 470-mile arc, with Germany establishing an eastern front against Russia as well.

The year 1915 witnessed battles at places like Ypres, Neuve Chapelle, Arras, the Vosges, Festubert, and Loos, idiotic frontal attacks in which brief, narrow penetrations of enemy lines failed disastrously when the penetrating forces moved too far forward and came under artillery and machine gun fire from the flanks; otherwise, attacks bogged down for lack of support, reserves, or supplies.

The following year, 1916, brought the realization, at a huge price, that the answer was not more men, more shells, more horses, more supplies, more of everything, when defensive positions could be reinforced and reentrenched accordingly; the result was simply more casualties with nothing gained. British, French, and Central Power governments were subsequently forced to draw more deeply from civilian manpower reserves to bring fresh troops to the line. As casualties mounted, morale fell among entente soldiers who no longer trusted their leadership.

While the men of the Fifteenth New York National Guard marched up and down Lenox Avenue with broomsticks on their shoulders, the British forces, under Gen. Douglas Haig, launched an attack on the German line at the Somme, preparing the way by shelling the German lines for a solid week, spending over 1.5 million shells and reaching a climax of 3,500 shells a minute. The British leaders assumed, incorrectly, that they were relentlessly pulverizing the German defenses, unaware that the Germans had dug their fortifications so deep as to be virtually unaffected by the bombardment. The shelling ceased at exactly 7:30 A.M., followed a minute later by 110,000 men going over the top in orderly rows and waves. One British captain, W. P. Nevill of the Eighth East Surreys, gave each of his four platoons a soccer ball and told them there would be a reward for the first platoon to kick its soccer ball into the German trenches, where a mere six German divisions awaited them. However, those divisions had one hundred machine guns and required less than a minute to set them up once the shelling stopped. Analysts later recognized that, had the British artillery paused a minute or two, then resumed shelling, the results could have been significantly different. Captain Nevill was killed instantly, with sixty thousand of his fellow soldiers dead or wounded in the first twenty-four hours. The stated objective that first day was to capture the railroad center of Baupaume, which would not fall for another 260 days.

French forces had fared no better. In February 1916, at the town of Verdun, one million German soldiers under the command of German minister of war Gen. Erich von Falkenhavn attacked a half million French troops led by Gen. Henri Philippe Petain at Fort Douaumen and Fort Vaux. Fighting along an eight-mile front with artillery, phosgene gas, and flamethrowers, Falkenhavn hoped to break the French spirit and nearly succeeded. "Soldiers of the Republic!" French commanders exhorted their men in response. "The hour has come to attack and to win. In the wake of a hurricane of iron and fire, you will storm forward together! You will fight them relentlessly until victory is yours! Fight wholeheartedly for the liberation of your country, for the triumph of Justice and Liberty!"

By the time the Battle of Verdun had ended in November, the *poilus* ("hairy ones," an affectionate term for French soldiers, who often sported shaggy beards and moustaches) no longer found such patriotic exhortations quite as intoxicating. Some compared Verdun to a "meat grinder" or a "slaughterhouse"; German fighters called it "the grave." Metaphors and figurative speech failed to express the reality: a horror of unimagined proportion, overwhelming violence beyond anyone's ability to understand or express. In the month of March, the town of Vaux changed hands thirteen times, and between June 23 and July 17, the town of Fleury was taken and retaken sixteen times, the line shifting over the course of the battle by as little as one thousand yards, at the cost, on both sides, of over a million men. "Humanity is mad," wrote a French lieutenant named Alfred

Joubaire. "It must be mad to do what it is doing. What a massacre! What scenes of horror and carnage! Hell cannot be so terrible."

By the spring of 1917, while Jim Europe's band marched and played in the streets of Harlem, rebellion was rampant among the French troops. Some regiments in the reserve lines agreed to return to the front on the condition that they would take up defensive positions only, while others refused outright to return at all. Men conspired in the billets, calculating that there weren't enough gendarmes to arrest them all or force them to return to the front. In the village of Coeuvres, an entire battalion turned on its officers, seized their weapons, and set up camp in the woods to wait out the war. Insurrection spread among colonial troops, among riflemen, in 113 infantry regiments and 17 artillery batteries. On May 27, at Chemin des Dames, thirty thousand French troops walked away from the line. Ultimately, 23,385 soldiers were tried and found guilty of mutiny, with over 400 receiving the death sentence. When General Petain replaced Robert Nivelle as the head of French forces and improved the conditions of the common soldiers, giving them better food, more rest, and longer leaves, the mutinies subsided, but the French fighting spirit had weakened past the point of recovery without help.

The British fighting spirit reached a similar state of despair. On the last day of July 1917, nine British and six French divisions launched a massive attack along a fifteen-mile front north of the Ypres salient, hoping to take a town called Passchendaele, four and a half miles away, and eventually to reach German submarine bases on the Belgian coast. Bringing three thousand guns to bear, the British fired four million shells over a ten-day period, plowing up fields where the water table was only a few feet below the surface and creating a quagmire that soon worsened with the fall rains. Thousands of men drowned in mud so deep it took sixteen men to carry a single stretcher. By mid-September, British generals were urging Haig to call off the campaign, but once again, Haig's stubborn refusal to alter his tactics came at a catastrophic cost in human lives. Over 160,000 men were killed or wounded; some were damaged more mentally and emotionally than physically, left dazed and incapable of speech, unable to understand where they were or what had happened to them. Suffering from neurasthenia, hysteria, and "shell shock," they were shipped home to English NYDN centers for men categorized as "Not Yet Diagnosed–Nervous."

By mid-November, as the men of the Fifteenth New York National Guard prepared to sail, tearing down "No Niggers Allowed" signs and arming themselves against Alabamans, 370,000 British troops at Passchendaele were dead or wounded, with German losses estimated at about 400,000 men.

A British officer, frustrated that the folks back home had failed to appreciate what the soldiers were experiencing, described it as best he could:

> leprous earth, scattered with the swollen and blackened corpses of hundreds of young men, the appalling stench of rotten carrion. Mud like porridge, trenches like shallow and sloping cracks in the porridge—porridge that stinks in the sun. Swarms of flies and bluebottles clustering on pits of offal. Wounded men lying in shell holes among the decaying corpses: helpless under the scorching sun and bitter nights, under repeated shelling. Men with bowels dropping out, lungs shot away, with blinded, smashed faces, or limbs blown into space. Men screaming and gibbering. Wounded men hanging in agony on the barbed wire, until a friendly spout of liquid fire shrivels them up like a fly in a candle. But these are only words, and probably convey only a fraction of the meaning to the hearers. They shudder, and it is forgotten.

For British and French troops at the end of 1917, hope lay not in themselves but in the Americans who were coming. "I was perfectly aware that the United States had just declared war on the Central Powers," wrote Frenchman René Naegelen. "The Army Bulletin and the newspapers printed President Wilson's address to congress. Phrases flared up inside me, lofty phrases: 'We shall draw the sword and fight for Justice, Civilization, Freedom, Peace, giving our lives, our fortunes, everything we have . . .' I knew victory was certain. And yet I was also aware that the United States had little more than sporting guns and that it would take them months and months of training before they would be able to come help us."

Gen. John Pershing said he would be ready when he had landed and trained a million men, perhaps by the summer of 1918. The French would simply have to hold on until then.

As Christmas of 1917 drew near, the USS *Pocahontas*, transporting the Fifteenth New York National Guard, crossed into the danger zone where German submarines were active. They were to be called the 369th Infantry Regiment, a fact they would not be apprised of until mid-March, and made part of the army's Ninety-third Division (Provisional). Typically, a division held 19,000 men; an infantry brigade, 7,000; a regiment, 3,000; a battalion, 1,000; a company, 250; and a corporal's squad, about 8. The Ninety-third Division included the 185th Infantry Brigade, the 370th Infantry Regiment, the 186th Infantry Brigade, the 371st Infantry Regiment, and the 372nd Infantry Regiment, with an authorized strength of 991 officers, 27,114 men, twenty-four 155 mm howitzers, forty-eight 75 mm guns, twelve 6 in. trench mortars, 260 machine guns, and 16,193 rifles—but in various stages of completion and training, they were still at Camp Stuart in Virginia.

One night aboard ship, they saw a red light about 150 yards off their bow, perhaps only a fishing schooner, but reports said German submarines had been disguising themselves at night by imitating the lights on schooners. Another day, lying seasick in his bed, Jim Europe heard a boom and ran up on deck, only to discover he had merely heard the guns of the *Pocahontas* at target practice.

"Jim—did you stop to put on your life preserver?" a colonel asked.

"No, sir," Europe replied. "I didn't have to stop. But when I calmed down, I found out I had mine on and Cheeseman's too." Jim Europe was not fond of traveling by ship. "When I get to Europe, I'm going to stay there. They named it after me, you know."

On Sunday, December 23, the band played "Nearer My God to Thee," "Rock of Ages," and "Holy, Holy, Holy" during an improvised service, which, as they lacked a chaplain, Colonel Hayward led. The band played, "Onward Christian soldiers, marching as to war . . ."

On Christmas Eve, the men went to bed with their clothes on, standard procedure in the danger zone. Hamilton Fish found the time to write home:

Dear Father,

Today is Christmas Day and as I may not be with you I am taking advantage of a few hours . . . to write and wish you, Tanta and Helena Merry Xmas.

Practically all our time is taken up with studying and taking military examinations. Lights are turned out at sundown which varies around 4:15 P.M. and not turned on again until about 7:30 A.M. This makes the day very short and the night horribly long.

Our routine consists of breakfast at eight o'clock, inspection of quarters at 10:30, lunch at twelve and examinations from 1:15 to 3:15, dinner at 3:30. In the morning we study our musketry bulletin for the afternoon exams which are always written and conducted just as in college under strict surveillance.

The nights are tedious and everlasting. There are no lights of any kind permitted and there are no diversions.

Smoking is forbidden after sundown but of course that does not affect me. There have been no new developments and no one knows what we are going to do in France. It will take five months to place this regiment in the fighting line and undoubtedly we will be sent to some big training camp in France. . . .

We have seen no subs and I hope they are home for Xmas. If they come around they will have a warm reception.

With love to all
Affect., Hamilton

On Christmas Day, the men on board ship ate turkey.

On New Year's Day 1918, in a howling gale and blinding snow-storm, with sirens shrieking and French soldiers cheering them in welcome, they put ashore at Brest and boarded boxcars for St. Nazaire. The men were excited to be in France and hoped to be sent to the front to find out for themselves what the war was all about.

four

Orphans

LA
MARSEILLAISE

Allons enfants de la patrie,
(Let's go children of the fatherland,)
Le jour de gloire est arrivé!
(The day of glory has arrived!)
Contre nous de la tyrannie
(Against us tyranny's)
L'étendard sanglant est levé!
(Bloody flag is raised!)
Entendez-vous dans les campagnes,
(In the countryside, do you hear)
Mugir ces féroces soldats?
(The roaring of these fierce soldiers?)
Ils viennent jusque dans nos bras
(They come right to our arms)
Égorger nos fils, nos compagnes!
(To slit the throats of our sons, our friends!)
Aux armes, citoyens!
(Grab your weapons, citizens!)
Formez vos bataillons!
(Form your battalions!)
Marchons! Marchons!
(Let us march! Let us march!)

Qu'un sang impur
(May impure blood)
Abreuve nos sillons!
(Water our fields)

Col. William Hayward gave an order for the band to play immediately upon arrival in Brest, a way of extending greetings to their new hosts. Jim Europe assembled his men and called for "La Marseillaise," the national anthem of France. As part of his preparation for service in France, Jim Europe had learned or obtained the sheet music for popular French songs, perhaps including patriotic anthems like "Chant du Départ" or "Sambre-et-Meuse" (*"All these proud children of Gaule . . ."*), as well as one by American songwriter Leo Woods called "Joan of Arc" about the mothers of France and their sacrifices. Contrary to the popular notion that colored men were natural rather than trained musicians, the members of the regimental band could both improvise and read scores. As Eubie Blake put it, "If a fly landed on the page, it got played." Europe had plenty of time, waiting to sail and aboard ship, to create new arrangements, transcribe charts for new instrumentations, and give the music his own personal spin. Customarily, soldiers in uniform snap to attention when their national anthem is played. It took the French soldiers ten bars before they even recognized Europe's "inspired, rhythmic interpretation," and, indeed, it was not until the Americans heard a French band play the same song in the more familiar style that they understood the problem. The French had never heard jazz before, and when they did, they were stunned and astonished. It's unlikely that Europe could have been aware of the extent to which some jaunty French war songs were wearing thin for the French soldiers. One soldier called "La Madelon," a song telling of happy *poilus* spending downtime drinking wine and romancing prostitutes, a "stupid refrain, a blatant lie which the infantrymen never sang." Europe's interpretations infused old songs with new life, revitalizing both the tunes and the listeners. His version of "La Marseillaise" represented a kind of music France had never experienced, winning audiences whenever he played it.

In the falling snow, the New Yorkers boarded trains for St. Nazaire, a town on the French coast two hundred miles from the action. They packed into livestock cars with nothing but straw to sit on, a new level of discomfort. "All over America," Noble Sissle wrote, "we had been riding in Pullman cars, or at least first class chair cars and day coaches, and here we are now riding in not even a first class freight car but horse cars. The stern reality of war and the placidity of peaceful America dawned on us."

Far sterner realities awaited them.

Horace Pippin, who had supplied himself with pencils and paper, kept a journal and wrote of the cold and the snow and of being loaded into boxcars like cattle. As a chronicler of his wartime experiences, Pippin was always ready to note the hardships and the things he wanted but didn't have, usually food or cigarettes, but it was unusual for him to complain, even when suffering from frostbite. "The box car were so packed that no one could lay down," he wrote. "At the time I did not want to for as it were some of them got frost bitten and I also. It were my right hand but it were not so bad off. I were so cold that I were growing stiff. I started to run in that doing it I made out all right by that time were time for mess."

As they rode the train, the leader of the American Expeditionary Force, Gen. John J. Pershing, headquartered in Chaumont, was considering an urgent request from British prime minister Lloyd George that America send its surplus troops immediately to be incorporated into decimated British and French units. Hostilities had been suspended on the eastern front since December 2, pending peace talks at Brest-Litovsk. Russian losses had surpassed staggering, an estimated 4.67 million dead or wounded, 1 million missing, and more than 2 million taken prisoner by the end of 1916. Once the Bolsheviks gained control of the Russian assembly in the November 1917 elections, they immediately sought a separate peace, which allowed the Germans to transfer troops to reinforce the western front.

Lloyd George warned, accurately, that the Germans intended to launch a major campaign, hoping to decide the issue before the Americans could arrive in sufficient numbers to affect the outcome. American secretary of war Newton D. Baker had long insisted, "No American troops should be sent to the front until they were fully trained." French prime minister Georges Clemenceau countered that nobody was ever really ready and that despite his promise of *la guerre jusqu'au bout* ("war until the end"), France would be finished before help arrived. Pershing wired Secretary of War Baker in Washington regarding Lloyd George's plea: "Do not think emergency now exists that would warrant our putting companies or battalions into British or French divisions, and would not do so except in grave crisis."

At this time, Pershing did not know what to do with his black troops. It was clear, by the beginning of 1918, that white officers would have difficulty serving under colored superiors; some white officers called the prospect "distasteful," even "impossible." If officers felt that way about serving under blacks, how would enlisted men feel? The policy of having colored soldiers serve under white officers was firmly in place, but the question remained as to whether white troops would accept black troops supporting their flanks. Pershing had seen with his own eyes, in Mexico fighting Pancho Villa's army and elsewhere, that black soldiers could make effective fighters. Yet, his advisers continued to dispute the fighting value of units comprising black draftees, as well as the wisdom of placing them in the trenches. Secretary Baker was advised by Col. E. D. Anderson, chairman of the Operations Branch of the General Staff, who shared some of Gen. Lytle Brown's concerns and biases:

> There remains a large percentage of colored men of the ignorant illiterate day laborer class. These men have not, in a large percentage of cases, the physical stamina to withstand the hardships and exposure of hard field service, especially the damp cold winters of France. The poorer class of backwoods negro has not the mental stamina and moral sturdiness to put him in the line against opposing German troops who consist of men of high average education and thoroughly trained. The enemy is constantly looking for a weak place in the line and if he can find a part of the line held by troops composed of culls of the colored race, all he has to do is concentrate on that.

The War Department's solution was to press colored troops into the Service of Supply (SOS), making the SOS about 30 percent black. Of the four hundred thousand African Americans who served in the war, only about 10 percent saw combat, while the rest were employed as stevedores, porters, cooks, waiters, and ditch diggers or in the construction and repair of cantonments, roads, and railroads, either abroad or at military facilities back home. The Marines had no colored soldiers. Only 1 percent of navy personnel were black, working as messmen or stewards. Upon their arrival in France, the men of the Fifteenth, at least the realists among them, would have had little reason to expect anything better.

After entraining to St. Nazaire, some men initially thought they were at the front and expected to be attacked momentarily. Instead, the 1,949 men and 51 officers of the Fifteenth New York, having crossed the Atlantic to fight, found themselves assigned to menial duties. They were put to work draining a swamp near Montois, building storage warehouses, and laying railroad tracks at a rate unimaginable to the French, who inspected the tracks to make sure they would hold up and commented, "Magnifique." The men took pride in their work, though they may have feared that by performing too well, they would be stuck in the SOS for the duration. They felt their morale sinking lower and lower as the days passed, "quite against our thoughts in the matter," according to Sissle, as their Springfield rifles were taken from them and replaced with picks and shovels, the band playing rag tunes each morning to cheer the boys up.

Hayward wrote a letter to Pershing, begging for frontline duty, with the help of Arthur Little, a former magazine publisher. In his letter, to underscore his men's combat readiness, Hayward noted that the regiment had not had a new case of venereal disease in three months. Good hygiene was something army headquarters seemed obsessed with. Hayward invited journalists to observe and write about his men, courted celebrities, twisted arms, bent ears, and proved himself a "master fixer," according to his officers. To curry favor with high command, he also sent Jim Europe and his band to the resort town of Aix-les-Bains, forty miles from Geneva in the French Alps, to entertain American troops on leave. He'd invested too much time and emotional currency to get the unit up and running, called in too many personal favors, solicited donations from members of his Union League Club and from names as well-known as Rockefeller—he'd come too far to let it all amount to nothing more than laboring in the SOS. It was more than ego. Hayward believed sincerely in what he might have characterized as the Negro cause. He wanted his men to do well, not for how it might reflect on him, or not for that reason alone, but for how it reflected on them.

British and French leaders continued to plead with Pershing and with President Woodrow Wilson. Their situation was critical. To the argument that American soldiers would arrive in France unprepared and untrained, they asked, Who better to train them than seasoned British or French officers? France's Marshall Ferdinand Foch argued that American troops would learn more quickly in France than they would back home.

Pershing replied, "I do not suppose that the American army is to be entirely at the disposal of the French and British commands. We must look forward to the time when we have our own army. . . . Moreover, the time may come when the American army will have to stand the brunt of this war, and it is not wise to fritter away our resources in this manner." Pershing insisted that American troops be allowed to complete their training in America and that he would not allow American troops to fight under a foreign flag.

At St. Nazaire, the men from New York stayed out of trouble, worked hard, tried to stay warm, bided their time, bore the monotony, and wrote letters home exaggerating the action they were seeing and describing the groans of the wounded. The regiment was understaffed, with only two officers per company (about two hundred men), when six was the norm elsewhere, an officer shortage difficult to correct when white officers were more likely to transfer out of black units than into them. The men of the Fifteenth felt severed, like a lone regiment with no division and no support, disconnected from the fighting forces. They hoped their colonel could pull some strings and get them to the show—how could they distinguish themselves, show the world anything, draining swamps and laying railroad tracks? Pershing was not unaware of the unit, asking Hayward to supply him with orderlies for his private railroad car.

Pvt. John Graham, who'd been a shipping clerk before the war, enlisted on June 2, 1917, trained at Whitman and Wadsworth, then took ill at Camp Merritt while waiting to sail to France; he was in the hospital when the *Pocahontas* finally left port for good. He left the hospital on December 15 and returned to Camp Merritt, where a Southern officer called the colored soldiers there to attention as they ate their Christmas dinner and announced, in the spirit of the holi-day, "There are some packages for you darkies and don't any niggers touch them until I give the orders." When Graham maintained to the officer, politely, that there were no niggers in the company, he was penalized with extra work.

He sailed for France on January 13 and caught up to the Fif-teenth New York at St. Nazaire, but experienced more prejudice and abuse from "Southern crackers" sharing the facilities. Waiting in line at the canteen to purchase cakes and candy, Graham, with his com-panion Sergeant White, was ordered by a Southern guard to step aside so that his fellow Southerners could be served first. When Gra-ham objected, the guard drew his gun and said, "You nigger sons-of-bitches move to the rear." Sergeant White quickly relieved the guard of his gun and, before the hostilities escalated, unloaded it, handed it back to the guard, and departed with Graham, downhearted and dis-gusted with how they'd been treated. Despite all the evidence to the contrary, they still believed things were supposed to be different in the army. Graham told his story to a captain named Robinson, who saw to it that the sentry was punished. Nevertheless, cohesion in a military unit customarily derives from a sense of us-versus-them, where "them" is a foreign enemy.

The task of building and maintaining cohesion was further compli-cated by the fact that the regiments' units and battalions were sel-dom in the same place at the same time, often fragmented by varying assignments and duties. The band, for which the regiment became promptly and widely known, found itself at the disposal of army headquarters and sent off independently of the regiment it was sup-posed to train with.

The band's public relations mission to Aix-les-Bains, where they played for generals and American troops on leave, went well. Jim Europe, requiring his drum major and principal singer's services, se-cured Noble Sissle's early release from the medical facility where he'd been hospitalized with the flu. The tour opened on February

12 at the Opera House in Nantes, to an integrated, packed house of people in evening dress. "The French people knew no color line," Arthur Little observed, unlike American theaters where colored members of the audience were restricted to the balcony, dubbed "nigger heaven." Europe's reputation as bandmaster for the famous dancing team of Vernon and Irene Castle followed him. When the band arrived at Aix-les-Bains on February 15, they were greeted by a band of French schoolboys who played a barely recognizable version of "The Star Spangled Banner," whereupon Jim Europe's band uncorked a jazzed rendition of "La Marseillaise" in response, then set about the business of entertaining the troops.

Aix-les-Bains was deemed, for troops on leave, a safe alternative to Paris, which had too many prostitutes capable of spreading venereal diseases. The army had printed a set of rules given to men on leave in Paris, with number seven being "The Military Police have been ordered to take the names and report all ranks, including Militarized Citizens, who permit themselves to be solicited on the streets." Racists within the army feared, more than they feared syphilis or gonorrhea, that white French prostitutes would provide services for colored soldiers on leave, thus "ruining" the soldiers, who would then crave white females upon their return home. The song "How You Gonna Keep 'Em Down on the Farm after They've Seen Paree?" took on political overtones when the "Negro problem" was considered: how were they to be kept down, on the farm or in the cities or anywhere else, after they'd seen "Paree," where there was a good chance that they would be treated with respect as human beings, as equals and men of worth? There was no telling what sort of "ruined" ideas they might bring home.

"Long previous to the war," wrote war correspondent E. W. Lightner, "thousands of blacks from various States of Africa were in France, most especially Paris, at the universities, in business and in the better ranges of service. Everywhere and by all sorts and conditions of whites, they were treated as equals. During several visits to the French capital I, an American, knowing full well the prejudices of whites in this country against the race, was amazed to see the cordial mingling of all phases of the cosmopolitan populations of the French capital. Refined white men promenaded the streets with refined black women, and the two races mingled cordially in studies, industries and athletic sports. White and black artists had ateliers in common in the Latin quarter."

Jim Europe proved an able ambassador, often opening his shows with the familiar "Over There" but playing a broad range of songs, impressing members of both the military leadership and the French community with his musical talents and magnanimity. One night, when a local Frenchman gave Europe a piece of music he'd written and asked if the regiment's band could perform it, Europe agreed and stayed up the entire night, transcribing the song and writing out the arrangements: "3,000,000 notes," he said the next day in exaggeration. At another concert, when Europe noticed a French child imitating his conductor's motions, he ended the song they were playing, gave the child his baton, guided him gently to the podium, and turned the band over to the child, who was thrilled to lead the ensemble (or to believe he was leading the ensemble, which was more likely watching Europe's eyes for direction) in a simple tune.

"Lieutenant Europe was no longer the Lieutenant Europe of a moment ago," Noble Sissle wrote of Europe's conducting style, "but once more Jim Europe, who a few months ago rocked New York with his syncopated baton. His body swayed in willowy motions and his head was bobbing as it did in the days when terpsichorean festivities reigned supreme. He turned to the trombone players, who sat impatiently waiting their cue to have a 'Jazz spasm,' and they drew their slides out to the extreme and jerked them back with that characteristic crack. The audience could stand it no longer; the 'Jazz germ' hit them, and it seemed to find the vital spot, loosening all muscles. . . . 'There now,' I said to myself. 'Colonel Hayward has brought his band over here and started ragtimitis in France; ain't this an awful thing to visit upon a nation with so many burdens?'"

"You will be going where no American soldiers have been before," the band had been told by American major general Francis Joseph Kernan after a concert earlier in Tours. "Upon the impression left by you on the minds of the French population will rest the reputation of American soldiers in general. The French recognize no color line—I beg you not to be the cause of the establishment of such a line. You are representatives of the American nation. The eyes of France will be upon you, and through France, the eyes of the world."

⁂

Back in St. Nazaire, the men of the 369th continued to build railroads, drain swamps, and wait in the hope of seeing actual combat. In camp, boxer George Cotton was attached to Headquarters Company, stationed at the Adjutant's Office as a member of the regimental police. Cotton's former sparring partner, heavyweight champion Jack Johnson, had written a letter from exile to New York congressman E. H. LaGuardia, asking for permission to join the army, saying, "All I ask is a chance to show my sincerity. There is no position I would consider too dangerous. I am willing to fight and die for my own country. I cannot offer any more. Will you kindly make my offer known to the proper authorities?" In the end, Jack Johnson's contribution to the war effort would be purely nominal: Allied troops called some of the heavy shells used during the war "Jack Johnsons" for the heavy punch they packed.

They saw the toll the war was taking on the besieged population of France. For George Cotton, it made the reason they'd come to France less abstract. Anyone who expected a man of George Cotton's bulk and occupation to be punch-drunk or simpleminded met instead a sensitive, articulate gentleman who, one evening after darkness had settled in and all was quiet, was moved to speak to his superior.

"Sir—did you ever stop to think about our blessings, over here? In the midst of all the poverty which the French people are suffering?

I saw a sight this afternoon which made me think of it. A lot. You know, I was on duty down at the dumping grounds, where the army trucks throw out the waste from the camps up here. There were hundreds of old men. And women. And children, swarming over those fields. To pick food, and fuel, from our refuse. Just think of it, Sir Adjutant, Sir. The stuff we throw away, as waste, supplies all the food and heat that those poor people have to keep themselves from starvation and cold. And some of our fellows kick. It makes me think."

It spoke highly of Cotton, who was far from home in a strange land and might well have been preoccupied with his own problems and circumstances, to feel such sympathy for those less fortunate. It also spoke highly of the unit that he could share his thoughts with a white superior officer.

"It was awfully cold and windy down there today," Cotton continued, "and there seemed to be a larger and hungrier crowd than usual. I noticed one young girl, who kind of got on my nerves. She was pretty. And oh so thin. I guess she was about seventeen. That girl didn't have nothing on, in all that cold wind, but a little calico slip of a dress. She was so eager to get something good to take home that she tried to beat the crowd by running out and climbing up on top of one of those big truck loads. To pick over the stuff before it was dumped out on the fields. And that's how I found out she was so thinly dressed. That she didn't have nothing on under that calico slip. When she got up on top of that truck, the wind caught hold of that thin dress and just blew it right up over her head."

"What did the poor girl do, Cotton?" the adjutant asked.

"Oh, Sir, Adjutant, Sir, the girl didn't do nothing. She just kept looking for food and wood. Except that she straightened up for a minute, to make a grab for her skirt, and said, in a funny little shrill voice, 'Ooh-la-la.'"

There was nothing salacious in his words, only compassion for a girl who was small and too thin, desperate, hungry, and cold, without a proper coat.

He was not alone in his empathy for the French people—for any-one fighting subjugation to the Hun. When an enlisted man asked a colored officer why he had joined and what he was fighting for, the officer's response was succinct, as he later recalled: "I told him I was fighting for what the flag meant to the Negroes in the United States. I told him I was fighting because I wanted other oppressed people to know the meaning of democracy and enjoy it. I told him that millions of Americans fought for four years [in the Civil War] for us Negroes to get it and now it was only right that we should fight for all we were worth to help other people get the same thing. . . . I told him this is our opportunity to prove what we can do. If we can't fight and die in this war just as bravely as white men, then we don't deserve an equal-ity with white men, and after the war we had better go back home and forget all about it. But if we can make America really proud . . . then I am sure it will be the biggest possible step towards our equalization as citizens. That is what I told him, and I think he understood me."

❧ ☙

On March 10, the hopes of the men from Harlem were answered. Pershing capitulated, ceding to the wishes of Hayward, or Foch, or both, and issued orders that the regiment join the French army and entrain to the town of Connantre, seventy miles east of Paris. There the men of the Fifteenth discovered they'd been given a new name: the Trois Cent Soixante Neuvième RIUS, now part of the Sixteenth Division of the French Fourth Army.

Colonel Hayward couldn't keep from crowing in a letter to a fel-low colonel back at Camp Wadsworth in Spartanburg:

The most wonderful thing in the world has happened. . . . A fairy tale has materialized and a beautiful dream has come true. We are now a combat unit. . . .

It is all so wonderful, especially following the monoto-nous tour of duty during our first two months in France. . . .

There are no American troops anywhere near us, that I can find out, and we are "les enfants perdu," [the lost infants] and glad of it. Our greatest American general simply put the black orphan in a basket, set it on the doorstep of the French, pulled the bell and went away. I said this to a French colonel with an "English Spoken here" sign on him, and he said, "Weelcome leelte black babbie."

Gazing from the train windows as they departed the coast, Henry Johnson, Needham Roberts, William Butler, Spots Poles, Elmer McCowan, and the others would have beheld strange scenery: acres of piled-up munitions, armored trains carrying camouflaged artillery pieces, airfields with great flocks of airplanes waiting to fly, barbed wire entanglements stretching for miles, wrecked homes and buildings, miles of shredded fields and scarred meadows, and vast burial grounds sprouting tens of thousands of small white crosses, some decorated with the tricolored French flag, others marked as German.

Horace Pippin was glad to leave the wet work of St. Nazaire behind. As they neared the front, he was surprised to see all the half-demolished buildings, the houses with big holes in them that let you see clear through to the other side. "The old women and old men came out of their homes to see us and they would cry for joy as we went by," he wrote. "That were the first town I ever seen to be in so much need. . . . The wind were so cold it would go through anything you could put on, and I felt for the old women and men to think how they had to get along in that friendless and helpless town."

They made their beds in dirty barracks with mud floors. Pippin remembered only cold and rain dripping through a hole in the roof, so much rain that, he wrote, "I did not know whether they had a sun there or not. I now will say that I have not seen the sun in more than a month."

Noble Sissle, traveling west on March 20 to Connantre from Aix-les-Bains, may have been the first member of his unit to reach the front itself, purely by accident, when the third-class section of the troop train he was riding in, along with the horn section Jim Europe had recruited from Puerto Rico, became separated from the first-class section, shunted onto a different track entirely in the middle of the night, while everyone aboard was sleeping. Sissle and his companions discovered what had happened the next morning when they stepped off the train at the first station, only to find themselves alone. Sissle's confusion was compounded by the fact that neither he nor the Puerto Rican horn section with him spoke French.

They got back on the train "very much bewildered" and ended up in Châlons-en-Champagne, a jumping-off town only a few miles from the front where the communication trenches leading to the front began. There, an American MP from the Twenty-seventh New York Division (the same division that sang them off at Spartanburg) told them where they were.

Sissle was unaware of exactly how close he was to the line until he heard "a shriek through the air like the screaming of a pheasant," followed by a tremendous explosion as a German shell landed nearby. The French soldiers in the area took the shelling in stride. Sissle and the Puerto Ricans considered it a baptism by fire: they had become the first members of the 369th to come under actual attack.

"I never saw such a scamper for cover as that exploding shell caused amongst those musicians," Sissle wrote. "In fact, they so completely took to cover that it was two days before we located all of them."

By March 21, the band and the regiment had been reunited. They moved from Connantre to the town of Heirpont, where the men of the newly coined Trois Cent Soixante Neuvième RIUS were met by about fifty French instructors, who gave the regiment its "finishing touches and specialistic training." Five French instructors were attached to regiment and battalion staffs, the rest to the enlisted men, about five per company or one to each platoon. The New Yorkers were allowed to keep their uniforms but traded their Springfield rifles for the French Lebel, with its longer rapierlike bayonet. They wore French ammunition belts, pouches, and helmets.

They were greeted by General Le Gallais, commander of the Sixteenth Division of France, with whom they were attached. Le Gallais warned Hayward that the enemy might not wait for them to complete their training.

"What would you do if the Germans came piling through here?" the general asked Hayward. Hayward vowed that his men would do their best, but one of his officers, after Le Gallais had left, gave a truer answer.

"If the Germans came piling through here," the officer said, "in four or five days, the 369th could be counted on to spread the news all through France."

In Heirpont, the band played and Noble Sissle performed "Joan of Arc" in French for Gen. Henri Gouraud, commander of the French Fourth Army, of which the Sixteenth Division was a part. Gouraud had first served to protect French colonial interests in Sudan, Niger, Chad, and Mauritania before rising to the rank of brigadier general at the age of only thirty-four. A lean man with a pointed beard, a bushy handlebar moustache, and an intense stare beneath the brim of his braided general's cap, Gouraud had lost his right arm at the Battle of Gallipoli in the 1915 Dardanelles campaign, but he had recovered to lead the French Fourth Army as of July 1917. "He looked weak and frail in his distorted figure, yet when he came close enough so that you could see the flash of fire that sprang from his eyes and that strong confidence and determined look," Sissle said, "you well realized why he was called 'The Lion of the Argonne.'"

His nickname was in fact "The Lion of France," but his den was in the Argonne sector. He was to lead the men from Harlem into battle and, in many cases, make decisions that would determine who lived or died. The men regarded him with instant respect, trusted him, and sought to earn his good opinion.

Training began immediately. Language barriers were not as insurmountable as had been feared. Frequently, a French soldier could demonstrate a task or procedure for the benefit of the American soldiers in pantomime, without having to explain his actions fully. There was much to learn.

They had to know how to read French maps. Each *secteur* had *sous secteurs* ("subsectors") and a *centre de résistance* (CR) composed of *points d'appui*, or garrisons, which contained several *groupes de combat*, comprising *grenadiers-voltigeurs*, *grenadiers*, and *mitrailleurs*. A *parallèle* was a trench parallel to the front. A *boyau* was a perpendicular trench. A fighting space was a *tranchée*, and a wider area was a *sape*. A parallel, or *doublement*, ran thirty to forty meters behind the front line.

They learned how to use and maintain the Lebel rifles, which were inaccurate at long range and carried only three bullets in the clip, to the Springfield's five. They learned how to take the Lebel apart and put it back together, under calm conditions and under fire. They learned how to use a grenade launcher called a *trombalian*, fitted over the muzzle of the Lebel, capable of throwing grenades as high as 250 feet in the air, the grenade potent enough to kill anyone standing within 30 feet of where it landed.

They learned how to wield the longer bayonet, how to fight from a hole in the ground, and how to use the heavier French weapons, the mortars and grenades. They also learned to use the Chauchat machine gun, with its semicircular magazine, similar to the American tommy gun, with wooden grips and of a contrary design, where the front half of the weapon recoiled against the stock, making the whole thing shake fiercely when fired and difficult to aim.

They learned how to use French radios, how to manage their dogs, and how to use their pigeons to carry messages. One pigeon, sent from Fort Vaux in 1916, had carried a message saying, "We are still holding out . . . relief is imperative . . . this is my last pigeon," and reached its destination before the gas it had inhaled killed it. The pigeon was subsequently awarded the Légion d'honneur.

They learned how to delouse themselves under trench conditions. The French called lice *totoes*. Head lice (*Pediculus humanus capi-
tis*) bit them on the backs of their necks and behind their ears, fed on
their skin and blood, and laid eggs in their hair. They had body lice,
or crabs, too. Lice are light-averse and like dark places; are spread
by human contact, shared clothing, and shared beds; and thrive in
unclean places, making the trenches a perfect environment for them.
Battling lice seemed as intractable and unwinnable a struggle as the
war itself. If you saw a jacket made of shearling or goat hide that
somebody had thrown away, and you thought it would be warm to
wear, the *poilus* may have warned you not to put it on—you couldn't
get the lice out of those things. Sgt. John Jamieson was inspired to
write a poem about them:

> *They ran wild simply wild over me.*
> *They're as reckless as reckless can be.*
> *No matter where I'm at, when I take off my hat,*
> *There are little ones and big ones, you could pick 'em off like that.*
> *Oh how they bite, oh, how they bite all over me.*
> *They made me just as sore as I could be,*
> *But at night when I lay down, each little coot would seek a crown,*
> *Oh how they crawls, oh how they crawled all over me.*

They learned what the different German shells sounded like—how
to tell explosive rounds from gas rounds, which made a soft *kerplunk*
sound, and how to cope with gas attacks, either mustard gas, phosgene, or simple tear gas. If your eyes burned right away, it was tear
gas. If the tear gas made you want to sneeze too, leave your mask on
because that was likely a gas the Germans fired to make you take
your mask off, usually followed by worse gases. Mustard gas, or
ypérite, as the French called it, made your skin blister. It didn't make
your eyes hurt right away, but some time later, they'd start to burn.
It smelled a bit like garlic in high concentrations, but it was toxic

even at low, nearly odorless levels, forming acid when it came in con-tact with the mucous membranes, the eyes, and lungs. Mustard gas could get into your clothes and hang around a long time, especially in wooded areas. Phosgene didn't hurt your eyes or skin at all and smelled like fresh-cut hay, or maybe grapes, and it was nasty, because you didn't really feel anything at first, but it got into your lungs and made acid that broke down the linings and ate away at your capillar-ies, until you started coughing uncontrollably and eventually drowned from inside out as your chest filled with fluids. You could get a dose without feeling a thing and be dead twenty-four hours later. Tear gas dispersed in the wind, whereas the other gases were heavier than air and sank into the ground or filled shell holes, such that sometimes if you jumped into a hole filled with gas, you were in bigger trouble than if you stayed in the line of fire. Red star. Yellow star. Green star. White star. The Germans marked their shells to know which ones they were loading, but this made them easier to defend yourself against because you could find a piece of shell casing and read the markings. Keep your mask handy, but never panic, because that made you breathe harder, which made you more susceptible.

They ate French rations. Garrison rations were pretty good, pre-pared in mess facilities in the reserve areas, adjacent to railroad de-pots, aid stations, or rest areas, with ample portions of vegetables, meat, bread, and wine. French field rations, prepared in portable kitchens closer to the front, were considerably less palatable, hauled to the front by the "soup man," whose job was considered as dan-gerous as any, or more so, considering that he was required to tra-verse perilous territories under fire carrying equipment that made him slower, less mobile, and more exposed. Menus included roasted meats, oversalted fish, pâtés made of meat products one did not want to ask too many questions about, vegetables, rice, and a variety of beans, often hastily prepared. Least palatable of all were the *vivres de reserve*, carried in the *poilus*'s packs, including two tins of boiled or corned beef, "Boeuf Bouilli," which the British dubbed "bully beef" and the French called "monkey meat"; a dozen *biscuits carrés*, or hard-tack, wrapped in waxed paper; boxes containing blocks of compressed or powdered vegetable, chicken noodle, or beef and rice soup; envelopes containing dehydrated noodle soup or *comprimés de bouillon*; foil-wrapped portions of coffee stored in refillable tins to prevent crushing (also good for keeping matches and cigarettes dry); two rations of sugar in small paper envelopes; and sometimes crystals of rock candy. The men were also given a daily portion of wine to fill their two-quart canteens, meant to last twenty-four hours, though some of the Americans mistranslated *vingt-quatre heures* to mean *dix minutes*.

"After this free indulgence," Sgt. John Jamieson recalled, "some of our boys thought they saw Germans in the trees, in the trenches, and in fact everywhere. Some of our sentries were firing at the twigs on the trees when they happened to be blown by the wind, and of course, there were numerous things which happened after the boys had drank their wine. So the precious wine had to die a natural death and we had to go without it."

"There sprung up," Sissle wrote, "a great comradeship. The French officers had taken our officers and made pals of them. The non-commissioned officers in the French army who held a little more elevated position than the non-commissioned officers in our army by virtue of their long military campaign, treated our boys with all the courtesy and comradeship that could be expected. Cheeriest of all was the good comradeship that existed between our enlisted men and the faithful old French *poilu*. You could see them strolling down the road, arm in arm, each hardly able to understand the other, as our boys' French was as bad as their English. In their souls and in their breasts there seemed to beat the same emotion. They were for one cause—liberty and freedom."

Strolling arm in arm, in broken English, the *poilus* spoke of the things they knew, practical things that might help.

When the ground was frozen, shell bursts could send splinters of frozen clay, sharp as needles. If you found yourself forced to take refuge in a shell hole, only to find a corpse in the crater, you didn't want to drink the water in the bottom of the hole, no matter how thirsty you got, because you would die of dysentery—you wouldn't be able to stop shitting. If you took shelter in a shell crater and men were already there, they would resent you because before they had been safe. Now, thanks to you, they may have been spotted and could draw artillery fire.

Sometimes when the shelling became particularly intense, there would be so much dust and smoke or gas in the air that it could seem like night in the middle of the day, and at night it was worse. It was often impossible to stay in contact with headquarters, and headquarters could not stay in contact with you either. Sometimes you could even lose contact with your own company, and when that happened, you might find yourself wandering, lost, until the next man you ran into in the fog and smoke was the enemy, who was just as lost as you. Then you had to fight him, hand to hand, and kill him before he killed you. Sometimes entire units could wander around lost all night and by dawn's light find themselves behind enemy lines, surrounded, and then you would be killed. To orient yourself, you needed to look at the stars, if the stars were visible, and if the North Star was in front of you, you had to turn around if you wanted to get back.

Without telephone lines, which were usually cut by the shelling, and without liaison personnel or runners, the regimental commanders often didn't know where their men were or where the front was. Even in the light of day, you might advance and retreat and advance and retreat so many times over the same repeating landscapes that you wouldn't know where you had started, where you were going, or where you were, and the maps headquarters used to drawn up battle plans often bore little resemblance to what the soldiers could see in front of them.

You needed to sleep when you had a chance, because at times you would go without sleep for days, and if you saw men stumbling as they marched, weaving and zigzagging from side to side as if drunk, it meant they hadn't slept, not that they'd had too much wine.

If you saw the entrance to a German latrine during the day, you could fire a few shots to register your rifle to the target, fix your rifle in place with a sandbag or two, then wait until after dark, when the Germans used the latrines. If you took a few shots then, you might get them on the crapper. And if you fought a man with bayonets, you needed to go for his nuts, because he was going to go for yours.

A nice breeze blowing on your face was dangerous because it meant that conditions were favorable for a gas attack. It was much better when the wind was blowing at your back.

The French taught the Americans practical things: to cut the tails off their overcoats, because then there was less material to soak up the mud and rain and weigh a soldier down, and to turn up their coat collars, because sometimes machine gun fire could be so intense that leaves and twigs rained down from the trees above.

You could make a lamp using a can, a sawed-off cartridge, and a strip of cloth as a wick, but you had to borrow a little gasoline from a *camion* driver. If you put it together right, you had a light that would burn for hours, which was good in a dugout when you wanted to write a letter home. You could also improvise a wall sconce by melting a candle onto the cross section of a bayonet, which could then be thrust into the wall of an *abri*, but leave any letters you've written behind if you're going over the top, because if you have them on you when you die, they will never be delivered. And don't go over the top with any money on you either, because the ambulance corps guys will go through your pockets.

They learned how to coil the barbed wire into balls during the day when there was time. At night they could carry the balls and throw them into the wire already set up in front of them for easy re-inforcement. They learned how to use a shovel to cut grooves into the trench walls to make climbing out easier, how to use a periscope, and how to hammer a horseshoe into a tree trunk to brace a tele-scope. They learned that it was unwise to take shelter behind the car-cass of a dead horse, mule, or cow, because depending on how long it had been there, the body cavity might be full of big, black, wet,

muddy rats, hungry, smart, and bold. The French told the Americans how the rats got into the food supplies and ate everything they
could sink their teeth into. One unit had locked a very large cat in a
dugout to exterminate the rats, but in the morning, the rats had eaten
the cat and dragged its bones back into their lair. "*C'est la vérité!*"

They learned that sometimes, from inside a dugout, constant
shelling made the sound of a whirlpool, of water rushing in and out,
and in a real barrage, you could feel the entire earth tremble and
shake, the air rushing all around you, explosions crashing and crashing, and then you might start to shake yourself, and your arms and
legs would tremble, just like the earth, until you couldn't tell what
was shaking, the earth or you.

The *poilus* had wilder stories, folklore passed up and down the
trenches since the war began and believed to be true: An angel had
appeared in the sky at Mons and watched over the troops below. The
Germans had a factory where they took corpses from the battlefield
and rendered them into candles and boot oils. They notched the
edges of their bayonets into saw blades, the Germans did, to rip a
man's guts open. They'd captured a Canadian soldier and crucified
him where his mates could view him, pinning him to a cross with
bayonets—everybody knew it. And the Germans had women in their
dugouts too. Men had found women's underwear during raids. And
some people said there was a ghost in the trenches, a German officer,
a captain or a major, wearing a monocle. People had seen him. He
would disappear behind his own lines and give enemy gunners your
location. That wasn't the worst of it. A band of deserters lived in
no-man's-land, some said, men of all nationalities, Frenchmen, Germans, Italians, Brits, Canadians. They'd been living there in caves
for years, wild and crazed and mad from the shelling, and they came
out at night to rob the dead and feed on their corpses. If you listened
carefully enough, sometimes you could hear them. Best if you found
yourself out and about in no-man's-land, not to go alone, or the can-
nibals would get you. And then, it was time to fight.

five

Baptism

La République nous appelle
(The Republic is calling us)
Sachons vaincre ou sachons périr
(Let us prevail or let us perish)
Un Français doit vivre pour elle
(A Frenchman must live for her)
Pour elle un Français doit mourir
(For her a Frenchman must die)
—Étienne-Nicolas Méhul and
Marie-Joseph Chenier,
"Chant des Guerriers," 1794

The shelling Noble Sissle heard, after getting separated from the band on the train from Aix-les-Bains on March 20, represented the opening shots of the largest battle in the history of the world: the 1918 German spring offensive designed to break through Allied lines, divide the French from the British, and end the war on German terms. With twenty German divisions transferred from the eastern front, the Central powers had gained numerical superiority on the battlefield and were successfully exploiting it in a campaign that would drive the British Fifth Army back forty-four miles in the

Somme and push the French back forty miles at Champagne-Marne, near where the 369th was stationed. The French needed to bring reinforcements forward as soon as possible.

After about three weeks of training in the reserve areas, the 369th moved to the front on April 13, marching from Givry-en-Argonne up a gravel road through Heirpont and Herpine to the village of Auve, where the regiment divided into two groups, with the Third and Headquarters battalions marching northeast to the town of Maffrecourt, where they established a regimental base. The British and French diplomats and generals who had petitioned for American aid at the end of 1917 had correctly maintained that troops would learn more quickly in France and would benefit from training by experienced French or British officers. The 369th had been the first American unit transferred to the Allies and ostensibly comprised the best-trained American troops in the field.

Jim Europe was glad to exchange band duties for combat training, no longer hampered by the bigotry that had interfered with training back home; his French instructors and interpreters showed no bias or resentment toward their black pupils. Writing home to Fred Moore, editor of the black newspaper the *New York Age*, Europe said of the French, "Their broad minds are far and free from prejudice, and you, as a great champion of our people, I am sure will be glad to know that despite their contact, despite the desperate efforts of some people, the French simply cannot be taught to comprehend that despicable thing called prejudice. . . . 'Viva la France' should be the song of every black American over here and over there."

They kept marching, moving forward. The First and Second battalions marched ten kilometers due north just past the village of Hans, stopping at Camp de Peupliers, about three kilometers west of Maffrecourt. They suffered no casualties, even though the trenches before them and the town behind them came under intermittent bombardment. The German shells passing overhead whistled sharply, reminding some of the men of the sound of the brakes on a trolley car screeching down a hill.

Fortunately, the first sector they moved into, Sector CR (*centre de résistance*) Melzicourt, facing the Hauzy Woods, was relatively quiet, which was why the French had chosen it for them. Their initial task was to familiarize themselves with the labyrinth they were to live and work in. Every sector was different, but the trench system had a basic structure: a framework of three parallel ditches with a support line six to eight kilometers to the rear of the front line and a reserve line eight to twelve kilometers behind the support line, with the three lines connected by a latticework of communication trenches running perpendicular to the front lines. In no case did any of these trenches run in a straight line for more than a few yards; instead, they zigzagged to lessen the damage done by direct hits from artillery shells. The German trenches had roughly the same structure. When not on duty, or for protection during heavy bombardment, men stayed in dugouts, hollowed-out rooms with bunks and rough furniture, and while some were fairly clean and well ventilated, most were dark, dank places and incubators for lice and vermin. French dugouts were relatively crude constructions compared to the German accommodations, which were generally deeper, roomier, and better ventilated. Both French and German lines had salients—shallower ditches used for observation posts or to launch raiding parties—extending out into no-man's-land, and both had laid long thickets of rusting barbed wire in front of them to prevent easy incursion.

A typical day began with a general morning stand-to roughly an hour before dawn, the time most attacks seemed to come. Each *groupe de combat* would be roused, with the men taking their places along the fire step, an elevated berm at the base of the front *parallèle*'s enemy-side wall. From there, officers and men could see over the sandbagged parapet, watching the German lines through the barbed wire for movement, rifles ready and bayonets fixed. Stand-down came at sunup, once it was clear that no attack was forthcoming. Men would then break down into smaller groups to eat breakfast, the rations having been up the night before, usually strong tea and baguettes, sometimes cheese or bacon fried in the *abri* over smokeless kerosene or paraffin fires, though sometimes the smoke from the bacon itself was enough to attract the attention of snipers.

After breakfast, the day presented a variety of duties and tasks. Weapons had to be cleaned and serviced. Repair parties set about fixing any section of the *parallèles*, *sapes*, and *boyaux* that might have been damaged the night before by shell fire. Men wrote letters home or took the opportunity to crawl into an *abri* to sleep. Men inspected their feet for swelling, numbness, or discoloration, early signs of trench foot, and they inspected their hair for *totoes*. Officers toured the trenches, inspected the repair work, chatted with the soldiers, and made out reports, noting ammunition stocks, supplies, and casualties. Officers used the daylight to read and censor the letters their men wrote, deleting any information that might give aid or comfort to the enemy were the letters to fall into enemy hands during an attack or raid. Officers wrote their own letters as well, either to their own families or to the families of men killed in action.

Evening stand-to came at dusk, a repeat of the dawn's performance. If no attack came, the men stood down and set about the more serious tasks best accomplished after dark. Wiring parties crawled out into no-man's-land to repair places where the wire had been damaged by shell fire. Digging parties took shovels and spades and made their way to the end of the salients to extend their trenches a few feet closer to the enemy, sometimes pausing in the night to listen to the sounds of German work parties digging toward them. Transport parties carried materials up from the rear: bread, water, tinned beef, occasionally fresh fruit or vegetables, mail, sandbags, timbers, duckboards, barbed wire, stakes, mauls and pickaxes, corrugated iron, tarps, pumps and drainage pipes, gas masks and replacement filters, ammunition, grenades, and flares. Combat groups manned observation posts or ventured out into no-man's-land as patrols or raiding parties—by far the most dangerous assignment. Parties from either side would venture out into no-man's-land at night to take prisoners, gather intelligence, or simply kill as many of the enemy as they could before the alarm sounded, forcing them to scamper back to their own lines. Troops were rotated at ten-day intervals, battalions and companies spending ten days in the support line, followed by ten days at the front and then ten days at the rear.

Horace Pippin was posted as corporal of the guard one night and assigned to enforce a curfew in a nearby town. He witnessed his first casualty when one of his guards shot a man who refused to obey an order to halt. They were about five kilometers from the front, by Pippin's estimate, but close enough to see the fire from the distant guns, batteries mounted atop far-off hills. Death was near. He was within range, not safe. He'd arrived at a place where men had agreed to kill each other. That first night, Pippin was terrified.

After two weeks, the orders came to move up. Though shocked to see how miserable the actual trenches were, Pippin figured if the French could live in them, so could he. The first dugout he found had wooden beams so waterlogged he could squeeze them like sponges. "I had a candle so I lit it and it went out. I tried it again and it did the same so I cut off the stem thinking I could get it to burn. I could not. I seen others do the same thing so I knew that this dugout were too damp for a candle." There was no opportunity to get clean or dry off, and the only article of clothing he removed for twenty days was his helmet, which he used as a pillow.

He made his first foray into no-man's-land shortly after that. A lieutenant, or "looey," asked for eight volunteers, and everybody's hand went up. The patrol was to leave at midnight. The lieutenant led them amid shells bursting "fast and plenty," one close enough to knock them off their feet, though it did no further damage. They heard bullets whizzing past in the darkness. They searched their sector for enemy raiding parties, tried to listen but heard only bullets and shells, and found no Germans. "We were in one of the worst places that any one ever went in," Pippin concluded. "We are in a bad place at that time . . ."

On April 20, General Le Gallais turned Sector CR Melzicourt over to the First Battalion, though for the first rotation, the 369th shared duties with French troops. Forty kilometers east of Reims and ten kilometers north of Maffrecourt, Sector CR Melzicourt was bordered on the right by the Aisne and on the left by the Tourbe, with the Hauzy Woods lying in between, on the western edge of the Argonne forest. The 4.5 kilometers assigned to the 369th represented 20 percent of all American-held territory at that time. In front of them was the German Third Army under the direction of Gen. Karl von Einem and the German First Army under Gen. Erich von Below.

All along the front, the Germans were pressing harder and harder, racing the clock and the calendar, aware that the Americans were slowly but surely joining the battle. American troops from the U.S. First Army suffered heavy losses seventy kilometers to the east of the 369th's position. Two hundred kilometers to the north, the German Fourth and Sixth armies pushed the British back twenty miles along the formerly intractable Flanders front south of Ypres, part of a colossal German drive to end the war. Along the Somme, between March 22 and April 16 the German Seventeenth and Second armies seized forty miles of British-occupied territory along a fifty-mile line, stopping fifty-five miles northeast of Paris. At the beginning of May, the German Seventh Army under Gen. Hans von Boehn advanced to the Marne, stopping a mere forty miles from Paris. No one doubted the French when they claimed the situation was dire.

Gen. John Pershing hesitated. American losses at St. Mihiel had convinced him that his troops were not ready (Lloyd George called their performance "wholly amateur") and that loaning them out piecemeal was "frittering away" his resources. General Le Gallais was nevertheless thankful for the "resources" Pershing had loaned him and, having seen for himself how his "leetle black babbies" handled themselves in training, trusted them to protect a sector the French deemed vital in preventing the Germans from making a southward thrust toward Paris's eastern flank.

Col. William Hayward told his men that their task was to hold the right flank against the German attack, should it spread to the east of Reims. During their first weeks at the front, the men of the 369th adopted a largely defensive posture, facing daily shellings of varying magnitudes and minor German offensives in the form of small raiding parties. Some days it seemed like the greater enemy was the myriad of rats that overran the sector, getting into the soldiers' personal gear and food supplies, sometimes climbing over them as they slept. With the spring thaw came yet more rain that made the trenches even muddier. Puddles overflowed the duckboards and sometimes poured down into the dugouts where the men sheltered. They were miserable, unaware that the worst was yet to come.

∽∂∾ ∽∂∾

Jim Europe, after ten days in the support trenches and ten days at the front with the Third Battalion, came into reserve and asked to see his friend Noble Sissle. Sissle found Europe in his barracks.

"Hello, Siss,'" Europe greeted his old friend. "How are you?"

"All right, mon lieutenant," Sissle replied. "How are you after twenty days in the mud?"

"Man, listen—old man mud turtle himself has never tramped in as much mud as they had us living in," Europe told Sissle. "Whatever man started this trench stuff, he must have been the meanest man in the whole world. Wonder where that orderly of mine is? Taylor! How that boy ever got in the army, I don't know. Lord, he'll drive me crazy."

Europe sometimes referred to his orderly, Private Taylor, a small, animated, cheerful, and somewhat featherbrained kid, as the "disappearingest boy in the army," one of the youngest in the regiment and a boy who never took anything seriously, but who had proven one of the finest sharpshooters with the Lebel rifle, which some considered more effective as a club than as a gun. Taylor entered the room with a broad smile on his face.

"Hello, Sergeant Sissle," he said.

"Hello, Taylor. How are you?" Sissle asked.

"I'll tell you how he's going to be," Jim Europe interrupted, "if he don't bring me some water so I can bathe. The Germans ain't got anything up there that will run him as fast as I'm going to run him."

Taylor laughed and grabbed a bucket to fetch water.

"That boy ain't worth a nickel as an orderly to me," Europe said, "but he is so young. I feel sorry for him. I could not stand to see him out there on the firing line, but I have to watch him, or he'll be right down in the post line. He's always looking for the 'Bush Germans.'"

"Bush" was the men's pronunciation of the French word for their enemies, *Boches*.

"What's going on up at the front?" Sissle asked, adding that he'd heard heavy artillery firing.

"Let me tell you what happened this evening, when I was bringing my section out of line. We started about dusk, and as we were walking slowly through the woods, an Austrian eighty-eight shell explodes. Whizz-bang! You never in your life saw such scrambling for cover, so sudden was our departure in different directions."

Europe had asked if anybody was hurt, calling his scattered men together. One of his men asked what that sound had been.

"'It's a Whizz-bang, but they never land in the same place twice,' I said, thinking I was dispelling their fear. Siss, you'd have split your sides if you had seen that boy," referring to his orderly, Taylor, "running back to the spot over which that shell exploded. 'What's the matter?' I said, thinking something was after him. 'Nothing,' he answered, all out of breath, 'but you said those shells never land in the same place twice, so I thought that the safest thing to do would be to run back to where the first one landed.'"

"Siss, I stretched out and howled. If another shell had come, I could not have moved for laughing."

Europe had a more harrowing tale to tell. The men and officers of the 369th had yet to initiate any offensives on their own and were still fairly green where tactics were concerned, but they had, in increasing numbers, accompanied their French counterparts during raids or patrols. Envious, or perhaps just anxious to prove himself, Jim Europe found himself "talking biggety" to his French counterparts, as he explained to Sissle.

Europe had taken a moment from his duties to visit with a gathering of four French officers in the next section over. They welcomed him with what he sensed was a degree of skepticism. The difference between an untested newcomer fresh on the scene and a seasoned veteran who had survived months or years of combat would have been nearly as great as the gap between a soldier and a civilian. Yet, the veteran soldiers knew that they depended on these new arrivals and could not win the war without them. Europe had developed a true affection for his French comrades. He may also have wanted to see action as a way of honoring his friend, Vernon Castle, who had been killed, Europe had recently learned, in an accident in the skies above Fort Worth, Texas, and Benbrook Field, where Castle had been serving as a flight instructor. Castle had flown more than one hundred reconnaissance missions over the German lines with the Royal Flying Corps, shot down a German plane, and been awarded the Croix de Guerre for bravery, before being shot down himself, after which, relieved of combat duty, he had served by training younger pilots. Castle was British to the core but, like the French, unbiased toward blacks, "one white absolutely without prejudice," Europe had said in a letter to Eubie Blake after hearing the news, asking Blake, "Can you imagine my grief? My one real and true friend, gone."

Europe's French comrades offered the American lieutenant a cup of wine and continued trading war stories with each other, now in English for the benefit of their guest. They had all been in service since the war began and were veterans of the Battle of Verdun, where the French had lost a number of men approximately equivalent to one-quarter of the population of Paris. Each Frenchman was one of only two or three men left from his original company. Entering his third month at the front, Jim Europe knew he had little to add to the discussion but felt expected to say something. He told Sissle, "I thought that a word expressed on my part as being desirous of wanting to witness the thrills of modern warfare would boost my stock and, being an American soldier, I thought also I should uphold the valor of the American army."

He shot his mouth off, telling his new friends, "One thing I wish to do is go on a raid. The general doesn't think we've been on the line long enough to pull off a raid."

"Bravo," one of the veteran officers said, jumping up and patting Europe on the back. "We are going on a raid tonight, and you can go with us. Just get permission from your colonel."

Europe realized at once that he might have spoken in haste, though now he couldn't take his words back. He wanted to go on a raid, true, but perhaps not so soon, not this way, not just yet. He worried that in the excitement of combat, his compatriots would begin speaking French, a language he didn't know, at a time when fully understanding what was going on around him would be crucial. He worried that when the order came to retreat, he wouldn't understand and would get left behind. His only hope was that Colonel Hayward would deny him permission, but Hayward was altogether too willing to let Europe acquire the experience.

At 7:00 P.M., Europe reported promptly to the French officers' *abri*, where he was given a French uniform to change into. He was told to leave behind all his personal belongings and anything that might be used to identify him, should he be captured. That unnerved him, as did the Frenchman who handed him a cloth cap to wear in lieu of a helmet, explaining that helmets made too much noise in no-man's-land. A bottle of wine was then passed around, and Europe noted with surprise how the Frenchmen drank with great zest. They seemed unconcerned about the mission they were about to undertake, though of course they'd been on many raids before and were no doubt used to such endeavors.

"They were happy as larks, just as though they were going to a picnic."

Europe wondered how it was that a man could actually get used to risking his life. He did his best to laugh and smile but could only force a pained grin.

As men readied themselves all around him, checking gear, cinching belts, retying bootlaces, Europe prepared himself.

"Lieutenant," a French officer said to him, interrupting his reverie. "The time has come to go."

The French officer handed him an automatic pistol, about the size of a child's cap gun. The Germans, Europe knew, had a gun the Allies were calling Big Bertha, a cannon the size of a redwood tree that had been shelling Paris from seventy-five miles away. If that was the biggest gun in the war, Jim Europe was sure he held the smallest. Even so, he gladly accepted the pistol and hoped it would prove sufficient.

The raiding party consisted of about thirty men. Silently and in single file, they moved forward down the *boyau* toward the front line. It was unfamiliar territory to Europe, who found himself stumbling frequently in the darkness. As he moved forward, following an officer, he passed dark forms huddled in the corners, waiting to take their place in line. It was eerily quiet. He wished someone would clear his throat or make some kind of human sound. He would have made a sound himself, but his mouth was bone dry, without enough saliva to lick a stamp. For a brief moment he felt like he was asleep, and this was a nightmare from which he couldn't awake.

Eventually, they reached the jumping-off point, the place, an officer whispered, where they would go over the top to venture into no-man's-land. As they waited for the rest of the raiding party, Europe looked up into the sky and noticed that it was one of the most beautiful nights he'd ever seen; there was no moon but a vast array of stars, with the Milky Way stretching from horizon to horizon, each star twinkling with an apparent mirth, as if none of this was happening. Europe worried that there was too much starlight—perhaps the raid should be postponed for some darker night. He whispered as much to one of the French officers, who whispered back that there was quite a bit of brush growing in front of the trenches to provide cover, and they'd be able to cut their way through their own wire undetected. Once they were upon the *Boches*, the officer explained, it would be to their advantage to have light to observe signs of resistance, should any be encountered. It sounded both logical and at the same time crazy. If it were darker, Europe reasoned, it would be harder for him to see the Germans but harder still for them to see him.

"I was not overanxious to see Mr. Fritz," he confided to Sissle, "and I was certainly most anxious that none would see me."

"S'il vous plait—step to one side," an officer whispered, and then, one at a time, the raiding party went over the top, moving quickly but quietly. Europe waited his turn with trepidation, frightened anew to see that the last two *poilus* to go over were carrying a stretcher. He was certain that he would be returning on it and asked himself again why he'd invited himself into this mess.

"Let's go over, Lieutenant," the French officer whispered, scrambling out of the trench. Europe followed. He crawled on his belly, hugging the earth, uncertain of how far he'd come until he reached a gap prepared in the French wire. He crawled through the gap and into the place he'd been hearing about for years, no-man's-land. He was soaked from crawling along the wet ground but too nervous to feel cold. He saw shadows, shell holes, blasted trees, brush, wire, men lying prostrate, and still the brilliant stars above. During the days he'd noticed the buds opening on the trees, the yellow and white flowers poking through the greening earth. He had no such appreciation in no-man's-land. Following his guide, he crawled past the soldiers lying to the side of the path like so many human railroad ties until they came to the place in the German wire where a preliminary raiding party had cut a hole the night before. There was always a chance that the Germans had discovered the hole and set a trap, a

machine gun just on the other side, ready to rip apart anybody fool-
ish enough to crawl through. The Frenchman indicated that there
was no danger.

No danger?

A soldier crawled forward, carrying a large ball of white tape.
The French officer whispered in Europe's ear, explaining that the
man would go ahead of the rest, using the tape to mark the shortest
route to the German trenches and, of course, the shortest route back
once the raid was over. Just as the tape layer returned, Europe heard
a series of booms from the rear—the French light artillery opening
up—and then watched as a half dozen shells burst not forty yards in
front of him. He dove for cover.

The night broke open in a storm of explosions and fire, with
shells thundering all around him, 77s and 105s and mortars, guns of
varying caliber pouring down on the German trenches. Europe
hugged the ground, dug his fingers into the clay, and tried to pull
himself closer as the bombardment swept the enemy lines. He heard
shells whizzing overhead before they exploded, and when shells exploded prematurely overhead, a rain of shrapnel fell on him.

After about two minutes, he heard the report of a flare pistol.
The officer next to him had fired a Veery pistol into the air, the red
flare signaling to all that it was time to attack. Every man in the raiding party jumped to his feet, crouched low, and scurried forward
through the hole in the German wire. They formed a line on the other
side of the wire, and when the French officer fired a second flare,
they leapt to their feet and made a mad dash for the enemy trenches.

"Come with me, Lieutenant," Europe's French officer shouted.
Europe slipped through the wire, gripping the tiny pistol in his hand.
He followed the tape until it ended, then jumped down into the German trench. Lights filled the sky, flickering and flashing, like some
Fourth of July fireworks display. The French artillery had continued
advancing, pushing back the Germans, who were either retreating
or preparing a counterattack. Europe heard men yelling as French

soldiers dashed to and fro in the trench, throwing hand grenades into any dugout they found until every nook and cranny, shadow and recess, had been blasted to bits. Europe expected a counterattack at any moment but instead saw only the French soldiers going about their deadly business. He saw no prisoners, no Germans surrendering with their hands over their heads, saying "Kamerad, kamerad!" Had the Germans anticipated the raid and abandoned their trenches? Were they lying in wait? Had they perhaps slipped back in behind them, blocking their retreat?

Then, the French officer fired a green flare into the sky, signaling the end of the raid. Though not three minutes had passed since he'd fired the red flare, it seemed to Europe like an eternity. One by one, the soldiers hurried back to the exit marked by the white tape. Some of them had scavenged the German trenches for souvenirs: pieces of paper, letters, a German coat, a helmet, anything that might have intelligence value, an insignia, a medal, discarded food rations, photographs. None of the raiders had taken any prisoners. Europe was startled to see the stretcher bearers return carrying a wounded man.

He climbed out of the German trench and ran for the gap in the wire. Where the surreptitious advance had been furtive and orderly, the retreat was loud and chaotic, every man for himself, a mad dash back across no-man's-land for the hole in the French wire. Europe ran like he'd never run before, glad not to be carrying a heavy rifle, which would only have slowed him down. Soaked with sweat, he dove into the French sap and was still running when the German return fire opened up on the French lines. Europe flew down the duckboards, hurling himself into the first *abri* he found to wait out the shelling, which lasted a full fifteen minutes. It took Europe's heart that long to stop racing.

When certain that the shelling had stopped and that he had his wits about him once again, Europe made his way to the French officer's *abri* to collect his things and thank the French soldiers for inviting him on the raid. Saddened to see that only two of the four brave officers had returned, he learned the next morning that the two absent officers had been seriously wounded in the bombardment following the raid.

"Goodness gracious, Lieutenant," Sissle said after his friend had finished his story. "It's all right to go where duty calls, but you are too valuable to go flirting with death like that."

"Don't worry," Europe replied. "I ain't lost nothing more out in no man's land. I found everything last night that ever existed out there. Next time I go, they will have to read orders to me with General Pershing's name signed to them. And re-signed."

Colonel Hayward got word of Lieutenant Europe's bravery just as he was composing a letter to Emmett Scott, special assistant to Secretary of War Norman Baker, who was in charge of tracking and documenting the performance of colored troops. Hayward wrote,

Dear Scott,

Am writing this from away up on the French front where the "Fighting Fifteenth," now the 369th U. S., is really fighting in a French Division. . . . I have two battalions in the trenches of the first line and the third in relief at rest just behind our trenches. The three rotate. Our boys . . . have patrolled No Man's Land. They have gone on raids and one of my lieutenants has been cited for a decoration. . . . Two questions of the gravest importance to our country and to your race have, in my opinion, been answered.

First: How will American Negro soldiers, including commissioned officers . . . get along in service with French soldiers and officers . . . ? Second: Will the American Negro stand up under the terrible shell fire of this war as he has always stood under rifle fire . . . ?

We have answered the first question in a most gratifying way. The French soldiers have not the slightest prejudice or feeling. The *poilus* and my boys are great chums, eat,

dance, sing, march and fight together in absolute accord. . . .
As I write these lines, Capt. Napoleon Bonaparte Marshall
and Lieut. D. Lincoln Reid are living at the French Officers' Mess at our division Infanterie School, honored
guests. . . .

Now, on the second question, perhaps I am premature.
But both my two battalions which have gone in have been
under shell fire, serious and prolonged once, and the boys
just laughed and cuddled into their shelter and read old
newspapers. . . . They are positively the most stoical and
mysterious men I've ever known. Nothing surprises them.
And we now have expert opinion. The French officers say
they are entirely different from their own African troops and
the Indian troops of the British, who are so excitable under
shell fire. . . . Do you wonder that I love them, every one,
good, bad and indifferent? . . .

Brother Boche doesn't know who we are yet, as none of
my men have been captured so far, and the boys wear a
French blue uniform when they go on raids. I've been thinking if they capture one of my Porto Ricans . . . in the uniform of a Normandy French regiment and this black man
tells them in Spanish that he is an American soldier in a New
York National Guard regiment, it's going to give the German intelligence department a headache trying to figure
it out.

⁓☙ ❧⁓

The German spring offensive continued to ramp up, with more
shelling and more raids. Pvt. Herbert White had moved up with
the Third Battalion on April 20 and was picked a few days later to
be part of a platoon that was going over the top, toward the Hauzy
Woods, where Jim Europe had gone. White considered himself "one
of the lucky ones." At 3:00 A.M., he climbed off the fire step and over

the parapet, looking for the opportunity to take prisoners or gather information in other ways. German sentries discovered them five minutes into the foray and opened fire on them, machine guns screaming. White and the others went to ground, laying still for ten minutes before they were forced to move for better cover when the Germans shelled the area. White crawled into a hole, where he found himself in the company of a French lieutenant and four comrades. They waited out the barrage. The shelling lessened around 4:00 A.M., just as a hard rain began to fall, and perhaps because of it, the German artillery stopped. White and his mates crawled back to their own lines and fell into their bunks to sleep in wet clothes.

A clash of greater significance transpired on the evening of May 15, two days after Maj. Arthur Little's First Battalion had rotated back to the front, on a night when Albany, New York's Henry Johnson stood watch at Observation Post 29.

At five foot seven, Private Johnson had a harder time seeing over the parapets than some of the men in his company. He stood on his toes, leaning against the dirt wall, his rifle ready, his eyes straining against the darkness for any sign of enemy movement. At nineteen, he knew less than some of the other men about the geopolitical forces that had converged to start the war; yet, coming from the "wrong side of the tracks" in Albany, he knew more about fighting than they did. Born in Winston-Salem, North Carolina, in 1898, he was the son of tobacco farmers, but he'd run away from home at the age of twelve, following the rail lines north past New York City to Albany, where everyone said there was lots of work to be had. At the time, he weighed only about 130 pounds, but he grew strong and muscled handling baggage for the New York Central Railroad. Between trains, Henry and some of the other baggage handlers liked to drink whiskey and play dice on a blanket on the floor. He was a charmer, a ladies' man, and a gambler.

He stood on his toes again, peering into the darkness.

Nothing.

The first time Henry Johnson stood watch through the night, the sound of a man's footstep on a loose duckboard or the wind rattling the barbed wire was enough to set him shaking. The second time he stood watch, he was a bit calmer, and the third time he was calmer still. Now, on his second tour in the trenches, he considered himself something of a seasoned veteran, nothing compared to his French babysitters but nevertheless hardened to false alarms, a professional soldier at not yet twenty-one years of age. He was a member of Company C, and his immediate superior officer was Lt. Richardson Pratt from Brooklyn. Pratt was well liked and capable, but when he'd suggested taking a squadron of inexperienced men with him into the forward observation posts, Johnson objected and volunteered to go in their stead. Inexperienced men fired their weapons and shot their Veery flares into the air if so much as a moth fluttered past. They made a lot of noise, drew attention to their location, and made everybody nervous.

Johnson rested his Lebel rifle on the parapet before him. As a weapon, the Lebel was a cut above throwing stones at the enemy, a "peashooter," the men called it. With only three bullets to a clip, you spent as much time reloading as firing, though to be fair, the Lebel was reasonably accurate at a range of ten or fifteen feet. Johnson gazed out across no-man's-land looking for any movement, listening for any sound, a twig breaking, the snip of a wire cutter.

Nothing.

The moon was waning, shedding enough light to make out shadows and shapes. Sometimes the moon was so full he could almost read a book by it. Other nights, when there was no moon, and no stars shone down, it was so dark he couldn't see to tie his shoe or read a pocket watch, and dawn took forever to come. It was worst just before dawn because then you knew that whatever was going to happen would happen soon.

Not normally an early riser, he'd never seen so many sunrises since joining the army.

He heard a sound.

He raised his rifle and held his breath, listening. He scanned the horizon, moving only his eyes.

Nothing. He lowered his rifle.

He thought of the men of the Second Battalion, back in Maffrecourt, enjoying ten days of rest. Johnson had been in the trenches at Montplaisir on his first rotation, sharing the battlements with French soldiers from Battalion Josse, but they were on their own for this tour. He was glad to be on familiar ground. In the dark, it was easy to get turned around.

Johnson looked to the rear, even though the German lines were in front of him. Two nights earlier, they'd been harassed by sniper fire, which was particularly worrisome because the snipers had somehow gotten behind the regiment's observation posts. Major Little had sent a squad on an inspection tour the next day. The inspection turned up the dugouts the snipers had used, as well as points along the front where the enemy could have slipped through. Rather than plug the gaps, they'd sent out three parties that night to lie in ambush where the line had been penetrated, hoping to meet the enemy and take prisoners when the Germans came back. The ambush parties had failed to make contact.

An illumination rocket went up to his right, but it was too far off to cast much light on the field before him. His station was Combat Post 29, fifty yards to the east of Post 28, where half a platoon waited under the command of Lieutenant Pratt. To Johnson's left, the Tourbe river ran high with the spring rains. To his right stood a line of trees forming the edge of a wooded copse, part of the Bois d'Hauzy. Before him, a field sloped gradually down to the northeast, part of Melzicourt Farm, the farmhouse about half a mile away, just up from the Aisne, which wound south.

Johnson strained to listen but heard nothing. Quiet was good. Three ambushes had been set again tonight, but none near Post 29, which lacked automatic rifles and consisted of a central dugout where two men and a corporal slept underground, safe from shelling, with a pair of lightly fortified listening salients radiating twenty yards into no-man's-land on either side. Each salient had a dugout of its own in case of shelling. Johnson stood sentry in the post on the left. On the right, to the east, his friend Needham Roberts from Trenton gazed out over the barbed wire.

Johnson turned his collar up against the cold. The temperature was still dropping into the forties at night.

The Germans came through at about 2:30 A.M., moving through a gap in the line and passing to the west until they were 150 yards to Johnson and Roberts's rear. At around 2:35 A.M., Johnson heard a noise and spun about to see Needham Roberts with his finger to his lips, indicating the need for quiet. Roberts gestured for Johnson to follow him.

When they reached Roberts's observation salient, the two men peered over the top, rifles ready.

Roberts pointed in the direction of the sound he'd heard a few moments before.

Johnson braced his rifle with his left hand, holding a Veery pistol in his right, ready to send an illumination rocket five hundred feet into the sky at the first provocation. He looked over his shoulder to locate a case of grenades resting next to the dugout door.

"There!" Roberts whispered.

"What?"

They waited again, staring in the direction of the field of barbed wire protecting the enclosure from the rear. Johnson's heart pounded in his chest, and it was hard to swallow.

They heard it again, the distinct clipped, metallic sound a wire cutter makes when the blades meet.

Johnson fired the rocket as Roberts began to yell.

"Corporal of the Guard! Corporal of the Guard! Corporal of the Guard!"

As the flare rose, Johnson saw the top coils of wire flash against the black sky and then something like birds taking to flight. It was a barrage of incoming hand grenades, or "potato mashers," as they were called for their distinct shape. Each German grenade carried ten grams of gunpowder ignited by a percussive cap set off when the handle plunged into the canister. Sometimes when a German grenade landed perfectly on its side, it failed to detonate.

Johnson hit the dirt and covered his head as the grenades landed, each the equivalent of a tenth of a stick of dynamite. His eardrums thundered as dirt rained down all around him. He felt a sharp stinging pain in his left leg, another in his side. When he sat up, he saw that Needham Roberts was hurt, bleeding from a head wound, but still throwing grenades out into the darkness from where he sat propped against the dugout door. Blood ran down the left side of his face; his left leg was soaked with blood from the waist down. Johnson had stood watch with Needham before and considered him a friend, above and beyond the bonds of common soldiers. Needham needed help. Johnson knew he was the only one in a position to render immediate assistance.

He called out "Corporal of the Guard!" again, even though the Germans were between the salient and the central dugout. The corporal and the two relief men waiting in the dugout with him were of no use, cut off by the raiding party.

Johnson got to his feet, raised his rifle, and fired at a shape in the night. Something moved to his left, so he fired at it too. He saw a German soldier rushing him from the right. He swung the rifle around quickly and fired his last bullet into the German's chest at point-blank range. He looked up and saw a half dozen Germans moving toward his right flank. To the left, he glimpsed an even larger group, perhaps ten or fifteen total.

"Corporal of the Guard! Corporal of the Guard!"

Another grenade landed and exploded harmlessly behind him. Needham was hurt badly but still pitching grenades into the darkness from a sitting position. Johnson looked up and saw a second German bearing down on him, firing a Luger pistol. There was no time to reload. A bullet caught him in the thigh just as he reversed his weapon to grab it by the barrel. He swung the Lebel in a three-quarters overhead motion, catching the German squarely on the skull with the rifle's butt. Like the French, the Germans also didn't wear helmets when they went on raids, lest the metal of the helmet brush against an unseen branch or strand of barbed wire and make a telling sound. Instead, they wore soft, gray-wool forage caps stitched in red. The Luger went off one last time. The bullet hit Johnson in the foot. The stunned German stood a moment, dazed, and managed to say, in perfect English with an American accent, "The little black son-of-a-bitch has got me!" before falling next to his slain comrade.

Johnson didn't know what to make of the fact that the man had spoken English with an American accent, but there were stories of Germans who'd grown up, lived, or gone to school in America and returned home to fight for the kaiser.

"This little black son-of-a-bitch'll get you again if you get up," Johnson replied. He called for the corporal again. Where was everybody? There were Germans everywhere. He heard shouts both distant and near: "Vorsicht! Gerade aus! Zurück!" He heard gunfire and grenades, accompanied by flames, smoke, and more shouts. Then he heard supporting machine gun fire from somewhere to the rear.

"Corporal of the Guard!"

He turned to see how Needham Roberts was faring and filled with rage. One German knelt at Roberts's feet, holding him by the ankles, while another knelt at his head, his hands clasped across Needham's chest with his arms hooking beneath Needham's armpits. They were about to carry him off as their prisoner. Needham was unconscious, unable to defend himself. There had been talk of what the Germans might do if they ever captured a black soldier. You would be better off dead, everybody said.

As he ran to help his friend, Henry Johnson unsheathed the bolo knife he carried in a canvas scabbard on his belt. With a nine-inch blade sharpened on one side and at the tip, the knife was more than a quarter-inch thick at the hilt, a three-pound piece of black steel as heavy as a meat cleaver with a wound leather grip. Bolos were more commonly issued to machine gun companies and used primarily to cut brush, but Johnson had always appreciated the heft of the thing and kept his sharp with regular honing. He leapt at the German who had Needham by the armpits. He raised the knife high in his right hand, adrenaline pumping through his veins, gave a scream, and brought the knife down on the German's head, driving the blade through the crown of the enemy's skull all the way to the hilt.

Blood spurted skyward as the man fell, staining Johnson's coat. He rolled off the body, withdrawing his blade, and struggled to his feet. Where was the second German, the one who'd had Needham by the feet? He heard shouts in the distance and gunfire from somewhere down the line. He felt no pain despite his injuries, too infused with the heat of the moment to notice anything else. He felt fear, yes, but not the kind of panic that might make a man take flight.

He looked at Roberts. He couldn't tell if he was still breathing. He was all alone now, and for all he knew an entire company of Germans was closing in on him.

He strained to catch his breath.

He heard a shout behind him. The German he'd clubbed with the butt of his rifle had recovered, a smear of blood running down the right side of his face. The German charged, smiling and firing his Luger. Johnson hated the man for the way he smiled. He felt a bullet strike him in the shoulder, another in his thigh. He fell to his hands and knees. When the German closed in, still firing, Johnson took the bolo knife in both hands and lunged, thrusting the knife upward into his enemy's abdomen. He twisted the knife, thrusting again to inflict the greatest damage, nearly lifting the *Boche* off his feet. He turned the point of the blade down and ripped at the German's bowels until the knife came free.

The man fell to the ground. Johnson thrust the knife in one more time, then withdrew it. He knelt over the man, ready to deal another blow, but saw that it would be unnecessary.

He stood again. The enemy patrol was in a panic, fully exposed behind enemy lines and taking casualties. Johnson saw Germans everywhere, swarming like the rats that lived in no-man's-land. He heard support coming from behind him but doubted it would arrive in time. He looked to the gap where the enemy had cut through the French wire and saw two Germans helping a third onto a stretcher, the injured man evidently a victim of one of the grenades Needham had thrown. If he was going to die, Johnson wanted to die fighting. He found the grenade box and threw one, then a second, then a third. The French had been impressed at how far the men from Harlem could throw hand grenades; Capt. Hamilton Fish had explained that most of them had at some point in their lives played baseball, several professionally, in the Negro leagues in fact. Johnson emptied the box, and when it was empty, he threw the box as well.

He listened. He heard words shouted in German, others shouted in English, and the boom of distant artillery.

He fell to his knees. He had nothing left—no strength, no ammunition—except the resolve not to be taken alive. He took his knife in his hand and sat back, leaning against the wall of the trench to wait for the Germans to come for him.

But the Germans had fled before American or French support troops could make their way down the trenches. When Lieutenant Pratt arrived from Combat Post 28, Needham Roberts was unconscious. Henry Johnson leaned against the side of the trench. He managed to say "Corporal of the Guard" one more time before collapsing into unconsciousness.

Medics loaded Johnson and Roberts onto stretchers and dressed their wounds as best they could, sterilizing them with tincture of iodine and packing them with clean gauze pads soon soaked through with blood. There was, in that sector, a rail line with mule-drawn flatcars used to move personnel and supplies to the front and, when necessary, to carry casualties to the rear, where a dressing station was set up just beyond regimental headquarters. While Johnson and Roberts were being moved, a Sergeant Major Hooper woke battalion commander Major Little from a light sleep at 3:30 A.M. to tell him of the regiment's first hand-to-hand combat. There was no official report as yet, Hooper related. The injured men were waiting for ambulances to take them to the hospital. Little threw on a pair of boots and a bathrobe over his pajamas and ran to catch up to the cart.

He found Johnson and Roberts at the dressing station. He'd been told they were both near death and probably wouldn't last much longer, so he was quite pleasantly surprised to see them awake and alert, talking as they lay on their stretchers. Capt. Seth B. Mac-Clinton had given them each a cup of rum, something each company commander kept on hand for just such medical emergencies. The doctor at the dressing station told Little that his men's prospects were good, all things considered. Roberts had taken shrapnel when a grenade exploded near him and been shot as well. Johnson had twenty-one wounds, the majority caused by gunshots.

Little interviewed the men and jotted down notes for the report he would have to write the next day. There were some inconsistencies that were hard to explain—Johnson was conscious when Pratt reached him but couldn't account for the fact that the Germans had managed to evacuate their dead, who, by Pratt's calculation, numbered at least four. Little knelt beside their stretchers and took their stories, finding their feats more remarkable with each added detail. When the ambulance arrived, Little stood to make room for the medics. Johnson propped himself up on one elbow and gestured to Little to come closer.

Little knelt again by Henry Johnson's side.

"Sir, Captain, Sir," Johnson began, using the form of address he'd been trained to use when speaking to a superior officer. His voice was hoarse. He smiled gently. "You don't want to worry about me," Johnson said. "I'm all right. I've been shot before."

Little made an inspection of Combat Post 29 at first light. The Germans, in their hasty retreat, had left a considerable amount of material behind. Little found forty potato masher hand grenades, seven long-arm wire cutters, three forage caps, and three Lugers. One of the gray-wool forage caps had a two-inch-long slit piercing the top, with a hank of hair matted to the inside by dried blood. Marks in the damp clay beyond the wire indicated where the Germans had set down two stretchers during the raid. There were numerous footprints in the clay as well. It was understood that German raiding parties ordinarily carried one long-armed wire cutter for every four men. Extrapolating from the number of wire cutters found at the scene, in addition to the stretcher marks, the footprints, and the fact that the Germans had evacuated at least four casualties, Little estimated that Henry Johnson and Needham Roberts had fought off a minimum of twenty-four *Boches*.

The trail left by the retreating Germans was relatively easy to follow. There were footprints, more abandoned equipment, and marks where stretchers had been set down to give the bearers a rest; most of all, there was blood. At the opening the Germans had cut in the wire, they found an unidentifiable pulp of flesh and tissue, a tatter of cloth from a German coat, and a blown-apart first aid kit. A hole in the ground where a grenade had landed was about the size and shape of a small washtub and nearly filled to the top with blood, so much that it took a week for the clay to absorb it. There were other pools of blood, blood smeared on trees and logs, and discarded, blood-soaked handkerchiefs and bandages for almost half a mile. The trail ended at the Aisne, where the raiders had crossed.

Little returned from his inspection and dictated the report from his notes. He recommended that both Roberts and Johnson be awarded medals for honor and valor.

Two weeks later, on May 31, the First Battalion was relieved and rotated back to the town of Maffrecourt, where they underwent a week of open-field warfare training, crawling on their bellies through the tall grass and learning infiltration techniques. Major Little found an opportunity during the battalion's respite to ride to the hospital where Johnson and Roberts were recuperating. Both men were out of danger, but it was evident from the severity of their wounds that both would be crippled for life. Little learned that the doctors had been forced to replace the shinbone in Henry Johnson's left leg with a silver tube where the tibia had been completely shattered; several of the metatarsal bones in his left foot had been crushed as well.

Johnson and Roberts both smiled as Major Little approached their beds. When he asked how they were feeling, they said they were feeling fine. The major tried to make small talk, but he found conversation difficult as their lives and backgrounds were too different to provide much common ground.

"Tell me then," Little asked. "How has it come to be that you're so proficient with a bolo knife?"

Johnson had to smile. It was no secret among his men that Little prided himself, if that was the word, on his associations with soldiers whose civilian pasts included criminal activities—lock pickers, brawlers, thieves, and the likes of Sergeant Bayard with his own private paddy wagon—though the men knew Little was not quite as "uptown" as he liked to believe.

"I mean," Little persisted, "have you ever been mixed up before in a fight where you used a knife?"

Johnson looked at Roberts. Roberts looked at Johnson, who tried not to laugh but failed. He tried to answer the major's question but had a hard time forcing words to come from his lips as he suppressed a guffaw. Laughing in an officer's face could be seen as insubordination.

"Sir, Captain, Sir," he said. "You want to know if I ever fought with a knife?"

Roberts laughed again from across the room. That set Henry off. The two men laughed at Little's naiveté, chuckling at first, but the laugh kept building, until both men roared. Johnson was laughing too hard to say another word.

Little laughed too, probably without a clear idea as to what was so funny:

> My question had been too ridiculous. . . . The walls of that
> hospital ward echoed with the sounds of revelry, as we all
> joined in laughter—the Americans, in appreciation of the
> comedy of the moment—the French nurses and patients, in
> sheer contagion.

◦◦◦

It's impossible to pinpoint exactly when the more colorful name "Hellfighters" was first applied to the 369th, since the enemy gave them the name, a fact ascertained after a German prisoner told his interrogators that his comrades were particularly wary of confronting colored American troops. The moniker was adopted and popularized by American newspapers carrying the story of what they called "The Battle of Henry Johnson." The account that brought Johnson to national attention was entitled "Young Black Joe," published in the *Saturday Evening Post* on August 24, 1918, and written by Irvin S. Cobb, whose presence was both serendipitous and planned. By some measures, Colonel Hayward worked as hard for his regiment as its public relations agent as he did as its military leader, and he had arranged, well in advance of the Battle of Henry Johnson, for a press junket to come to the front to write stories about his colored regiment. He could hardly have staged a better performance by one of his men for them to report on and review.

The morning after the battle, Colonel Hayward arrived on the scene with Cobb, Martin Green of the *Evening World*, and Lincoln Eyre of the *New York World* in tow. Of the three, Cobb was the best known, described in the *Saturday Evening Post* as "one of America's chief assets. . . . More people read him than any other contemporary writer—to be both amused and informed. He may not be the funni-est man in America, but if he isn't, who is? . . . He skimmed the cream off the European War in the first three months, and has made nearly everything written since seem dull and trite." Cobb made his first tour as a correspondent for the *Post* in 1914, then returned for a second tour and paid a visit to the 369th at the invitation of Hay-ward, where Cobb, Green, and Eyre toured the trenches and at-tended a band concert. Cobb was morbidly obese and ugly by his own account (he'd written a humor piece entitled "The Advantages of Being Homely"), with a cigar often lodged amid his jowls and eye-brows bushy as a machine gun nest. Hayward had arranged both a reception and a band concert for his visitors on the night before Henry Johnson went to work with his bolo knife. At the concert, in the town square, Noble Sissle, standing in for Europe who was at that time stationed in the front trenches, determined that the band would play a selection of songs familiar to the famous Southerner. They began by playing "Stars and Stripes Forever," then a medley of "plantation melodies," including Stephen Foster's "Old Folks at Home" and "Way Down upon the Swanee River," which Cobb later wrote made him want to cry. For an encore they played "Dixie," softly at first, building to a dramatic finish, while a brilliant full moon shone above the shell-shattered steeples of Maffrecourt.

The reception for Cobb, Eyre, and Green did not go as well. Many of the regiment's noncommissioned black officers made them-selves scarce or refused to shake Cobb's hand. Several turned their backs to him, avoiding eye contact. Sissle's selection of plantation music was a conscious effort to "soften his views such that his poi-soned pen would be at least modified, if not stilled forever." The men were aware that before the war, Irvin S. Cobb had been one of the foremost perpetrators of racist stereotypes, a Southern "humorist" from Kentucky writing essays and portraits of life in America and in the reconstructed South. He had published in such places as *McClure's, American Magazine,* and the *Saturday Evening Post,* writing in a "Southern" prose style that might charitably be compared to Mark Twain's, with long, winding sentences, self-congratulatory vocabulary choices, and a tendency to delay getting to the point for as long as possible. His essays frequently included condescending caricatures of black people, ridiculing their speech and culture. To be fair, it was much the norm for white writers, and black writers too, to transliterate African American dialects, using "dems" and "does" and "I'se gwine." A commentator named Robert H. Davis wrote in the May 1917 issue of *American Magazine*, "It is a safe wager that there is not a man living today who has ever heard Irvin Cobb utter a disagreeable phrase about any human being, among either the quick or the dead." All the same, when the 369th's noncommissioned black officers turned their backs on him, they had good reason to do so.

Cobb asked if Little could think of any interesting experiences his readers might enjoy reading about. Little allowed, coyly, that things had been rather dull of late, with a few amusing anecdotes from time to time and constant shelling and sniping more or less all the time.

"We did have a little fight this morning that was good while it lasted. If you're interested in that sort of thing. A couple of our boys had a real pitched battle, for a few minutes. I've just finished writing the report—I'm trying to get them the Croix de Guerre. Would you care to read it?"

As soon as they read the report, the visiting journalists knew they had one of the better stories of the war. When they asked to have a look at the grounds to get a better sense of what had happened, Little said he'd be delighted to show them. Making their way to Combat Post 29 was difficult. The day was warm enough that the portly Cobb was soon winded and asked three times to stop to catch his breath, mopping his brow with his sleeve. Little was particularly eager to show them the grenade hole full of blood. Cobb and the others were duly impressed. From there, Little indicated the path the Germans had taken to reach the river and described what they'd found along the route, though to travel any further was surely to invite a sniper's bullet.

At lunch, back at Major Little's command post, Cobb had a question.

"I know it's against your rules to talk shop at the table," he said, "but how much special training for this trench fighting did Henry Johnson have before he licked those twenty-four Germans?"

"Same as the rest of the regiment," Little replied. "No more than three weeks. In theory. In practice, taking away the time spent changing stations and the ordinary routine of our early days with the French, I'd guess the special training our men have had would equal about a week of what the draftees are getting in the cantonments back home."

"Seems to me," Cobb replied, "that if he'd had the normal training our men at home are getting today, by tomorrow night Henry would have been storming Potsdam."

A few days after their visit, an article by special correspondent Lincoln Eyre appeared on the front page of the *New York World* describing what Eyre called "The Battle of Henry Johnson." New York's evening papers quoted from or reprinted Eyre's story later that day. By the following morning, the Associated Press had syndicated the story of the first two colored American soldiers to receive the Croix de Guerre from coast to coast, the phrase "The Battle of Henry Johnson" proving rather catchy. The story offered a modicum of good news during a month in which American papers had carried mostly bad, giving accounts of the German spring offensive, which to that point had been fairly successful. It also provided Harlem with its first African American war heroes, as mothers read to their sons and daughters accounts carried in the black newspapers of Johnson's inspiring heroism.

"Your husband," Colonel Hayward wrote to Edna Johnson in Albany, "Pvt. Henry Johnson, is in my regiment, the 369th United

States Infantry, formerly the Fifteenth New York Infantry. He has been at all times a good soldier and a good boy of fine morale and upright character. To these admirable traits he has lately added the most convincing numbers of fine courage and fighting ability. I regret to say that at the moment he is in the hospital, seriously but not dangerously wounded. The wounds having been received under such circumstances that every one of us in the regiment would be pleased and proud to trade places with him."

Hayward told her the details of the battle without getting too graphic, saying, "Henry laid about him right and left with the heavy knife." He told her that Gen. Henri Gouraud had offered one hundred francs to the family of the first man to be wounded heroically. Accordingly, he was sending her half the reward, the other half going to Needham Roberts's family. "It is my hope and prayer to bring him back to you safe and sound."

The story gained national attention after "Young Black Joe" appeared in magazine racks from coast to coast. It was the first mainstream article to treat the experience of black American soldiers in full, describing their courage and discipline, rather than resorting to the minstrel-show jokes and comical anecdotes other journalists found themselves compelled to use. Running a full three pages, between ads for Mennen's shaving cream and the Ceebynite ("see-by-night") compass with its luminous, radium-coated needle and dial that soldiers could read in the dark, Cobb's story, illustrated with a half-page photograph, limned the experience to the best of the writer's ability, quoting a "stumpy private with a complexion like the bottom of a coal mine" as saying, "Henry Johnson, he done right well, didn't he? But say, boy, effen they'll jes gimme a razor an' a armload of bricks an' one half pint of bust-haid licker, I kin go plum to Berlin."

"They're all like that boy with the bolo, and some of them are even more so," Hayward was quoted as saying.

"If ever proof were needed," Cobb concluded, "which it is not, that the color of a man's skin has nothing to do with the color of his soul, this twain then and there offered it in abundance. . . . They were soldiers who wore their uniforms with a smartened pride; who were jaunty and alert and prompt in their movements; and who expressed as some did vocally in my hearing, and all did by their attitude, a sincere heartfelt inclination to get a whack at the foe with the shortest possible delay. . . . I am of the opinion personally, and I make the assertion with all the better grace, I think, seeing that I am a Southerner with all the Southerner's inherited and acquired prejudices touching on the race question—that as a result of what our black soldiers are going to do in this war, a word that has been uttered billions of times in our country, sometimes in derision, sometimes in hate, sometimes in all kindliness—but which I am sure never fell on black ears but it left behind a sting for the heart—is going to have a new meaning for all of us, South and North too, and that hereafter n-i-g-g-e-r will merely be another way of spelling the word American."

Cobb's article was picked up and widely reprinted in the black press, giving the story a second life after its initial run, to the extent that Cobb was astonished to find African American porters and redcaps, waiters and servants, coming up to him upon his return home to thank him for telling Henry Johnson's story. Gratitude from black Americans was not something Cobb was used to. He had created a hero, perhaps intentionally; unintentionally, by virtue of his being read by more people than any other contemporary writer, he had seeded a myth.

six

Summer
in Hell

For 1,360 days, the war had raged along a more or less stable front, with ground taken, ground lost, the conflict confined to a narrow band of land between the entente positions and the German Hindenburg Line. On May 27, the greatest battle ever fought in the history of the world entered its third phase when four thousand German guns opened fire along a twenty-four-mile line between Soissons and Reims, thirty miles to the west of the 369th. Within twenty-four hours, German forces annihilated eight French and four British divisions, driving a wedge fifteen miles deep and forty miles wide through the Allied lines in what was dubbed the "Third Battle of the Aisne."

There was now reason to believe that things were finally changing, that the stalemate had been broken. For German commander Gen. Erich Ludendorff, it was the last chance to break through before the Americans filled the trenches in numbers sufficient to halt any further German progress. Some called the strategy a "peace drive," for it was intended to strengthen Germany's position at future peace talks, short of winning the war outright.

On May 30, the Germans reached the river Marne near Chateau-Thierry, stopping only forty-six miles from Paris. They'd taken about forty-five thousand prisoners in the drive. Marshall Ferdinand Foch appealed to Gen. John Pershing to give him more troops, and Pershing, sensing a true emergency, gave Foch four white regiments to use as he saw fit.

Arthur Little was in his *abri* with a few fellow officers, waiting out one of the twice-daily shellings meant more as harassment than as prelude to an assault, when a medical officer new to the front entered the dugout and said shrilly, "My God, Captain. This is no place for troops! This is positively dangerous!" Little and the others could only laugh.

In fact, the Hellfighters had had it relatively easy so far, with a little more than a dozen fatalities, mostly sergeants, buried in a section of the Maffrecourt churchyard cemetery designated for *les soldats Negro*, which they called Sergeants Hill.

June saw an increase in shelling, more explosive rounds, more gas rounds, and in particular more yperite, delivered in shells marked with yellow crosses on the casings and leaving a yellowish powder where the chemical dried in the summer sun.

In the lines, men tried to establish a semblance of normalcy despite the extraordinary circumstances in which they found themselves. Men gathered for crap games in the dugouts or out of view behind the cook shed. Garbage details carried the company's trash to incinerators, where the smoke stung their eyes. After it rained, men formed lines to dredge the water and muck from the trench, passing buckets hand to hand. Carpenters hammered and sawed wood, reinforcing parapets, reframing the portals to the *abris* loosened by the shelling. There were sandbags to fill and holes to repack where bombs loosened the parapet. Men used the fire step as a bench to oil the bolts and breeches on their rifles, pulling strips of oiled flannel through the bores, cleaning the sights, preparing their weapons for inspection in the quiet of midday.

They wrote letters on paper purchased in the village *papeterie*, letters that would arrive home bearing French postal designations, marked *correspondance militaire* or *contrôle postal militaire*. They talked about friends back home, girls they had left behind, and what they missed about their mothers' cooking. About how long the war might last and where they might meet again when it was over. About what good soldiers the French *poilus* were. About who was favored by the colonel, the major, the captain, lieutenant, or sergeant, who was in and who was out of the doghouse, who was the biggest kiss ass and who never would suck up, no matter what. About how the German boots were better than the French or American ones. About rumors of where they'd go next, who was going to be promoted, and who was going to be transferred.

At evening stand-to, it was time again for vigilance, eyes riveted on far-off knolls, clumps of trees, curves in the land, watching for motion along the ridge. They listened, watching the setting sun rim a far ridge in red and gold, with flocks of blackbirds flying home to their nests.

Waiting for the moon to rise, they tried to remember, would it be full, half, quarter, maiden? What would it mean if the moon was full? More light for mayhem, or too much light for it, too much light to fight?

Then if all was quiet, the order came to stand down, post sentries, and wait.

Jim Europe and Noble Sissle rotated to the rear for ten days' rest in Maffrecourt, managing to borrow a piano from a local family and move it to their barrack, where they could play songs and look out the window at the countryside, a golden field of mustard plants, and, beyond that, rolling hills of windswept summer wheat extending to the horizon beneath clear blue skies. Europe had even managed to bring a chaplain's pump organ to the front trenches, where he would pump the pedals to fill the bellows and play tunes in the dugouts to entertain the men. On the piano in the barracks at Maffrecourt, Europe played Sissle a song he'd written at the request of an officer who wanted a song about missing home. He sang,

In the blue of the skies,
I see the blue of your eyes,
In the thrilling song of the bird,
Your voice is heard,
It thrills me, stills me,
With love anguish fills me,
I find the white fleur-de-lis
An anthem of your purity,
As the bees kiss the vine,
I feel your lips touching mine,
The breath of the rose
Your perfumed tresses disclose . . .
Everything reminds me of you.
Everything reminds me of you.

Perhaps because he was in France or on the continent named after him, the lyrics Europe wrote were of an elevated tone and lacked the conventions of black dialect found in plantation songs; there were no "dems," no "dese," and no one played the banjo, pining for days of yore. He'd been preaching the sermon of jazz everywhere he went, or rather he'd let the music speak for itself, making converts, opening eyes and ears, but France had been speaking to him too, a conversation that went both ways. He'd received a new level of respect, and it invigorated him. Europe had been prolific *en repos*, penning other songs, including "I've an Observation Tower of My Own" ("*Night and day, whether near or far away/I see every little thing you do*"), one called "Trench Trot," and another called "I've Got the Map of Your Heart."

They played on the spinet piano and wrote songs for a few days, then Europe was rotated back to the trenches. Sissle said goodbye, went about his own duties, trained and drilled, and prepared to move up again to the reserve lines when his own turn came. He didn't see his friend again until he learned that Europe, while commanding his machine gun company, had been gassed and taken to a hospital in the town of Gizaucourt, five miles to the rear of Maffrecourt.

Sissle got permission and, accompanied by one of the Puerto Rican horn players in the band, hiked to Gizaucourt along a dusty road until a soldier near the hospital directed him to the gas ward. It was common, at transport stations or hospitals, to see gas victims, blinded with bandages over their eyes, walking in single file behind a sighted leader. It took Sissle a moment to find a nurse who spoke English. He wrote,

> I will never forget the terrible scene that greeted our eyes as we went from the vestibule into the interior of this gas ward. In the first place there were rows of cots and little improvised partitions were made of pieces of sheet pieces torn and hung on strings to shut off one patient from the other, but as you walked down the aisle by the rows of cots, you could see how the different ones were suffering. Some of them in places where their eyes were, were just large, bleeding scabs; others, their mouths were just one mass of sores; others had their hands up, and there were terrible burns under their arms, where the gas had attacked the moisture there. They made a pitiful sight. Others, their nose had been burned so terribly that they could only breathe through their mouths and the sound of them gasping for breath resembled the sound of the croak of frogs that you hear at night passing down the country road.

As they neared Europe's bed, they heard a dry, hacking cough from behind the screen. They feared the worst.

Instead, they found Jim Europe sitting upright with a notebook propped on his knees, writing a song. Europe smiled to see his friend Sissle, his eyes bright and undamaged behind his thick tortoiseshell-rimmed eyeglasses, but instead of talking about his injuries, he said,

"Gee, I am glad to see you boys—Sissle, here's a wonderful idea for a song that just came to me, in fact . . . last night during the bombardment."

Sissle was impressed as ever by the man's strength, his indefatigable nature. He was a force.

Europe had written, making the best use of his convalescence, what would become his best-known song, "On Patrol in No Man's Land," a jaunty, jittery melody and lyrical treatment juxtaposed against a dark situation:

> *There's a minnenwerfer coming, Look out! Bang!*
> *Hear that roar! It's one more.*
> *Stand fast. There's a Very light.*
> *Don't gasp, or they will find you all right.*
> *Don't start to bombing with those hand grenades,*
> *There's a machine gun! Holy spades!*
> *Alert! Gas! Put on your mask.*
> *Adjust it correctly and hurry up fast.*
> *Drop! There's a rocket for the Boche Barrage,*
> *Down! Hug the ground as close as you can,*
> *Don't stand! Creep and crawl.*
> *Follow me, that's all.*
> *What do you hear, nothing near.*
> *Don't fear, all's clear.*
> *That's the life of a stroll when you take a patrol*
> *Out in no man's land. Ain't life grand,*
> *Out in no man's land.*

His answer to the question in the penultimate line, "Ain't life grand?" would have been, Yes, life is grand, though war is not. It was not in his character to wallow in self-pity or dwell on the negative. He had always been the responsible one in his family, supporting his mother and sister and supervising his alcoholic older brother. Jim Europe never dwelled on setbacks, focusing instead on the rosy future he knew was coming.

From Gizaucourt, Europe was evacuated to a hospital on the outskirts of Paris to convalesce. The doctors classified him as unfit for frontline duty but still able to serve. He was, at first, saddened to miss combat duty, though he could now give his full attention to the band and start thinking about the future. He wrote a letter to Eubie Blake in New York. Blake had written him to complain that business was slow because of the war. Europe didn't have much sympathy:

> Eubie, the thing to do is to build for the future, and build securely and that is what I am doing. When I go up I will take you with me, you can be sure of that. . . . At present I am a soldier in every sense of the word and I must only take orders and be able to stand all sorts of hardships and make untold sacrifices. At the moment I am unable to do anything. My hands are tied and tied fast but if the war does not end me first as sure as God made man, I will be on top and so far on top that it will be impossible to pull me down.

Europe's band played a Fourth of July concert led by Eugene Mikell at Gen. Henri Gouraud's headquarters in Chalons. Gouraud requested plantation songs, and specifically hoped to hear the young Jenkins Orphanage percussion twins, Steve and Herbert Wright. Noble Sissle sang "Joan of Arc" (*"they have borne the burden of grief for many a day,/now other mothers' sons enter the fray"*), which always left Gouraud misty-eyed. The music was temporarily interrupted by an aerial dogfight overhead, which sent stray bullets down to scatter the crowd below. Gouraud made a speech saying he was grateful for America's support. Only forty-six years old, he was France's youngest general, close in age to his men, and quite popular with the New Yorkers as well as his *poilus*, who appreciated his frequent visits to his troops at the front. He had seen for himself what the conditions were, unlike other rear-echelon armchair generals who'd decided the fates of millions without ever leaving the safety of their offices. Gouraud enjoyed the concert but had other things on his mind, having received intelligence that he could expect up to forty German divisions headed his way, with the 369th directly in their path. The attack would come in the Champagne-Marne region, on a fifty-mile line between Reims and Verdun, with the Argonne forest in the middle.

The question was when. Gouraud and his staff believed the two most likely days were either the Fourth of July, America's Independence Day, or Bastille Day, July Fourteenth, with German military strategy guided not by a sense of poetic irony but rather by the idea that the enemy would drink too much on the holiday and be too incapacitated to fight back.

Gouraud hoped to induce the Germans to attack on his terms, then set a trap for them. He planned to evacuate the forward trenches and move his battalions back to the second line. Only a holding platoon, or "camouflage squad," of thirty men would remain, strung out along a two-mile sector, with about one man every three hundred yards. The holding platoon's job would be to lob grenades and run from machine gun to machine gun, firing off a few rounds to make it look like the front trenches were still occupied, then cut out and retreat at the last minute, fending for themselves, by and large, spaced far enough apart to be virtually cut off from each other. French artillery would be accurately registered on their own abandoned trenches prior to the attack so that when the Germans reached the evacuated French line, they could be shelled effectively. If they continued the attack, they would meet fresh, rested troops on the second line. Capt. Hamilton Fish volunteered to lead the camouflage squad and wrote a farewell letter to his father, saying, "I do not believe there is any chance of us surviving the first push."

The Hellfighters spent the Fourth of July playing baseball, holding a round-robin tournament, with the first round determining battalion champions and a final round to crown the regiment champion. A betting man might have wagered on whatever side Spot Poles played on. General Le Gallais visited and warned the men of the impending battle. He told them that their task would be to launch the counterattack, once the Germans fell into Gouraud's trap. Then, Le Gallais laughed and deployed what he knew as an American expression, saying he hoped the *Boche* would "get what's coming to them."

They manned their posts, with the First Battalion on a hill north of Courtemont, the Second on a hill on their right flank between Maffrecourt and Courtemont, and the Third at Bersieux. No attack came, and they stood down around 3:00 A.M. From then on, they kept their movements as hidden as possible from German observation planes and balloons, staying in the barracks during daylight hours and moving in small groups. The main event was yet to come.

On June 6, Col. William Hayward joined Hamilton Fish's K Company in the front lines and, perhaps mistaking heavy German machine gun fire for the opening shots, refused to retreat when a French general gave the order to retire. Hayward purportedly said, "My men never retire—they go forward or they die!" While leading the charge, Hayward was wounded in the knee, whereupon he neither went forward nor died but instead hastened to the rear to attend to his injury.

Gouraud sent them a letter on July 7:

> ORDER
> TO THE FRENCH AND AMERICAN SOLDIERS
> OF THE 4TH ARMY
> We may be attacked now at any moment.
> You all feel that never a defensive battle was engaged under more favorable conditions.
> We are informed and we are on the watch.

We are powerfully reinforced in Infantry and Artillery.

We fight on the ground you have transformed by our persistent work into a formidable fortress—invincible fortress if all passages are well guarded.

The bombardment will be terrible; you will stand it without losing courage.

The assault will be fierce, in a cloud of dust, of smoke, of gas.

But your poison and your armament are formidable.

In your breasts beat brave and strong hearts of free men.

Nobody will look back, nobody will fall back one step.

Everybody will have only one thought—Kill, Kill many until they have enough of it.

And it is why your General tells you: That assault, you will break it, and it will be a beautiful day.

GOURAUD,
General Commanding the 4th Army

They waited, then grew tired of waiting, of false alarms.

On Bastille Day, the French invited the New Yorkers over for a modest celebration, with one bottle of champagne for every four soldiers to limit the potential for drunkenness. They toasted success, America, and France.

At midnight, the Germans commenced a massive shelling on the abandoned trenches, resulting in few casualties. It was clear after about half an hour that this was the major battle they'd been waiting for. Colonel Hayward showed up at the command post on crutches. Capt. Arthur Little sent a runner to Maffrecourt with an urgent message, calling for room service and asking the mess sergeants to bring up the kitchens because they'd be eating breakfast in the trenches.

Private Herbert White recalled the night:

On July 14th, the Germans made another determined effort to win the war. This fight was known as the second battle of the Marne. About midnight the Germans threw one of the heaviest bombardments of their four years of warfare. Our third battalion was ordered to the front lines and the night was terrible. For miles and miles all you could see was the flash of the big guns and the continuous roar of cannon and bursting of shells. We finally started for the front but had an awful time getting under the German barrage. Shells were bursting all along the roads, killing men, horses, blowing up wagons. As we moved towards the front we could hear nothing but our comrades lying on the ground crying, "Help me boys." As the battalion got nearer the front at the cross-road stood Maj. Spencer directing and encouraging the boys. Shells were dropping all around him, but he never moved a muscle. Shells were falling very fast and it was so dark that the platoons were losing each other. At daybreak shells were still falling fast as ever. Nevertheless we reached our position and, together with our French comrades, we not only held but drove the Germans back a few kilometers to Belleou-ridge [Belleau Ridge] which the boys held for some time.

All night, an artillery duel raged. At 8:00 A.M. on July 15, the regiment rendezvoused at a place called Camp Bravard to prepare for its counterattack. The men were massed on a shelf of land behind a steep hill that temporarily afforded protection. It was safe enough that some men found a place in the morning sun to close their eyes and sleep, knowing that so far, the line in front of them was holding. If it gave way on either side, or if it had already, allowing the enemy to flank them, surely somebody would wake them.

At 2:30 P.M. on July 15, Capt. André de Fouquiers, aide to Gen. Helie d'Oiselle, commander of the French Eighth Army Corps, arrived to tell the men that Gouraud's trap had worked. Over three-quarters of the distance from Verdun to Reims, the Germans had not made it past the evacuated "slaughter pits" of the French first line. In the few places that the Germans had broken through, the second line had held, save for a few narrow salients. It was time to hit back, while the Germans were vulnerable and before they could reverse the fortifications in the occupied trenches.

The 369th marched west to join the French 161st Division under General Lebouc to attack the Germans at Sous Secteur Beauséjour, facing a high ground called Butte Mesnil, where two hundred thousand German and French soldiers had died during the first two years of the war. Butte Mesnil guarded the towns of Ripont and Sechault and the fertile bottomlands along the Dormoise river. The Germans had taken it again and needed to be dislodged. Before dark, the regiment moved again, marching four kilometers west of Laval and occupying new positions with the First Battalion on the left, the Second in the center, and the Third on the right. To the regiment's left was a regiment of Chasseur Alpins, and to the right, Moroccans.

The nearly constant shelling now worsened, and the 369th's new trenches were so shallow that they were vulnerable to indirect hits and shrapnel. They lost about sixty horses and mules, which meant that bringing up supplies would be difficult—which meant they would go hungry. It was the first war in history in which artillery fire killed more men than bullets from small arms.

The prevailing feeling was helplessness. Soldiers feared that death could come without warning, a lone bullet whistling through the darkness, fired by an unseen enemy, finding its target more by luck than design. Men became superstitious, feeling their luck had run out, or else they engaged in a sort of reverse magical thinking, believing it wouldn't happen to them. They also feared the shot that wounded or maimed but didn't kill, that left a man senseless, permanently damaged, no longer in control of his life. Each feared dying a coward—or discovering that he was a coward but not dying, then having to live with that knowledge for the rest of his life.

Finally, each feared getting killed or wounded without proving anything, dying neither nobly nor ignobly but just going, instantly, making nothing of his life in the way of his dying. Better to die heroically, taking large numbers of the enemy with him or saving someone else, but too often that was not the case.

With each incoming shell, the soldier held his breath, tightening his grip on whatever he had in his hands, flinching at the deafening noise. Another shell would land, and the soldier would feel vibrations and tremors and the rain of pebbles and bits of things—then he would exhale. Wooly Bears and Flying Pigs and Jack Johnsons. The earth would burst skyward in fountains of dirt and spouts of mud, while black smoke filled the air.

Sometimes the explosions were so constant that the soldier couldn't tell them apart or identify them anymore—"drumfire," some called it. Percussionists like Steven and Herbert Wright could hear patterns in the bombardment: a paradiddle, a rat-a-pa-tan, a press roll getting faster and faster until there were no moments of non-shelling between shells. By one estimate, in the peak of battle, German guns fired about nine thousand shells in forty-five minutes, or a little more than three shells per second.

Horace Pippin watched Gouraud's trap unfold as the French feint lured the Germans into a counterattack while the French retreated from their own lines. "As we were waiting ready," Pippin wrote, "the French artillery knew right where they were by the airplanes that were circling around them. Then a red light came out of the airplane. It did not go out before the French artillery opened up on them."

The French artillery punished the Germans for half an hour. Pippin counted about five hundred dead Germans when he joined the French troops reoccupying their former positions. There was no time to rest. They pressed the attack.

It was a terrible night to fight. "It were raining the hills were like ice it were all you could do to stand up," Pippin recalled. "The mud were so thick and slippery that you could not make fast time up the hill but we did not let that get the best of us. I ran and some time I would be down. Then I would creep along."

They came to a road and found themselves pinned down. German artillery and machine guns blocked the road. Pippin felt overcome by emotions, sad and angry at the same time. He saw his comrades lying on the road and in a field beyond. He found a good friend, lying still. "I looked to see if I could do him any good. I could not for he were done for."

They stayed off the road and moved along the ditch next to it. The shelling increased. Pippin found an old church to take refuge in, though the building was half demolished. He had one more field to cross, but the German gun batteries had the field well registered. He and three others from K Company ran as fast as they could. When the shelling increased, they ducked into a hole and waited. After they felt the shelling abate, they ran again and dove into a ditch at the far side of the field. "We laid down once going then we came to the trench that we had so much trouble to get to and found the body of men that were on the line at the time. I did not see anyone that were in my Co. K but I fought on. When the battle were over and we were back and seen what were there of my platoon I yet say to myself sometimes how did I ever do it that were the trying time."

The next morning he saw shells piled up like cordwood and more trucks coming with more shells: "truck after truck of shells would be going and coming all along the line. They had shells as far as you could see piled up."

It was difficult for the men to know—when there were no wirelesses or land lines and the only means of communication was runners or pigeons—where they stood strategically. Soldiers were unable to tell if they'd been placed in the proper position and the next move was to attack, or if they'd been placed in the wrong position and were taking a senseless beating. They knew only one very small piece of the

war. Rumors passed up and down the trenches. The enemy is in retreat. The enemy is about to attack. We are winning. We are not
winning. Nobody knows what's happening—pass it on.

Fortunately, Gouraud was masterful at keeping his men informed and encouraged. He sent a letter on July 16:

> July 16th, 1918
>
> SOLDIERS OF THE 4TH ARMY
>
> 4th Army
> Staff—5th B
> No. 6954/3
>
> During the day of July 15th, you have broken the effort of
> fifteen German Divisions supported by ten others.
>
> They were from their orders to reach the Marne in the
> evening; you have stopped them where we wanted to give
> and win the battle.
>
> You have the right to be proud, heroic infantrymen and
> machine gunners of the advanced posts who have signaled
> the attack and who have subdivided it, aviators who flew
> over it, battalions and batteries who have broken it, staffs
> who have so minutely prepared that battlefield.
>
> It is a hard blow to the enemy. It is a beautiful day for
> France.
>
> I rely upon you that it will always be the same each time
> they will dare to attack you and with all my heart as a sol-
> dier I thank you.
>
> GOURAUD

On July 17, three days after Gouraud's trap stymied the Germans' Bastille Day attack, the defensive battle turned into an offensive one. The Hellfighters received orders to move to a first-line

quarter-sector called CR Balcon-Reverchon. They moved at day-break on July 18, following a map, along roads and cross-country and at last through the towns of Laval, Wagemoulin, and Minau-court, where they took cover when enemy scout planes appeared, and where they experienced light but harassing artillery fire.

They eventually met guides from the Forty-seventh Battalion of Chasseurs, whom they were relieving, and were conducted to Centers of Resistance Beauséjour and Crochet, opposite Butte Mesnil, where the Germans had taken French positions evacuated during Gouraud's trap. Here, the trap had failed; instead of leaving when the French guns opened up, the Germans had dug in with every intention to stay. The French 163rd, 215th, and 363rd regiments of General Lebouc's 161st Division were already engaged in the attempt to dislodge them.

The 369th RIUS battalions received their assignment and learned that they would move into their attacking positions that evening. The men emerged from their shelters around 6:00 P.M. on July 18 and moved as soon as it got dark.

Some felt like each step toward the front was taking them further away from civilization, from everything human society had been creating and building for the last five thousand years. The front was a world of fire and smoke and life in caves, where the strength in your arms and legs, the acuity of your eyes and ears, and how hard you were willing to fight for the right to keep breathing determined how long and how well you lived. At the same time, they held dear the sense that there was something noble in the drama, a cause larger than themselves, something to fight for, not just against—that something righteous, maybe not here and now, but at the end of it, waited on the other side.

Bodies flapped, equipment clanked, boots scuffled, and men coughed. Commands were spoken softly. "Keep your head down. . . . Keep moving." Legs and backs ached. Men readjusted their rifle slings where the straps dug into their shoulders.

The First Battalion had precise orders as to what route to take and when to depart, but when they followed their orders, they found themselves in a traffic jam. Another battalion had been assigned the same route, along an exposed stone road leading across a ridge of hills where, in daylight, the men would have been clearly silhouetted against the skyline. They were somewhat safer in the dark, but the darkness could be illuminated with flares. In the previous years of fighting, German observation balloons had thoroughly surveyed the road; German batteries could easily rain down a storm of accurate fire if they chose to. Night also brought along the road an unbroken convoy of supply trucks moving ammunition and provisions to the front. Arthur Little, recently promoted to major, knew his men were vulnerable, stalled at the bull's-eye of an obvious target, but he could think of no military strategy to prevent the catastrophe he was certain would come. Believing God would not fail him, as military planners had, Little prayed for deliverance.

A few seconds later, they heard a squadron of German planes, and then on the horizon, behind the German lines, Little saw a set of signal lights lit as beacons to guide the planes to the airfield where they would need to land. There would be no artillery fire until the squadron had passed lest the enemy shoot down their own planes.

"Some of our people were of the opinion that it was the hand of God that saved our regiment that night," Little wrote. "Some others seemed to feel that it was mere coincidence that the Germans did not shell the road on account of the squadron of airplanes over our line. I believe that we owed our safety to the guiding hand of God."

When the Germans commenced shelling between 2:00 A.M. and 3:00 A.M., they were too late. The regiment had reached its destination, PC Wilson in the Vilquin sector, where they were hustled into shelters, machine guns positioned, horses unhitched.

The next morning, they waited for the whistle that would signal the counterattack. When it came, they scaled the parapet and launched themselves over the top into no-man's-land, dodging hole after hole and running from crater to crater. Geysers of earth shot skyward where the shells from the French batteries fell ahead of them, and a blue haze hung in the air. There was the smell of gas. They ran, advancing for about two kilometers, creeping forward, then dashing, not so fast as to run into the supporting barrage rolling before them but fast enough to get behind the German barrage coming toward them. They ran past the dead and the wounded, beardless blond Germans in *feldgrau* uniforms, past scattered equipment, broken guns, and punctured helmets.

"God damn, let's go" became the new battle cry.

Wounded men fell, cried out, groaned.

Men lost their way, panicked, found themselves again.

Charles Jackson, Henry Johnson's brother-in-law from Albany, ran until a shell tore his right foot off. He was one of fifty-one wounded in the counterassault. Fourteen men died.

On the evening of July 20, Charles Fillmore led Company B into position reinforcing a French battalion. Company C, led by Captain MacClinton, took heavy casualties while reinforcing the French company holding PA Christopherie, the leftmost strong point of CR Crochet. One platoon was saved from annihilation only when a sharply angled bend in the trench absorbed the energy of a direct hit, but the explosion was still sufficient to knock the lead men in the platoon violently to the ground. Shrapnel killed 1st Lt. Oscar Baker, the first officer to fall, as he led a machine gun company covering Company C.

That night and the next day, German prisoners passed through, marched by their guards to French prison camps. When the prisoners paused, the men from Harlem offered them biscuits, chocolate, and cigarettes from their own short supplies, which the "Bush Germans" greedily devoured. They were hungry and tired of fighting. They were not the relentless brutish Huns the prewar propaganda had made them out to be, just scared kids, glad to be out of the fight.

Hamilton Fish found time to write another letter home:

July 21st, 1918

Dear Virginia,

We have been having a sleepless time of it for the last two weeks preparing and waiting for the German attack but when it came we were ready for them and gave the Boche a bad beating which I hope will hasten the end of this fiendish war. My company was in the front lines the night of the attack in force. However they smothered us with shell fire and my company lost three dead, six wounded and four badly gassed. It was quite an ordeal and the men stood it well. I had several narrow escapes being hit on the helmet with shrapnel and being covered with dirt from a big shell in an open field. My horse was killed a few days ago while in a barn several miles in the rear. He was a fine powerful Bay and more or less trained to shell fire.

I hope to get my permission on Aug 1st or as soon as this Battle has become stabilized and look forward to seeing you in Paris. We are now acting as support for a French regiment in an active sector and the shells are constantly cracking over head.

Affec., Hamilton

At 2:00 P.M. on July 21, Little's First Battalion was ordered to move again to CR Fortin on at the east flank of Sous Secteur Beauséjour, recently retaken from the Germans. A team of officers went to reconnoiter the new position and figure out where they wanted to position their men. The reconnaissance team saw a shorter route than the one on the map, but it involved moving cross-country through open land. They were out of rifle range, but within range of German 77s, effectively being sniped at by cannons, shells forcing them to scramble as the German batteries tried to anticipate their next move, firing ahead of the reconnaissance team but without result.

Captain Fillmore's Company B, occupying a support command on the Marson Road, was closest to CR Fortin. The road was hidden from the Germans by a long hill with a swamp on the other side, leaving anyone who used the road relatively safe from explosive ordnance, where only a direct pinpoint hit would do damage. As the light faded, the Germans shelled the swamp, filling it with gas that formed a low fog hugging the wetlands below the road. A few of the officers on the reconnaissance team, as well as a few officers and platoon leaders from Company D, took a gassing and discovered that the substance used was not lethal, neither yperite nor phosgene but some variety of lacrymator or sternutator, merely irritating to the eyes and throat and causing headaches and nausea.

For the men, gas was gas, and they had yet to face it in such quantities. How could one know for sure whether it was lethal or not? Gas was a weapon that demoralized. Veterans thought it was not as bad as it had been made out to be—nasty for sure but something you could anticipate and protect yourself from by properly using masks and antigas procedures. To someone experiencing gas for the first time, it was terrifying. The urge was to run, not pass calmly through it.

As Charles Fillmore moved his company through the swamp to the relative safety of the higher ground and the Marson Road, he knew his men felt a growing panic. Observing the scene, Arthur Little wrote, in what was most certainly an understatement, "A number of the men yielded to various forms of extravagancies in expressions of distress." He also observed Fillmore removing his mask and intentionally taking a gassing to show his men that it was all right, then calmly and with extraordinary courage and patience guiding his men to their destination. Little and Fillmore had had a difficult relationship and a number of run-ins ever since Fillmore had complained about the lice at Camp Whitman and Little apprised him of the proper way to speak to a superior officer. Every time Little corrected Fillmore, he did so in the belief that he was acting for the good of the regiment, unable to convince Fillmore that it was neither personal nor due to his race. It was to be expected that white officers would associate with other white officers during their free time, just as black officers were more likely to form friendships with other black officers, but all the same, Charles Fillmore could well have seen Little's promotion to major as an act of racial patronage or favoritism. Fillmore's regiment had already been taken from him, and he continued to resent the demotion that came with his removal as head of the Fifteenth. Fillmore's actions on Marson Road won him the Croix de Guerre. It was Arthur Little who wrote him up for the citation.

In the third week of July 1918, they occupied the trenches at CR Fortin, renamed CR Vilquin (the renaming of sections, sectors, and centers of resistance frequently confused anyone already having trouble reading the French maps), which Germans had occupied during Gouraud's trapping maneuver, and which bore evidence that the enemy had left in a hurry. They found five-gallon vacuum food containers, rifles, bayonets, belts, helmets, machine gun barrels, a pair of fine Goetz binoculars, ammunition, overcoats, emergency rations and canned goods, gas masks, packs, shovels, picks and lanterns, and accurate German maps that explained how the German artillery batteries so often found their targets. The men from Harlem made use of what they found in the trenches or collected as souvenirs items they had no other use for. They also found the bodies of perhaps twenty dead Germans. It would have been too dangerous to seek out an open burial ground. They buried the bodies in the side wall of a trench.

By the end of July, it was clear that the German spring offensive and "victory drive" had been stopped, but at a high price in French and British lives. Pershing wrote a letter to Washington relating his opinion that the Allies were done for and could not win without American help. The French wanted to turn the defensive victory at Champagne-Marne into an offensive one that would start the Germans running and keep them running all the way back to Berlin. However, as had happened so many times during the war, reversals and counterattacks stalled at the enemy's fortified fallback positions. German morale had flagged, and they knew they were not going to reach Paris, but they still wanted to hold as much ground as they could.

Upon arriving at CR Vilquin, the Harlem regiment made preparations to stay. They repaired the damage done in the previous battle, dug out collapsed trenches, and sent teams out under the cover of darkness to repair the barbed wire entanglements protecting their lines. They sent out patrols to reduce German resistance one piece at a time, take out snipers and machine gun nests, and capture prisoners to gain information from them. Fresh troops brought in to replace the regiment's losses had to be assimilated, brought up to speed, and taught the considerable difference between Service of Supply and frontline infantry duties. Often the new men came from other colored units that had experienced strained relationships between black enlisted personnel and white officers. They brought their distrust with them. During one patrol assigned to dislodge a German machine gun, men panicked when the machine gun opened fire, dropped their weapons, and ran, which was uncharacteristic for seasoned troops. There was, in some quarters, a new grumbling in the ranks.

"Rumors and underground reports came to me," Arthur Little wrote, "that mutterings were being indulged in to the effect it was a pity that the officers of high rank couldn't be made to go upon some of these dirty missions which they seemed to be so fond of ordering for others."

It was a complaint as old as war itself, and one answered in the usual way when, as July ended, a new lieutenant named Worsham was killed. He had been leading a raid on a machine gun nest and marching at the head of a column when the machine gunner surprised him, killing Worsham and six of his men. Worsham had only joined the regiment two days earlier but was already well liked with a promising career. The men brought his body to a ruined stable; it was then carried by caisson to Valmy, ten miles to the rear, and laid to rest in a churchyard with a service at which the band played solemnly and Frank Debroit blew taps on his cornet. Arthur Little wondered at "the unhumanizing of the soldier's heart," how it was that men of God could go to war and be killed by other men of God. Perhaps the preachers and teachers of the world who spoke of war did not understand their subject matter as well as they should.

Their position at CR Vilquin again faced Butte Mesnil, where the enemy could look down on them, bringing the regiment under frequent sniper attack. Horace Pippin took an assignment one night to go after a German sniper who had been wreaking havoc on Hellfighter positions. The sniper, wherever he was, had zeroed his sights on the communication *boyau* the "soup men" were using to bring the fighting troops their food, a job that had to be done two or three times a day. They had tried adding a layer of sandbags to protect the trench, to no effect, such that the soup men got through on some days but not others, and the troops went hungry. The sentries at the observation posts were on the lookout, day and night, but could not determine where the sniper's fire was coming from. Someone had to go get him. Pippin and one of his fellow corporals volunteered, knowing their mission was akin to looking for a needle in a haystack—and dangerous, given that while they looked for him, the man with the high-powered rifle could well be looking right back at them through his telescope.

They searched all night, moving quietly, staying low, getting a feel for the ground and for the places where a sniper might hide, somewhere high enough up the hill for him to see into their lines. They heard him fire off a few rounds, his sniper rifle making a distinct sound, and they knew they were close, but they still could learn much more than that. Pippin whispered to his friend that they might have some luck at daybreak, when the sniper working the night shift would likely be relieved. Maybe, Pippin whispered, they would be able to see and kill both of them. The German snipers were the best in the war, Pippin knew. To kill one would be quite a prize.

It started to rain, and it felt like morning would never come. When daylight finally arrived, Pippin could discern the outlines of trees in the valley below where his own men were sleeping. He felt he must be close to the sniper's position. He searched the trees with his binoculars, but it was still too dark to see anything. For a moment, at a spot near a river, thinking he saw a possible sniper post, he handed his buddy the binoculars and pointed, but his buddy saw nothing. He saw another, even more likely spot.

"Out in No-Man's land there were a big tree but we could not see it good where we were at the time so I told my buddy to look out for me that I were going to get a better view of that tree," Pippin wrote.

He circled back and found a trench he knew would take him closer to the tree. Crawling out of the *boyau* and into the death zone, he found a place to hide in view of the tree he had spotted. He waited, alone, knowing that the sniper was likely to reveal himself and take a few shots at the mess sergeants as they brought up breakfast. Perhaps the sniper knew he was being hunted, or maybe he had fallen asleep; for whatever reason, no shots were fired that morning. Pippin had been up all night. He was cold and wet and exhausted and wanted to sleep, but he waited.

The rain picked up. He didn't want to be out another night in the rain. As the noon hour approached, Pippin considered abandoning his vigil and making his way back to the nearest *boyau* when he heard the sniper fire. He saw the leaves move in the tree, branches parting, then returning to their original position. He aimed his rifle at the spot in the tree where he'd seen the leaves move and fired.

He saw nothing. By firing, he'd given his own position away. If he'd missed, the sniper was likely now aiming his rifle at him. He heard the sound of someone rushing toward him, then turned to see his fellow corporal breaking through the brush. The corporal told Pippin he'd seen the sniper's body fall from the tree.

They slogged back to their dugouts, where Pippin collapsed, having nothing left. "They told us to take a good rest that night if we could get it, for they may need us for some strong work that is to come of sometime soon," he wrote. In his dugout, men were busy passing buckets of water to bail out the shelter. He made for his bed, was asleep before he knew it, and was woken up for what he thought would be dinner but which was in fact breakfast. He took a moment to appreciate the man who had woken him up for looking out for him, for making sure he had something to eat. "There is one thing about that old 15th New York infantry and that is they never fear danger and they always give one another. If there is one he looks downhearted they would cheer him up some way and that is the way we all did with one another and that way we all were in good standing."

He went outside, found a soup box to sit on, took a letter from his pocket, and reread it. The letter soon had the desired effect. "When I thought of home I would look for the letter," he later wrote. "It took all dread away of thinking about home. It made me feel good to read it. I went over it the second time, then put it away in its old place again then I go to mess."

One life Pippin may have saved by taking out the sniper who'd been firing on the supply lines was that of Pvt. G. J. Williams.

"I was detailed to what is known in the French army as the 'Train-de-combat,'" Williams recalled. "This is a little unit of the regiment that you never hear much about, but one in which men very often work all day and even all night. You have to do all sorts of work, such as carrying food, ammunition and clothing to the boys in the front line trenches even though the roads were under heavy shell and gas attack. Nothing must hinder your work, for it is very necessary for the men up front to have food and ammunition. I have seen men and horses blown right from their wagons. . . . My next move was to get caught in a bombardment of shells while working on the ammunition train. I saw men and beasts alike blown hundreds of feet in the air from exploding shells, but fortunately I came through the whole thing without a scratch."

こめ そめ

They maintained their rotations at Butte Mesnil, ten days in reserve, ten days at the front, then ten days of rest. They marched to the front and then away from it, faced danger, and turned their backs on it, marching side by side in columns of two, route step, jumping over ditches, stepping over obstacles, slipping, falling, helping each other up. They walked in the rain toward the front, passing weary French soldiers marching in the opposite direction, forage caps and greatcoats caked in mud; they made eye contact but said little beyond the usual questions replacements always asked.

"What's it like up there?"

"Ça va bien. Ça va bien."

"Forward for France!"

"Replacements," a French soldier was once heard to mutter. "For the cemetery."

They marched away from the war, up and out of the trenches, past farms and open horse stalls filled with dirty straw, chickens scuttling away at their approach, perhaps a pointy-eared sheepdog stretching and sniffing the wind, and skittish livestock kicking their hooves against their wooden stalls, a sound like distant cannons. They walked on roads grooved and rutted by the wheels of trucks and hay wains, roads pocked by horses' hooves and men's boots, between fields without hedges to mark their boundaries.

They might see, on a farm building, white numbers painted on a plank, map reference markings. Buildings hit by shells, roofs damaged, patched roughly and temporarily with boards, buildings where the plaster on the sidewall was pocked and knocked to the ground until the building's ribcage showed. On the door of a barn there might be chalk markings left by previous occupants, other units and battalions, the graffiti indecipherable. They grouped themselves in platoons and kept intervals between them, lest a single shell fall and take out the lot of them.

Away from the war, they found villages where it had been set aside, if not forgotten. In town squares, men in uniforms slept in the backs of wagons, winding themselves in waterproof ground sheeting, while girls with colorful scarves on their heads carried baskets, and old women in black garments blended into the shadows. They passed through intersections where men too old to fight shoveled stone rubble into holes in the pavement. They felt as if they'd returned to the world, where not everything was the color of mud or olive or khaki, and where people still had gardens in their yards and bean plants crawling up their poles in the heat of summer, and if a soldier passed close enough, he could reach and pull a green bean from where it grew and pop it into his mouth.

In open-air cafes, they saw officers in clean uniforms smoking tobacco in briar pipes and reading newspapers. Boys hauled water in flexible canvas buckets or sold two-day-old copies of the *Daily Mail*, sometimes even New York papers, and then the men could pause to read the headlines and see how the Lincoln Giants were doing, or the Yankees.

While at rest in villages, men were asked not to gather in groups larger than four to minimize the potential damage in the event a shell should find them. Everything was within range—the Germans had guns that could and did reach Paris—but the equation held that the farther from the front you were, the safer you were. In the rear village of Hans, a shell wounded four men from the First Battalion as they were washing themselves and their clothes, filling their bodies with fragments of sharp, jagged metal. "Such incidents were accepted as part of a normal day's activities," according to Arthur Little. "They would arouse no excitement, and but a moderate degree of interest, much less interest than that aroused by the report of an arrival of mail from home."

At rest in the villages, the men saw French girls, perhaps even exchanged a few words or a smile, but seldom more than that. Of life at the front, British writer Sir Basil Liddell-Hart wrote, "Under such tiring and chilling conditions, sexual desire was not very strongly felt by most men—contrary to the picture painted in some of the war novels—and only a small minority sought the local brothels when out of line. But many more of us missed, and felt a longing for, the sight of some attractively feminine women. That was not so much an actively sexual desire as an esthetic desire for the beauty and grace of womanhood." The U.S. Army's position on men availing themselves of prostitutes was clear. It was a restriction that, while true for white men, was doubly true for black men, even if they were serving with the French army and not the American Expeditionary Force (AEF).

"Rest" did not mean idle time or inactivity. Sometimes there were barracks to stay in, but other times, the men slept in pup tents. German planes would occasionally fly over and give them a casual strafing. Training-camp regimens still needed to be followed, with 5:00 A.M. reveille, calisthenics, breakfast, inspection, hospital call, morning reports, first call for drill, assembly, reports of the day, more drill, physical training, manual of arms, rifle instruction, parading in company, lunch and rest, bayonet drill, lectures, close order drill, final review, chow, after-dinner lectures, recreation, a 9:15 P.M. call to quarters, and taps by 9:30 P.M. Of the regiment, 40 percent were now replacement troops who were not good soldiers, "so green in their knowledge of soldierly bearing that we wondered what the officers of home training camps could be doing with their time," according to Little. They drilled and stood for ceremonies that the new replacement troops probably thought pointless, but the purpose was to inculcate group cohesion and camaraderie, in which sense the collective activity of complaining about ceremonies was as useful as the rituals being complained about. They played baseball every day and made the game part of the schedule of activities. In Hans, a rest area about ten kilometers behind the lines, they had hot showers and even a place to sterilize their clothes, rather than having to do it by hand, holding their shirts up in the sunlight to search for *totoes*, or "seam-squirrels."

Eventually, the order would come to move up again. They would gather their gear together and fall in at the jump-off point, while the officers reviewed their marching orders, the setting sun making their shadows stretch and climb the hills. They marched past the same farms they'd seen ten days earlier, past other units, men bivouacked in a field, tarps, tan canvas tents only partially camouflaged, candles inside them turning them into luminarias, casting silhouettes against the canvas of men bent to their tasks, writing letters, arranging gear, praying on their knees beside their cots. Sometimes they had French guides; other times they followed maps past places marked as villages, but where only rubble and stone remained.

They marched over pitted roads in the darkness, toward distant thudding sounds and a flickering horizon, past sentries huddled beside walls of sandbags. The only other light came from the stars overhead or the moon. Sometimes ambulances passed on the roads with their lights off, carrying the wounded to dressing stations. The men marching rarely knew how far they had come or how far they had yet to go. They put one foot in front of the other and said the few necessary things there were to say: "Watch the hole." "Watch the wire—telephone line." "Stretcher coming through." Far away, they heard the straining of a locomotive. Closer, the metallic banging of trucks bringing up rations, the squealing wheels of a supply tram.

Approaching the reserve lines or the front lines, they left the open ground and sank into the earth. They moved forward now along half-collapsed ditches, which could be seen only briefly in flickers when flares lit the black sky. Sometimes the trenches were well drained, but in other places they weren't, so they marched and sloshed through water that deepened with each step, stumbling over a submerged board that became looser every time someone stepped on it. They lost more and more of the real world as they marched, where the sandbagged walls of the trenches afforded no peripheral views. When the walls narrowed or contracted, they could see even less sky, fewer stars, until their noses gave them more information about their surroundings than their eyes did, smelling gunpowder here, gas in the gullies and hollows or where the earth was freshly disturbed.

Closer to the front, they might have seen, if there was enough moonlight, the silhouettes of trees with their tops sawed off by shell fire, forests cropped and trimmed like an army haircut, denuded and skeletal branches hanging by just their bark, swiveling and swaying in the wind, dangling from what used to be an oak or a birch, but with nothing left to catch the sunlight. The men may have wondered how many bullets it took to shoot the leaves off a tree.

Finally, the order would come to fall out. Men dropped their packs, collapsed, crouched, hugged their knees to their chests, sank into the ground to dream of sleep and wait while officers met to decide where in the labyrinth they were to be posted.

There were quiet times in the trenches when men found ways to amuse themselves. On one occasion a private named Peter Sands was playing craps in the foremost line when a German shell dropped into a nearby trench. No one was wounded, but the explosion blew their only set of dice out of the trench and into no-man's-land. Sands made a private sortie over the top to retrieve the dice and resume the game.

Another private named Nichols (possibly William O. Niccolls of F Company) was said by Maj. Lorillard Spencer to be the champion crap shooter of the outfit, so accomplished at craps, or "African golf," that he somehow kept winning money even when the regiment had gone eleven months without pay. Out of gratitude for the many things the French had taken the time to teach them, the men from Harlem returned the favor by teaching the *poilus* and Moroccans how to shoot dice. They took to the game "like ducks to water," and the money they lost tided the New Yorkers over until the paymaster showed up. The Moroccans were a tough crowd, in their khaki-yellow uniforms sporting the red shoulder braid of the Legion of Honor and the star-and-crescent spahi insignia on their collars. They were part of the "Iron Corps" that fought at Nancy, in Joseph Joffre's Champagne offensive in 1915, at Verdun, Fleury, and Thiaumont. Strict Muslims would not have partaken of alcohol, but "African golf" was another matter. The men of the 369th had great respect for the Moroccans, "one of the greatest and bravest fighting troops that I have ever come in contact with," Sgt. G. J. Williams said. "Their one belief is that in going to their death, is going to Heaven, and that is one reason of their recklessness in fighting the enemy. . . . We boys did not share this belief, altogether."

Thirty-three-year-old Pvt. Lionel W. Rogers of Company L (enlisted September 25, 1916) became one of the best hand grenade throwers in the regiment by practicing on rats, throwing light grenades at the trench vermin to improve his accuracy, even though his comrades told him the rats were "altogether too big a target." He was engaged in this activity one day while he was eating. He got butter on his fingers and lost his grip on a grenade as he threw it, dropping it at his feet, where it exploded. The charge was small but enough to send him to the hospital.

Some days, the war was more of a spectator sport. Horace Pippin recorded a dogfight overhead:

There were nothing in the sky that I could see but clouds when all at once I heard planes. I looked up and seen that it were German planes came out of the clouds over our line.

I seen another airplane coming right for the German planes then the German planes went up for the clouds. Then I seen the other one were a French plane that came from the left of there and he started after the Germans. I think that the German seen that he could not get away from the French plane so he made a down drop I think about two hundred feet then he started up. At that time the French made a circle around him and as he got over the strip of road he opened up on the German plane and all at once he were on fire and he came down to rise no more.

I went over there to see it and it were a sight to see. You could not tell what it were it were in pieces and you could not make them out. There were two men in it and they looked like mush.

That day I seen three German planes come down and one French. There were not a day that there were not a fight in the air. Some times if a bunch of men were out on the road or in a field or walking or working any place the Germans would come down in a plane and would deal out death to them.

Some men hated the trench life. Others found they loved it— and loved fighting. Some soldiers admitted freely that even though battle was generally a horrible, traumatizing experience, it could be thrilling too. The body's response to danger could result in a jolt of adrenaline that heightened the senses, sped perception, and created a feeling of tremendous power that lingered and resonated after the danger had passed. The soldier who emerged from the field successful and undamaged sometimes relived the action with more pleasure than pain. Robert E. Lee (whose grandson, Dr. George

Bolling Lee, had helped Colonel Hayward organize the regiment) had said during the American Civil War, "It is well that war is so terrible—otherwise we would grow too fond of it," a sentiment seconded by Winston Churchill, first lord of the Admiralty and a battalion commander during World War I, who said, "There is nothing more exhilarating than to be shot at without result." Pvt. William Jackson was so fond of battle that he was brought before a court-martial for refusing a direct order to participate in a parade review for General Gouraud, which was to be followed by a chicken dinner and all the wine he could drink. In his defense, Jackson said he didn't want to attend the review because it would have meant missing the opportunity to kill Huns—that was what he was there for, and he didn't want to miss a day. Colonel Hayward, who presided over Private Jackson's hearing, not only let him go but gave him a new bolo knife and a whetstone to keep it sharp.

The feeling Jackson craved, the feeling that followed victory in combat, was a just reward that came to those who saved their own lives and those of their comrades. "Watching another man die is a terrible thing," Noble Sissle had written. But to survive, to prevail— that brought an entirely different feeling, terrible in the pleasure it gave to cause another man's death.

Sgt. William Butler learned the feeling on the night of August 12. A slight, good-natured nineteen-year-old from Salisbury, Maryland, with narrow features, thin lips, and an aquiline nose, he was manning a machine gun post at Sous Secteur Beauséjour. Men had received letters from loved ones back home asking questions: Was it true that Negro regiments were being abused by their white officers? Was it true that the colored regiments were being assigned to the most dangerous sectors? (Though being assigned to a "dangerous sector" meant you were going where you were most needed.) There were rumors in Harlem that the Germans had vowed to torture all captured Negroes. Another claimed that over two hundred black soldiers had been found wandering in no-man's-land with their eyes gouged out and their arms amputated. According to the story, having been taken prisoner by the Germans, then turned loose and sent back to the American lines as a warning, they were now being treated at the Columbia Base Hospital No. 1 up in the Bronx. Yet another rumor held that the Germans loved colored people and that if they won the war, they were going to set up a colony for Negroes somewhere down south, a place where colored people could make their own rules. The rumors were the product of German propaganda, perpetrated by provocateurs, but many found it hard to separate truth from fiction.

William Butler only knew that there were Germans in front of him who were trying to kill him. There had been an increase in artillery activity on the night of August 12, which often signaled an attack or raid would soon follow.

Then Butler heard a skirmish coming from a combat post behind him, where Lt. A. M. Jones had been taken prisoner just as he was lighting a star shell, along with five of his men.

Butler turned to see a group of men headed his way. Someone to his left fired a Veery pistol, sending a flare high in the air. In the dim light of the flare, Butler saw a squadron of Germans, a raiding party of about twenty or thirty soldiers, who'd captured the five colored enlisted men and their officer. They were headed straight for Butler, using a communication trench to return to their lines. Butler calmed himself, knowing he needed to wait until the raiding party was directly in front of him.

The Germans were twenty yards off, the prisoners grouped together in the middle, prodded along by guards with bayonets.

"Look out!" Butler shouted.

"Don't fire, Sergeant," Lieutenant Jones called back.

"Not yet Sir, but soon," Butler replied.

Jones and his men fell to cover.

"Now, Sergeant," Jones called back.

Butler opened up, first taking out the Germans leading the column, then, seeing a German lieutenant aiming his pistol, swinging the barrel of his "sho-sho" around and firing to clip the German at the knees. The raiding party fled in various directions. Butler squeezed off a few more rounds, then ran to rescue the American prisoners. He captured the German lieutenant alive, but the man later died from his injuries. Butler was believed to have killed perhaps as many as ten Germans and wounded countless others, for which he was awarded the Croix de Guerre.

"I must have run amuck," Butler said later.

⁓⊘ ⊘⁓

By the end of the summer of 1918, Horace Pippin felt inured to danger, not reckless but increasingly fearless. One night he went out with a small raiding party to get Germans, just because there were too many of them, and he planned to bring them back as prisoners or leave them dead in no-man's-land. It was a typical miserable night in the killing zone, cold and rainy and dark, but Pippin saw this as an advantage—there wasn't a man in France who wanted to be in no-man's-land that night, he reasoned, whereas he was largely indifferent to the conditions. The terrain was difficult, with the topography of an egg carton, all holes and hills, barbed wired and ankle-high trip wires. When a flare lit the sky from the German side, they laid low, waiting eagerly, not in fear, knowing the flare might mean a German patrol was coming. "Now it were to get Gerry's patrol if they were out."

Gerry was out. As if to prove it, a machine gun opened up on them, sending them scurrying for cover.

"We all laid low for a short time until the Looey told us to get that man so we made for him one by one until he were in the middle of us and then we closed in on him. He did not know we were up until a gun were at his head and he never said a word but threw up his hands and he were taken to our line."

One prisoner wasn't enough. They decided to lie in wait at a place where a German patrol was likely to pass. Pippin was cold, soaked to the bone, the water running down his rifle.

"It were not long to wait. I could hear voices but I could not see anything and we did not know how strong they were. Out of the blackness of the night came a sound like an owl. Hoo hoo, three times. It were not answered by any other for he were not there. They were looking for that man on the machine gun. They knew he were near there, so we answered him back. Hoo hoo that went back the sound of the owl. It were not long before I could hear them close at hand. We all knew what to do. There were nine of them in all. When they came up every man were covered so when they were told to throw up their hands they did so at once."

By the time they returned to their own trenches, multiple German machine guns were firing on them, bullets ringing off the barbed wire. Pippin wrote, "It sounded like birds chirping. They kept at it until day break."

꧁ ꧂

It would have been difficult enough, had they only Germans to fight. The 369th was, however, fighting a battle on two fronts, and all was not quiet on the racial front. There was discontent within the officers' ranks for reasons common in military units of any color, where ambitious officers occasionally feel they're being unfairly held back, or someone else is being unfairly promoted, or officers simply lose respect for one another or realize they can't get along. There had been tension between Charles Fillmore and Arthur Little over the lice situation at Camp Whitman and elsewhere, as well as between Fillmore and his fellow black officer Lt. James Lacey.

Both Fillmore and Lacey asked for transfers. Hamilton Fish, ever the politician, did not ask Hayward for a transfer but went over his head and wrote an exploratory letter to the commander of the white Seventy-eighth Division asking if there was a place for him. The officers of the 369th did not necessarily feel that things were unsatisfactory within the regiment; rather, they believed there might be better opportunities elsewhere. For colored officers, "elsewhere" meant one of the other regiments (the 370th, the 371st, or the 372nd) within the Ninety-third Division (Colored), no longer stateside but recently arrived. The 371st comprised largely poor, rural, colored draftees from Southern states—Georgia, Alabama, and North and South Carolina—where the draft had been postponed to accommodate the cotton harvest, and it was led entirely by white Southern officers who "knew how to handle blacks." The 370th and 372nd regiments, however, had black officers ranking all the way up to colonel. The four regiments from the other colored combat division, the Ninety-second, had also arrived and presented potential occasions for advancement.

For some of the officers within the 369th, advancement seemed remote. Other commanders from other regiments had sent non-commissioned sergeants stateside to attend officer training schools. Hayward, already shorthanded with only about one-third of the officers the army recommended, did not want to lose the leadership already in place and did not send anybody stateside. When company commanders recommended two sergeants, Henry Cheatham and Ben Cheeseman (the sergeant whose lifejacket Jim Europe had accidentally donned on the trip across the Atlantic), for promotion in the field, Hayward declined, explaining that he needed them where they were, particularly because they were in combat and under attack, holding their own, and, considering the setbacks and handicaps they'd had to overcome, doing well. Colonel Hayward did not care to tamper with what was by all accounts a healthy regimental morale or to fix something that was not, in his opinion, broken.

The War Department was, however, quite willing to do so.

The most die-hard pragmatists within the military would have been forced to admit that there had been problems with getting black men and officers to work together with white officers, enlisted personnel, and civil authorities. The riot in Houston was only the most publicized example. The trouble the Fifteenth New York National Guard had at Camp Dix or Camp Mills had been repeated at other camps (in Manhattan, Kansas, a black soldier tried to buy a movie ticket in a theater and was officially reprimanded for being in the wrong place). In training camps, segregation was inconvenient but theoretically feasible, where the army built separate barracks and separate mess facilities—such separation was not feasible on the battlefield. What would happen, in the chaos of battle, if armed black and white men found themselves fighting side by side?

The die-hard racists within the military had been undermining black troops and sabotaging their chances for success from the start. Instances of black units being given inadequate housing, clothing, equipment, or training were almost too numerous to count. There had been bias in selective service procedures, where eligible colored men were not granted the same exemptions as whites, such that in some Southern states, more blacks than whites were inducted. At camps where blacks were forced to train near white troops, the War Department made sure there were always twice as many whites as blacks, keeping what it considered a "safe ratio." Biased intelligence tests concluded that the African Americans had a "mental age" of about ten—whites had a mental age of about thirteen, but perhaps that's what you get when you let someone with a mental age of thirteen design an intelligence test. The perception persisted that colored troops had inadequate physical stamina to serve in combat, despite the testimony of white officers who had actually served with black troops.

"Of my knowledge I can testify that the impression so frequently expressed to the effect that the colored man cannot or will not stand physical hardship is just buncombe," Arthur Little wrote—strong language, for him. "If our men believed that going without food was unavoidable, they would never complain of hunger. If our men were satisfied that new shoes were unavailable for issue they would march all day (and cheerfully) with their bare feet touching the ground through the broken soles of their old shoes."

Black officers were not regarded or treated much better than black enlistees by the same die-hard racists within the military, many of whom came from the same stock as the hotel proprietor in Spartanburg. None of the fourteen officer training schools extant in 1914 admitted blacks, and when one was built especially for them in Des Moines during the war, none of the 639 officers commissioned received a rank higher than captain. The army was committed to preventing whites and blacks of equal rank from serving together. Sometimes white junior officers refused to salute blacks of higher rank and said instead, "Howdy, Uncle." Other times blacks of superior rank were ordered to salute whites of lower rank.

Despite Fillmore's complaints, black and white officers had worked together well in the 369th. In other units, they did not. In other units, black accusations of favoritism among white officers drastically undermined morale (in one regiment, white officers who shared a common barracks with blacks hung a curtain across the room and took the larger portion), as did accusations by white officers that black officers were unqualified, the result of tokenism, and required too much supervision. In the 369th, the white leadership did not expect their black officers or enlisted men to be perfect and forgave them when, to recall Spartanburg, they formed armed bands and surrounded police stations. In other units, racist white officers seized upon the slightest excuse to punish black junior officers or enlisted men, and too often, peers accused any black soldier or officer trying to make accommodations or avoid misunderstandings of Uncle Tom–ism or of collaborating with the enemy—not the German enemy, the other enemy. Officers distrusted each other, and the enlisted men had little faith that they were being led wisely by competent leaders.

If the behavior of French military officers held a mirror to racist factions within the U.S. War Department, those factions chose not to look in the mirror. Some within the American military establishment were unhappy about the relationships developing between French officers and civilians and black American soldiers; rather, they were unhappy *that* relationships had been developing between them, cordial collaborations based on concepts like mutual respect and fair treatment, those silly French notions of *fraternité, egalité,* and *liberté* ("Liberté chérie," "La Marseillaise" said, "Combats avec tes défenseurs . . ."). The French had repeatedly been observed saluting black officers, allowing black enlisted personnel to shake their hands, look them in the eye, and talk to their women. It had to stop, the white racists thought, before the black Americans got the wrong idea. Perhaps the French simply didn't know any better.

To that end, a document entitled "Secret Information Concerning Black American Troops" was drafted at AEF headquarters but disseminated by a French colonel named Linard on August 14, 1918 (shortly after William Butler had single-handedly fought off a German raiding party and rescued five prisoners and three months after "The Battle of Henry Johnson"). Linard explained the situation to his fellow French officers: as there were fifteen million black American citizens, America stood the risk of "race mongrelization" and interbreeding. The document essentially forgave France, a country without a large black population and therefore with no reason to fear miscegenation. Thus, the French were friendly and tolerant toward colored people. The document advised them not to try to superimpose such subversive notions on the Americans, because in America, the situation was different.

"The black man is regarded by the white American as an inferior being with whom relations of business or service only are possible," the document explained. It put in writing all of the malicious stereotypes that had victimized black Americans for centuries: blacks lacked intelligence, discretion, conscience, and morals, and they had a "tendency toward undue familiarity" with women. "The vices of the Negro are a constant menace to the American who has to repress them sternly. We may be courteous and amiable . . . but we cannot deal with them on the same plane with white American officers without deeply offending the latter."

"Qu'elles ne gâtent pas les nègres," Linard warned. "Don't spoil the Negroes." Doing so could, he cautioned, hurt the war effort by reducing American public support for the French cause. The document suggested that the French not eat, meet, or converse with black soldiers, shake hands, or do anything "outside the requirements of military service."

The French assembly later investigated the release of Linard's "Secret Information" and considered it actionable; in that sense they took it seriously. The French officers who worked beside the black American soldiers in the field did not take it seriously, nor did they change their un-American friendly ways.

⁓❧ ☙⁓

After the German Bastille Day initiative had been stopped, Pershing decided to restructure his colored troops and give black units either all white or all black officers, ordering in mid-July that the 369th's black field officers be replaced by whites. Capt. Charles Fillmore, 1st Lt. James Lacey, and 2nd Lt. Lincoln Reid were transferred to the all-colored 370th Regiment. Capt. Napoleon Marshall was sent to the 365th Regiment of the Ninety-second Division, where it was hoped his leadership would bring stability and order to a troubled group. Lt. Jim Europe was also transferred to the Ninety-second Division. Hayward protested to AEF headquarters, arguing that his men had been through too much together in the heat of battle to shake things up now, but he successfully retained only Jim Europe after explaining that he needed Europe to conduct the band.

"Our colored officers," Hayward later wrote, "were in the July fighting and did good work, and I felt then and feel now, that if colored officers are available and capable, they, and not white officers, should command colored troops. . . . There is splendid material there. I sent away forty-two sergeants in France who were commissioned officers in other units. I would have sent others, but they declared they'd rather be sergeants in the Fifteenth than lieutenants or captains in other regiments."

Negro war correspondent Ralph Tyler took a balanced view, filing in his report,

> To one who is here on the scene, and who knows of countless number of white officers who are daily being transferred to units and assignments which they would not themselves have selected, and of some having been peremptorily shorn of their rank on the field of battle, the "rule" carries no evidence of "exception" due to racial discrimination. *So far as I have been able to ascertain all transfers are made for the good of the service, regardless as to whether the ones transferred are white or colored.*
>
> The number of colored commissioned officers discharged, or transferred from their units, has been negligible when compared with the number of white officers honorably and dishonorably discharged and transferred, even when the proportionate number of each is considered.
>
> This is war over here—actual, not theoretical war, and its prosecution to the earliest conclusion is so urgent that commanding generals have no time to consider racial problems, even if they were, ordinarily, so inclined to do.

The enlisted men were privy neither to Pershing's private thoughts and strategic decisions nor to Hayward's. A copy of Colonel Linard's "Secret Instructions" was sent to members of the black press in Harlem and did not stay secret after that, but the men in France remained unaware of the document. The enlisted personnel—Henry Johnson, Needham Roberts, William Butler, Horace Pippin, G. J. Williams, Herbert White, John Graham, James Turpin, John A. Jamieson, Peter Sands, Lionel Rogers of Company L, Pvt. William Jackson, eager to kill Huns, and Pvt. James Henry Jackson from Huntington, Long Island—knew only that men they liked and respected were gone. In their place were strangers, white men who had yet to earn their trust and respect, white men who had spent less time at the front than they, who had not endured what they had at Spartanburg or at St. Nazaire, who had neither suffered what they had suffered nor seen what they had seen.

Captain Fillmore, the "Old Man of the Regiment" with his familiar white moustache, was gone, replaced as the head of Company B by a Capt. Aaron T. Bates. There was a fresh young lieutenant named George Robb, and another professional baseball player, Leon Cadore, a right-handed pitcher for the Brooklyn Robins, had been transferred to Company G. How would he do pitching against Spots Poles? some must have wondered.

They knew little about why their colored officers had been replaced. In any event, they would have to soldier on.

For some of the new white officers transferred to the colored regiment, leading black men was a new experience. First Lt. Herbert Schabacker from Nebraska wrote to his parents, "I do my share of translating French orders that were turned over to me . . . but a good deal of my time is spent with the men on post. Being Colored men, they are a little scary but let them see that their officers are willing to go there with what they must they will follow him thru anything and you would be surprised at their confidence in me. . . . I have heard when this Regiment went over the top and one of the officers was wounded and fell, twelve men rushed up to him to help him in spite of the fact that the earth was being churned up by machine gun bullets."

The men had held the sectors assigned them against the German spring offensive and the Bastille Day attack. They had become an effective fighting force. Though not sure what would be asked of them next, they had heard rumors, and one in particular excited them: the American First Army—eight hundred thousand men with another half million on the way—was going to make a major assault on Metz, near the southern terminal of the Hindenburg Line, where they would hopefully retake the St. Mihiel salient southeast of Verdun. According to the rumor, the well-seasoned 369th, having seen 130 days of combat, was going to be part of the assault, transferred from the French Fourth Army and reunited with their own army.

Hamilton Fish thought that, rather than join the regular army, the 369th would receive a well-deserved vacation. He wrote to his father,

> I hope to get to Paris towards the end of Sept. There is nothing to do here but attend lectures, study maps, and take exams. We get no more news about the war than you do. I believe the Regt. will be taken from the line soon and sent to the South for a six month rest but I hope that I will not be ordered to join it again. I have had all I want of certain persons.

The certain person Fish refers to was probably Colonel Hayward, who had blocked all of Fish's efforts to gain promotion.

On the night of August 25, the regiment was ordered to assemble in the town of Somme-Bionne, a small village well south of the fighting lines, where they were loaded onto canvas-topped trucks driven by Singhalese drivers and told to prepare for a "secret mission." They were prepared to kill more Huns, despite the leaflets the German airplanes were dropping over their lines:

> Hello, boys, what are you doing over here? Fighting the Germans? Why? Have they ever done you any harm?
>
> Of course some white folks and the lying English-American papers told you that Germany ought to be wiped out for the sake of humanity and Democracy. What is Democracy? Personal freedom; all citizens enjoying the same rights as the white people do in America, the land of freedom and Democracy, or are you not rather treated over there as second class citizens?

Can you get into a restaurant where white people dine? Can you get a seat in a theater where white people sit? Can you get a seat or a berth in a railroad car, or can you even ride in the South in the same street car with the white people?

And how about the law? Is lynching and the most horrible crimes connected therewith a lawful proceeding in a Democratic country? Now all this is different in Germany, where they do like colored people; where they treat them as gentlemen and as white men, and quite a number of colored people have fine businesses in Berlin and other German cities. Why, then, fight the Germans?

seven

The Guns
of Autumn

*We were all down in the dugout smoking and telling stories from one to
the other and I were on my bunk taking it easy and looking at the smoke
going up and thinking of the good old U.S.A. and wondering about
Broadway. I thought I could see them bright lights shining when a boy
said to me I wish I were home so that I would see my mother for I have
not seen her now for fifteen years or more so I said there is no one in
France that would not give anything just to have one hour for homeward
to use to see her. I would give it myself if I had a chance to do it.*
—HORACE PIPPIN

Lt. James Reese Europe's war, at least the combat portion of it, was
over after the gassing he took while leading his machine gun
company. His lungs were expected to recover, but not to the extent
that he could bear the rigors of combat. Noble Sissle mentions nothing of damage to Europe's eyes, which indicates he probably inhaled
a mild dose of phosgene rather than mustard gas. The early symptoms of a phosgene gassing include a gripping feeling in the chest as
the gas penetrates the cell walls in the lung capillaries to produce
acid in the corpuscle membranes where it interacts with water. It
causes bleeding in the lungs and, in fatal dosages, a suffocating,

drowning sensation. Lighter doses still cause lung damage and leave a man weakened, often suffering from malaise, though Europe evidenced no sign of that. He was glad to learn that, thanks to Col. William Hayward's pleading with American Expeditionary Force (AEF) headquarters, rather than being transferred to another regiment, he would be allowed to stay on as the leader of the band.

On August 18, however, Europe was asked to take the band to Paris to participate in a concert at the Théâtre des Champs-Élysées. The band performed jumping syncopated tunes, new versions of the familiar songs "Over There," "When I Get Back to the USA," and "I Don't Know Where I'm Going but I'm on My Way," and jazzy songs the listeners hadn't heard before. They likely performed some of the arrangements Europe had been working on in the hospital, such as "On Patrol in No Man's Land," "I've an Observation Tower of My Own," and "Everything Reminds Me of You." The band played so well that their stay in Paris was extended for another eight weeks at the request of AEF headquarters. Hayward complained that the AEF was acting as if the regiment's handpicked band was its own private orchestra.

Entertainment restored morale, and the troops on leave in Paris were going to need all the restorative entertainment they could get for the fall counteroffensive. The band played for American soldiers, British, French, Italians, Belgians, striking up each country's national anthem and rousing the patriotism of their listeners. They played for celebrities as well, played their swinging version of "La Marseillaise" for French prime minister Raymond Poincaré, for the British ambassador Lord Derby, and for Mrs. Theodore Roosevelt Jr., who shook Europe's hand after the show.

"Everywhere we gave a concert, it was a riot," Europe told a reporter from the *New York Tribune*, "but the supreme moment came in the Tuileries Gardens, where we gave a concert in conjunction with the greatest bands in the world—the British Grenadiers' Band, the band of the Garde Républicain, and the Royal Italian Band. My band, of course, could not compare with any of these, yet the crowd, and it was such a crowd as I never saw anywhere else in the world, deserted them for us. We played to 50,000 people, at least, and, had we wished it, we might be playing yet."

At the Tuileries Gardens concert, they played "Dixie," "St. Louis Blues," and W. C. Handy's "Memphis Blues," a tune Jim Europe had once played solo and slowly on piano during intermissions at Vernon and Irene Castle shows. The forms were new, the rhythms exotic, the dynamics and the pure showmanship astonishing—even the sounds the instruments made seemed strange and inexplicable, the trumpets seeming to buzz, the trombones making quacking wah-wah sounds as if trying to speak French. Afterward, the French musicians who'd heard the show wanted to examine the band's instruments, certain they must have been modified—there had to be a trick. The bandmaster for the Garde Républicain asked to see the sheet music for "Memphis Blues" and examined it, hoping it would reveal the secrets of Europe's sound, then taught his band to perform the music and asked Jim Europe to listen. The French band played the notes superbly, and yet the music lacked that . . . *je ne sais quoi* that the men from Harlem brought to the score.

"The piece doesn't sound like we heard it," the French bandmaster said, whereupon Europe picked up a horn and demonstrated how to mute the bell, how to shape the embouchure and swirl the tongue—how to make the instrument speak a whole new language.

It is impossible to pinpoint the single moment when jazz arrived in France, but the concert at the Tuileries Gardens remains a prime candidate.

Jim Europe felt pangs of guilt for not being with his men in the line, but he was glad to be safe. In mid-September, he wrote his sister, "I am very contented that I am with the band. . . . I spent five months in the trenches and God was with me, for I had some miraculous escapes, for unless I walk into some lost stray shot I'll come back to you and ma."

Noble Sissle's combat days were over as well, at least temporarily. He had accepted an appointment from Colonel Hayward to attend officer training; yet, he managed to find time to perform with the band, and wrote to Eubie Blake in New York, "Well old boy hang on then we will be able to knock them cold after the war. It will be over soon. Jim and I have Paris by the balls in a bigger way than anyone you know."

"Anyone you know" may have been a reference to Willie "The Lion" Smith, a ragtime piano player from Harlem and a champion cutter in the carving contests at the Marshall Hotel who'd been making a bit of a name for himself leading the Ninety-second Division's 350th "Black Devils" regimental band.

Back home, Eubie Blake was only one of countless African Americans trying to follow the progress of their special troops as reported in the black newspapers, which followed the progress of the war in general but focused on the home team, particularly the exploits of the 369th. Baltimore's *Afro-American* said of William Butler, under the headline "Trenton Has Nothing on Salisbury,"

Trenton, New Jersey, may have her Needham Roberts, but it takes Salisbury, Maryland, to produce a William Butler. Roberts had his comrade, Henry Johnson, to help him in repulsing a raiding party of Germans, but Butler took care of a German lieutenant and squad of Boches all by himself. Herbert Corey, a white newspaper correspondent, in telling of the incident said that Butler came "a-roaring and fogging, through the darkness with his automatic, and nobody knows how many Germans he killed. It was for this that General Pershing awarded him the Distinguished Service Cross recently and the citation read: 'Sgt. William Butler, Company L, 369th Infantry (A. S. No. 104464). For extraordinary heroism in action near Maison de Champagne, France, August 18, 1918. Sergeant Butler broke up a German raiding

party which had succeeded in entering our trenches and cap-
turing some of our men. With an automatic rifle he killed
four of the raiding party and captured or put to flight the re-
mainder of the invaders.' Home address, Mrs. Jennie Butler, Water Street, Salisbury, [Maryland]."

The rest of the State of Maryland and the whole United
States now has its hat off to Butler of Salisbury.

News of Henry Johnson's struggle of the previous May had
spread nationwide after Irvin Cobb's story "Young Black Joe" appeared in the August 25 issue of the *Saturday Evening Post*. The magazine was still on the newsstands when the New York papers, the
New York Age and the *New York World* in particular, told of Sgt.
William Butler's solo heroics, charging the German raiding party
and rescuing several of his mates. The *New York Times*, reporting on
the troop buildup in anticipation of a fall counteroffensive, mentioned the Negro soldiers fighting side by side with the French.

It was not only the Northern newspapers that were noticing and
acknowledging the contributions being made by African American
troops. An editorialist for the Raleigh, North Carolina, *State Journal* wrote,

Troop trains that weekly go through Raleigh . . . have been
accustomed along the route to drop the heroic boys down
in the cities where the populace could briefly see them and
cheer them as they leave their country. . . .

But there is one black hero who goes through every
time two whites do and we hear nothing of him. That is
the chocolate soldier who sits wedged into a stuffy day
coach and waits until the snail-like trains back him from
the station to put out on the main line. Nearly all of these
black boys have been drafted and put into uniform to fight
across the trackless waste of water for an abstraction which

is well-nigh stranger to them at home. A few colored friends may know of their coming and there is a short good-bye at the stations. But the great heart of a municipality is lost to them and they must go to war without any of the cheers that so freely and lovingly are given to the white men with whom they eventually will fight.

It isn't right and it should be ended this day.

The colored boys should be allowed to get off the cars, march through the city and receive the plaudits of all the people for whom they fight. . . . If there be whites who withhold their own enthusiasm lest it spoil a "dam [*sic*] nigger," then let the colored soldier have the streets for a moment while his own cheer him.

W. E. B. DuBois used military imagery when he spoke of the relations between the races as the war drew to what all hoped would be a prompt and permanent close, saying, "Let us, while the war lasts, forget our special differences and close ranks shoulder to shoulder with our white fellow citizens. . . . We make no ordinary sacrifice, but we make it gladly and willingly with our eyes lifted to the hills."

The regiment did not know what sorts of unordinary sacrifices they would be asked to make when they departed on the night of August 25 on what they were told was a secret mission. The French were moving them somewhere—or else giving them back to the AEF. Something big was happening. Rumors claimed that the Allies would attack the Germans in a fall offensive that would include, for the first time, the full American complement. The 369th had been in the front lines for about 130 days and were in no hurry to get to the next battle.

Departing Somme-Bionne, they boarded about 150 camions, or canvas-covered trucks, formed battalion convoys, and headed south-southwest, a direction those who consulted their compasses knew would not take them to Metz or the St. Mihiel salient. Each convoy was led by a French guide who would speed ahead in the darkness in his touring car to direct traffic at the unlit intersections. They arrived in the town of Courtisols, about ten kilometers to the east of Chalons, at 3:00 A.M. and bedded down at daybreak. They marched sixteen to eighteen kilometers south on August 27, billeting by battalions in the towns of Sarry and Sogny. On August 28, they marched twenty kilometers south again, some of them perhaps recalling those early days two years before when they'd paraded with broomsticks in the streets of Harlem. They divided up to billet in small villages— Vatry, Bussy-Lettrée, Compertz, Fontaine-sur-Coole, Vésigneul-sur-Coole, and Faux-sur-Coole—where they stayed all the following day, resting, attending to blisters, and writing letters, having been advised that rather than reuniting with the American army, they could look forward to a month of "drill and peaceful pursuits."

On August 30, 1918, they marched another thirty kilometers south through the villages of Coole, Humbauville, and Dompret, down a long, arrow-straight road marked "Ancien Chemin des Romains," to St. Ouen Camp, where they settled in, expecting to stay for a while. The numerous new replacement troops required intense rifle training if they were going to be effective in the trenches. They drilled, told the new men who'd transferred in from Service of Supply battalions the things the French had told them, got them up to speed. The new white officers who'd replaced the regiment's black officers caught up on their paperwork and tried to get to know their noncoms. They attended religious services led by visiting "colored clergymen of high standards" who "valiantly set about the missions to move the hearts of men—who for months had been trained to do the business of the devil—to the worship of God." St. Ouen Camp offered, by several measures, the most pleasant accommodations the men had had since arriving in France. It was the sort of place a man could get used to, though after spending four months in the trenches, they knew better than to get too comfortable.

A dust-covered French courier on a motorcycle arrived in the afternoon of September 7 bearing orders that confirmed it was indeed too good to be true. The regiment was to move again to the front to join the fall offensive. The next day brought a long, hard march north, moving more than thirty kilometers, past a prison camp where German prisoners stared at them through the wire, regarded the *blutlustige schwärzen*, many seeing them up close and in daylight for the first time. They passed through the city of Vitry-le-François, singing as they marched, according to Arthur Little, who did not record exactly what they sang, but one song attributed to colored soldiers in France went

> *Roll, Jordan, roll—roll, Jordan, roll—*
> *Soldier, you'll be called on*
> *To shake that thing you're sittin' on,*
> *There's a battle being fought in the Argonne,*
> *Roll, Jordan, roll*
> *Pray for forgiveness, Pray for forgiveness—*
> *Pray for forgiveness—*
> *That's all a poor black sinner can do*

On the evening of September 9, they boarded camions again to move by wheel, passing through Chalons in the wee hours of the night, to La Croix-en-Champagne and finally to barracks at Somme-Bionne, where they received orders to relieve a battalion from the 215th French Infantry at CR Crochet, one quarter-sector west from Vilquin in Subsector Beauséjour. Having come full circle, they were back where they finished their last tour and no longer entertained hopes of rejoining the AEF.

By September, the Allies, led by Allied Supreme Commander Ferdinand Foch, believed the Germans could finally be dislodged from their fortifications and pushed back across the Rhine. In the German spring offensive, German troops making rapid advances

had stopped not because they'd outdistanced their support lines but
because they'd lost heart. They paused to loot villages when they
could have taken more ground—German morale was believed to be
faltering.

With the addition of American forces, the Allies finally outnumbered the Germans. On the *L*-shaped front, the British held the
upper portion of the long arm, the French manned the tangents at
the axis, and the AEF was given the far end of the lower arm, near
Verdun, a section that was still active but not at 1916 levels. The
369th, with the French Fourth Army, manned the western portion
of the lower arm, abutting the AEF at the Argonne forest, a ten-by-
thirty-mile landscape of broken woodlands, ridges, ravines, and thick
copses, bounded on the east by the Aire river and on the west by the
Aisne. West of the divide between French and American sections,
the 369th faced Butte Mesnil, the town of Ripont, the Dormoise
river beyond that, then Bellevue Ridge and the town of Sechault.
East of the Argonne, the AEF faced German fortifications at Mont-
faucon, high ground commanding a view of the battlefields below
and of Verdun, fifteen miles further east, with the St. Mihiel salient
beyond that, a bump in the line that Gen. John Pershing had to
smooth out before he could move forward elsewhere. Pershing's
forces outnumbered German troops by a factor thought to be as
high as eight to one, but outnumbered German troops had withstood
assaults before, in a war that had long favored defensive over offensive positions. Furthermore, railroads behind the German lines allowed them to move reinforcements, supplies, and guns rapidly and
efficiently to where they were needed, while the Allies had to rely
on roads that grew more and more impassible during an unusually
rainy September.

The Americans brought more than numbers to the front—they
brought faith and a renewed energy. Yet, the British and French had
learned, very much the hard way, that battles were seldom won by
dint of team spirit alone. With the AEF to the east and the French

Fourth (joined by the colored 369th, 371st, and 372nd regiments) to the west, the two great armies each had the other's flank, presenting traditional problems of military strategy where if one of the Allies allowed the enemy to penetrate, the other would be left vulnerable to attack from two sides, a situation that could be mirrored if one faction advanced rapidly but the other did not keep up. In other words, Pershing would have to rely on his black troops, whether he liked it or not.

The First Battalion moved into the forward trenches of Quartier Secteur Crochet to replace the Fifth Battalion of the French 215th Infantry soon after dark on September 11 and managed to get a good night's sleep. A French commandant named Salerou turned over his command at noon the next day, September 12, but left his adjunct, a Captain O'Byrne, to stay on as liaison and adviser. O'Byrne and Little spent the day visiting the various companies and apprising them of the situation, which in Quartier Secteur Crochet was a precarious one, with no redoubt positions and no reserve troops to call upon if the First Battalion found itself overwhelmed or overrun. The mud was anywhere from two to six inches deep, making it difficult to walk, let alone fight.

All was peaceful until 6:15 P.M., when the Germans loosed what was known as a "projector attack," two or three hundred close-range mortars firing all at the same time, projecting gas shells onto the entire length of the front line, with the intention of catching and killing as many men as possible at evening stand-to, followed by a heavy shelling with explosive ordnance in a three-part sequence: first on the trenches at the front to kill or scatter anyone the gas shelling hadn't killed, then shelling the communication trenches to kill any reserves rushing forward, and finally firing heavily on the second lines to kill or pin down reserves scrambling to assist the troops at the front line, who would fall under attack from German infantry once the first barrage in the sequence had done its work.

The German infantry assault failed to even reach the trenches where the 369th had dug in. The Hellfighters were, by now, as tough and seasoned as anyone on the line, and they lived up to their nickname.

Within a few minutes, the French batteries answered, 75s and 90s flashing fire each time they discharged. French gunners calculated their angles, plotted trajectories, and scribbled logarithms on soggy paper. There was a brief moment of panic when an errant signal flare appeared to report the presence of Germans in the trenches.

Maj. Arthur Little had cracked a pair of ribs and was recovering in his *boyau* with bandages wrapped tightly around his chest when a Lieutenant Webb told him some of his men from Company D had captured some German prisoners. Little said to send them in as he wanted to interrogate them. Something was lost in the communication. Two prisoners were indeed sent in, but no guards from the regiment accompanied them. Little's pistol hung in its holster from a nail at the foot of his bed. The prisoners were huge men, one with his arm in a sling. Little could hardly move and, for a bad moment, realized there was nothing to stop the Germans from taking his pistol and shooting him.

Then a guard entered, the smallest private Little had ever seen, and pressed his gun to the spine of one of the prisoners. Relieved, Little asked the private what had happened.

"You see, Sir Major, Sir," the soldier replied, "I was sent out on a patrol with Lieutenant McNish, and pretty soon, out in front of . . . C Company . . . we sees a patrol coming towards us. It was pretty dark, and the lieutenant, he motions for us all to keep quiet and to lay down. The other patrol just kept coming, and pretty soon we all sees these Bush Germans, and then the lieutenant gives the order to fire, and we all let 'em have it good. Some of 'em was hit. We could all see it. And some run away. And then we closed in and took some prisoners. I don't rightly know how many there was altogether. The lieutenant just tells me to bring in the prisoners and I came. When we started, there was five of 'em, but they was such big fellers, I just thought I'd better clean 'em out a bit."

Horace Pippin drew an assignment to go after a machine gunner. Now a corporal, he was put in charge of the raid. He found the men he wanted to take with him and had them ready by 9:00 P.M. It was dark but still too early to move. He lit a cigarette and had a smoke, realizing his men, some of them young replacement troops, were looking to him for leadership, and he knew he needed to set a proper example.

"I knew we did not have much time by now. I never gave danger a thought. I always try to keep in good cheer in danger and every one that is to go with me tonight do not fear it or go bad for we always look for a good part on the bad part of everything," Pippin later wrote.

They wondered how to get the German machine gunner to open up and reveal his position. It was solved simply enough. He fired on them the moment they went over the top. They moved forward, one by one. It was a moonless night, so dark they could hardly see each other.

"Now we were in for it," Pippin wrote. "It were all we could do to make it from one shell hole to another and we did it one by one. I can't say how far we were from the boyau that we were to go to, but we already made some distance, every minute the German's machine guns kept up. They knew that there is something up that night and they kept on feeding us bullets yet no one as yet met one although they were thick at times."

Pippin crouched low in a shell hole with three other men and was about to move forward to the next hole when he heard one of his men groan. He turned to the man and rolled him over, but it was too late. The man was dead.

In the next shell hole, Pippin found his sergeant and told him of the casualty.

"Well that's three gone then," the sergeant said. "Two were hit some time ago, and I thought one were you." There were only five of them left.

"Not yet," Pippin replied.

"Do you see that light ahead of us that looks like a line of new dirt?"

"I do."

"Well that's the boyau we're after."

Pippin and the others crawled forward, while "the bullets were singing their death song through the air, and they would hit the wire and glance off and hum like a bee every minute I thought would be the last of us. I listened all the time to hear some groans from some-one and I'm glad to say I did not hear any."

He heard sounds coming from the trenches ahead of them, and then his sergeant placed his hand on Pippin's shoulder and whis-pered, "Germans."

Pippin understood that at this range, they would engage in hand-to-hand combat.

"Every heart were beating fast. All at once a shot. Then every man had a German to himself in the boyau. It were then more groans were heard in the boyau but not a shot were heard. It did not take long to clean up that patrol."

They took one man alive. The other Germans were dead. On their way back to their own lines, they gathered up their dead and carried them home.

"It were the hardest job I ever had to drag a dead man over that rough nomanland. We went from shell hole to shell hole trying to buck them bullets from the German machine guns. I helped to drop the third man in the trench and believe me, we were all in."

Pippin retired to his bunk in his dugout and tried to sleep, but no sooner had he laid down than a feeling of overwhelming home-sickness came over him. He thought of home. He could picture it clearly, his memories flooding back, and he wondered if he would ever see home again. Lying in his bunk, he thought of the letter he'd lost, and he could have kicked himself. He wanted to read it, but it had fallen out of his pocket somewhere in the Argonne. He hadn't gotten another letter in months. He craved a word from someone, until his craving became more than he could bear.

He stepped from the dugout. Everything seemed to be in order, so he went and got some food. Eating made him feel better, as did the cigarette he lit, exhausting the last of his tobacco but needing a smoke. Five of the boys from his company asked him if he had any more tobacco, and he told them he did not but shared his cigarette with them, passing it around, trying to keep it dry. He was happy to share, but that was all he was happy about. He had to stand guard duty that night, and he'd hoped the rain would stop, but it hadn't. None of the boys he was to stand guard duty with had overcoats, so they wrapped themselves in blankets.

He manned his sentry post.

He felt spent, emotionally and physically exhausted.

"There is no man can stand that again," he wrote. "No matter how good he is, I will say this much, if any man were in the front trenches for eight months or more he will and can not do it again."

He realized he hadn't taken his shoes off for a month. Usually, a man might go twenty days in either the second or the first line and then when he had ten days in the reserve, he could take his shoes off. He'd gone thirty days. Feet were not meant to wear shoes for thirty days. Men were not meant to do this.

"He may have the will but his body can not stand it."

He really needed another cigarette. He looked up and down the trench to see whom he could borrow one from, but he couldn't find anybody who smoked. Everybody was out, and everybody wanted a cigarette. Everyone he saw asked him for one, unless he asked them first.

Now he wished he hadn't shared his last cigarette because he wanted more. It had been five or six days since anybody had had tobacco, come to think of it, but he knew they'd be going into reserve soon, and then he'd see if he could buy some American tobacco. French tobacco was too strong. Usually that was all you could get. U.S. tobacco was better. "But I could smoke anything right now and I were glad to see another day for it meant so much to me."

⁓ ♧ ♧⁓

For Horace Pippin and the others, it would be a short stay at the front. Sixteen men had been killed or wounded by the gas during the projector attack, bringing the total to about two hundred men killed during the 369th's second assault on Butte Mesnil. On the same day, September 12, about fifty kilometers to the east, the AEF under General Pershing commenced its attack on the St. Mihiel salient. On September 15, the 369th was relieved by a French fourragère regiment and marched to the rear, to the villages of Somme-Tourbe and Somme-Bionne, about fifteen kilometers west of Ste.-Ménehould. They concluded that they were not likely to rejoin the U.S. Army for the fall offensive and might even sit out the offensive itself, given the direction they were traveling.

The next day, September 16, the U.S. Army back home carried out the death sentences for the remaining six black soldiers who'd been convicted for their part in the Houston riots.

The fall counteroffensive was scheduled to begin on the morning of September 26. The hope was, of course, for immediate success, but realists allowed that the fighting could possibly continue into the summer of 1919. The Allies had about 3.5 million troops poised to attack the Germans in waves, first at the ends of the L-shaped battle line, then in the middle. Pershing had about 250,000 men, with another 400,000 in reserve. Gen. Henri Gouraud brought about 450,000 men to the battle, though he didn't think this was enough and asked Pershing if he could spare any troops to use in reserve. Pershing had more black troops he was willing to do without and gave Gouraud the 368th Regiment from Pershing's Ninety-second Division, knowing the French had already been fairly successful using men from the Ninety-third, his other colored division. He held the Ninety-second in low regard, considering them neither well led nor well trained. Perhaps the French would know what to do with them.

Once it was dark on the evening of September 24, the 369th RIUS moved forward to support the French frontline troops, waited out the day, then moved again on the night of September 25, marching to the village of Minaucourt, with Butte Mesnil on their left. The Third Battalion, led by Maj. Lorillard Spencer, and Capt. Frederick Cobb's Second Battalion were given the first line, positioned with French infantry and fierce Moroccan troops opposite. Their goal was to drive the Germans from the village of Ripont and take an elevation called Bellevue Signal, making it safe to move on the town of Sechault, beyond which lay the town of Challerange and the rail lines the Germans were using to resupply and reinforce their troops. Cutting those railroad lines was the ultimate goal, but there was much work to do to get there.

They had elements from the 372nd Regiment for support on their right. A mere twenty kilometers further east, a young colonel named Douglas MacArthur led the Forty-second Division, which would fight its way north along the far side of the forest. The tacit goal of every American unit was to reach the Rhine first, to be the first to kick the Hun back into Germany. It was a race for glory the 369th held out little hope of winning.

The newly loaned 368th Regiment from the Ninety-second Division, with a Col. Fred Brown as its commanding officer, moved forward in the middle of the night after a long slog through the rain to plug a two-mile-wide hole between the U.S. Seventy-seventh Infantry to their east (manning the western edge of the Argonne) and the Eleventh Cuirassiers of the French Fourth on their left flank. Up to then, the 368th had seen little action and, after a brief and inadequate training period with the French, had manned only patrols in quiet sectors; thus, they had gained little or no experience with the sort of heavy shelling that, in pitched battle, could disorient or panic even seasoned troops. They lacked not only the heavy-duty cutters needed to snip through the German wire defenses but also flares and grenade launchers. Nor did they have their own artillery batteries or accurate maps. Most of all, they lacked trust, among the officers and between the officers and the men, having suffered from racial discord in all the ways the 369th had by and large managed to avoid. Without trust, officers would second-guess and blame each other, eroding morale and destroying esprit de corps, and enlisted personnel would respond halfheartedly to (or outright disobey) orders from leaders who, in their opinion, didn't know what they were talking about.

The men of the 369th RIUS crouched in the trenches on the night of September 26, waiting for day to break and for the attack to begin. They studied rough pencil-sketched maps of what the attack would look like and what their objectives were. They drafted letters to loved ones back home that began, "If these words come to you, it will be because I have fallen. . . ." Often before a major battle, a priest or clergyman passed down the lines, offering absolution to individuals and to entire units, for what they'd done and for what they were about to do.

Stretcher bearers assembled in the communication trenches with ambulances waiting behind them. Whispered questions and messages passed down the line: "Do you have enough water? Five minutes—pass it on."

The men tightened the straps on their helmets. For the first time, they'd been resupplied with American helmets, which had broader brims than the French helmets they'd been wearing, the American helmets shaped more like a pan than a bucket, probably better for keeping flying debris from falling in their eyes. More to the point, now they looked like Americans. They were Americans. They wanted people to know it.

They waited for the signal. The replacement troops were mostly nervous, the veterans mostly calm, some miraculously calm. Sometimes, waiting to go over the top, men felt an odd burning sensation on their foreheads, even in the cool early morning fog.

They double-checked everything, refixed their bayonets, straightened the gear on the man next to them, and caught each other's gaze but said little.

Pippin waited in the stillness. The Moroccan troops on his right flank (he called them Algerians) made him nervous.

"They were a good lot of fellows with us but they did not care for the French much. If we were with one of them and a French man came by us the Algerian would say '*Pardon Dar French*,' he meant that the French were no good for him." Pippin considered his "Algerian" comrades ruthless, unlikely to give an enemy a second chance or show any mercy. They carried eight-inch knives, went over the top holding them between their teeth, not even carrying rifles, and returned with knives bloodied.

"I have seen them do it. But when they come back do not look for a German for they would not have any with them. That is the way they would handle the Germans."

At the signal, "the Algerians broke the still air like a pack of mad men for the German line. They did their work fast and good in their way doing it. The next day I seen them they had no prisoner."

The Moroccan colonial troops led the charge into Ripont with their French comrades. Maj. Lorillard Spencer's Third Battalion and Capt. Frederick Cobb's Second were right behind them. They crossed the Dormoise, swollen by the month's rain, using three footbridges. At the far side of the stream, the Second Battalion engaged in ferocious, hand-to-hand fighting, with bayonets and bolo knives, rifle butts and teeth flying.

Spencer's battalion approached to the right of Cobb's men, eschewing the footbridges upon which men made easy targets, and tried to ford the stream instead. Lorillard Spencer walked along the riverbanks to lead and encourage his troops, acting much the good

Boy Scout, stalwart and strong and quite in view of the German machine gunners, who quickly cut him down, shooting him in the leg and wounding him six times. One of his fellow white officers considered Spencer's parading in plain view asinine. Spencer was carried off on a stretcher and replaced by Capt. David L'Esperance upon Colonel Hayward's orders. Three hours after the assault was launched, the Third and Second battalions of the 369th were ordered to halt their advance and dig in, just north of the river, with Bellevue Ridge ahead of them.

At midnight on September 25, Pvt. Herbert White, serving in his battalion's third replacement company, heard the bombardment begin. Big guns on both sides of the front fired fast and furious. The next morning, at 5:00 A.M., his battalion was ordered to advance. His company held back, helping to carry the wounded and repairing roads damaged in the shelling so that the artillery could move into new positions as the attack advanced. They were given picks, spades, and shovels and worked under heavy shell fire. An air battle raged overhead. They paused to watch two German planes fall from the sky, went back to work, and were strafed a few minutes later by another German plane.

Herbert White and his mates scrambled for cover, waited, then returned to work, only to see a shell land in the middle of a group of cavalry horses, killing eight of the animals, their bloody carcasses blocking the road. White sent for more men from his company to help drag the dead horses into the ditch, where they would rot or get blown up again.

They saw a bridge on the road where they were working take a direct hit. They repaired the bridge, and the artillery kept moving. They were then asked to assist a group of stretcher bearers.

"It was here," Herbert White said, "I got the worst feeling of my life."

They marched across the blasted ground, among the dead and wounded, men with legs torn off and skulls half missing, injured soldiers crying for help. Many of the wounded were lost before they reached the aid station. White and the others carried the wounded to the rear, passed another colored regiment moving up, and returned to the front. A French officer ordered them to go back, but they ignored him to take up the fight. White saw a platoon advancing nearby and watched as a shell fell in the middle of it, killing everyone but a sergeant and three privates.

White's company stopped. They were hungry, starving, having gone without water or bread for longer than anyone could remember. Finally, they ran into some French *poilus* who had with them some captured bread and some bulls they'd taken from the Germans. The French shared their bread cheerfully and told White and his company to follow them to their dugouts. There, they knocked one of the bulls in the head with a hammer, then skinned and cooked him. It was their first real meal during the drive. They were at a place called Snake Hill, which the French had been trying to take and hold for years.

"Our boys did the job in one day."

White lost two friends at Snake Hill, Frank Demsy, "a comedian," and William Stout, "a comedian and boxer." Later hospitalized, Herbert White was treated for the grippe and rheumatism, then diagnosed as having been gassed. For using a shovel, pick, and spade, Herbert White was cited for bravery.

Pippin had a run-in with a German plane that strafed him while he was trying to get something to eat. Quite suddenly he felt a "gush of air," and then the pilot opened fire on him. Pippin fell to the side of the trench he was in, taking cover, and stayed down until the pilot was gone—it was as close a call as he'd had during the war.

"I said to myself he near had me that time. But it were my quickness that saved me that time." When he told his comrades in the dugout about his near-miss, they thought he was joking. He found solace in a French cigarette and watched the rainwater drip drop by drop from the ceiling of the dugout to a pool on the floor.

Sometimes men got cocky—or just grew tired of being cautious and scared. After a while in the trenches, they believed they could anticipate events, that they could watch a German gun fire a ranging shot land a thousand yards behind them, with the next shot falling five hundred yards short, and gauge how much time they had before the gunner zeroed in and they'd have to take shelter. This illusion of control over one's destiny derived in part from the way the German shells often announced themselves before landing, their 77s and 155s making long, drawn-out screeching sounds before hitting the earth. The veteran soldier could turn his head, echo-locate the incoming shell, and with reasonable accuracy predict his degree of danger, taking cover only when necessary. The Austrians, however, had an 88 mm shell the Allies had dubbed the "Whiz-bang" for the brevity of its warning—a quick zipping whistle and then an explosion.

"If you are within the zone of dispersion, you are (as our men used to say) 'a poor boy.' There is no possibility of avoiding the penalties of that dispersion by dodging temporarily into cover," Arthur Little wrote.

It was possibly a "Whiz-bang" that found Pvt. James Turpin.

Private Turpin and his friend Sgt. John A. Jamieson, from Pippin's K Company, were attached to the Observatory Department, stationed at a forward observation post assigned to survey German operations at PC Marson, near Ripont. Jamieson was looking through his binoculars, watching a German squad repairing the wire in front of their trenches. He warned Turpin not to put his head out the door. When the Germans started shelling their sector, using gas, they put their masks on to wait out the bombardment. Jamieson commented that because of the shelling, they probably would not be able to return to the rear in time for dinner. Turpin agreed.

The shelling kept up for three hours. When it seemed to have halted, Turpin said he wanted some water and headed for the door. Jamieson tried to stop him, at which point Turpin said, "Are you afraid, Jimmie? Those are only little ones, and none of them have my name marked on them." Turpin handed Jamieson the binoculars he was carrying and stepped outside, when a shell struck about forty feet away.

Jamieson felt something warm slosh over him. Turpin's body—
or most of it—lay at Jamieson's feet. The concussion had severed
his head, which lay to one side. Turpin's limbs, torn from his body,
were scattered about the dugout. Jamieson was covered with his
blood. The shelling continued for another twelve hours, during
which time Jamieson was alone with his friend's remains. Jamieson
had known Turpin as a good kid, a soldier who had never refused an
assignment or hesitated to carry out an order, no matter what the
danger. He had loved his country and his flag and believed in what
they were fighting for.

Jamieson witnessed similar events twice more during the next
few days. A corporal from D Company named Stevens ventured
from his dugout one morning to see who was throwing grenades at
them, only to turn a corner and walk straight into an Austrian 77
shell, which "broke him into wee bits." Another comrade from
D Company took a direct hit from a German *minnenwerfer*, or "min-
nie waffle," after which "we were forced to shovel the poor boy up,
as the pieces of his remains were too small to put together."

Jamieson himself was shot twice. The first time, he was able to
dig the bullet out of his flesh with a penknife, dress his wound from
the first aid kit in his pack, and keep fighting. The second time, he
was hit by machine gun fire and took shrapnel as well, fracturing
the upper part of his left arm, an injury that permanently rendered
the wounded arm two inches shorter than his right.

Pvt. Elmer McCowan, formerly of 669 Lenox Avenue, was another
member of Pippin's K Company, led by Capt. Hamilton Fish.
McCowan was a fit young man, fleet of foot and well rested, suited to
the task when Captain Fish asked him to serve as liaison with the
French troops at their left flank. McCowan recalled,

The captain asked me to carry dispatches. The Germans
pumped machine gun bullets at me all the way, but I made

the trip and got back safely. Then I was sent out again. As I started the captain hollered to bring him back a can of coffee. He was joking but I didn't know it. Being a foot messenger I had some time ducking those German bullets. Those bullets seemed very sociable but I didn't care to meet up with any of them, so I kept on traveling on high gear. None touched my skin, though some skinned pretty close.

On the way back it seemed the whole war was turned on me. One bullet passed through my trousers and it made me hop, skip and jump. I saw a shell hole six feet deep. Take it from me I dented it another six feet when I plunged into it. In my fist I held the captain's can of coffee. When I climbed out of the hole and started running again a bullet clipped a hole in the can and the coffee started to run out. But I turned around stopped a second, looked the Kaiser in the face and held up the can of coffee with my finger plugging up the hole to show the Germans they were fooled. Just then another bullet hit the can and another finger had to act as a stopper. I pulled out an old rabbit's foot that my girl had given me and rubbed it so hard the hair almost came off.

It must have been the good luck thing that saved my life because the bullets were picking at my clothes and so many hit the can that at the end all my fingers were in use to keep the coffee in. I jumped into shell holes and wriggled along the ground and got back safely. And what do you think? When I got back into our own trenches I stumbled and spilled the coffee.

McCowan rested for half an hour, caught his breath, then ventured out into no-man's-land to help recover the wounded, working until he was gassed. McCowan shrugged off the effects of the gas and continued his work, amid shell and machine gun fire, saving the lives of his injured comrades by bringing them to safety. He was assisted by a Cpl. Elmer Earl from Middletown, New York. Of the fifty-eight members of K Company in that particular part of the sector that day, only eight survived. McCowan and Earl made multiple trips, and for their courage, both were awarded the Distinguished Service Cross.

On September 27, 1918, Colonel Hayward and his men pressed the attack, moving on the heights of Bellevue Ridge, which had to be taken before Sechault, the town below, could be assailed. The ridge was well protected by numerous machine gun emplacements, forcing the men to inch forward, crawling up the hill. Capt. John H. Clark from F Company led a squad to the top of a side crest but had to turn back after being spotted and fired upon. The regiment took heavy casualties. Yet, persistent work by the assault squads and rifle platoons eventually blew holes in the German line. Darkness fell, but the battle didn't stop.

It was another dreary night, and in the advanced positions, there were no dugouts in which to take shelter. Men stretched tent canvas over the tops of the shallow trenches where they lay and tried to stay warm. They ate their emergency rations and kept their heads down. Others found shelter beneath the camouflaged roofs of abandoned artillery positions. At the regiment's dressing station, Dr. Willis H. Keenan and Dr. G. Franklin Shiels couldn't get to all of the wounded, which numbered somewhere between three and four hundred casualties that night.

Hayward's orders for September 28 were to continue his attack, move down off Bellevue Signal, and cross the relatively flat farmland to take the town of Sechault. The attack was to be renewed at 7:00 A.M., preceded by artillery preparation. By 9:00 A.M., the 369th's Second and Third battalions were fighting off a German counterattack. At 2:00 P.M., they were back on the offensive, driving from west to east up the southern slopes of the plateau, where they stopped and dug in. At 6:30 P.M., the French 163rd Infantry stepped up their attack from the left, while the 369th moved forward at the center, with the French 363rd patrolling Mont Cuvelet to the right. By dawn on September 29, Bellevue Signal had fallen. Hayward's Second and Third battalions were depleted and spent, shot to pieces, forcing him to call up the First Battalion of Arthur Little.

Little's battalion had orders to relieve the French Battalion Favre at Bellevue Signal, descend the hill with Bussy Farm on their left and Mont Cuvelet on their right, and advance a little more than a kilometer to Sechault, the last German stronghold before Rosier's Farm, Challerange, and the rail lines. Little's final objective was Rosier's Farm, where he was to establish a new base and await further orders. It didn't help him move his men into position when he learned that the French guide he'd been sent had no idea where Battalion Favre was.

He spent September 27 and 28 moving men and equipment into position, a job complicated by the muck and mud that made boots, wheels, and hooves slip and sink into the earth. By the evening of September 28, Little was ready to make his assault. To stay in contact with Regimental HQ, he posted runners every two hundred yards to form a kind of Pony Express relay. Though it was an expensive way to use men needed at the front, one of his French instructors had told him, "Communication is more important than ammunition," which was particularly true when you were trying to advance behind a rolling barrage from close artillery.

Pippin's battalion—what was left of it—waited in support of Little's assault. Pippin watched the trees blow up:

> For two nights they gave us shell fire and the gas were thick and the forest looked like it were ready to give up all of its trees every time a shell came crashing through the forest. Trees would snap like a pipe stem. There were a big tree that stood by my dug out, it were a fine one but when the shell fire started the shells tore the top off of it. We barely knew

what to do for we could not fight shells, but we could the Germans. We would rather face the Germans to come over the top than to have their shells so all we could do were to not let them hit us if possible, for at that time we needed all the men that we had.

The 368th did not fare nearly as well as the 369th and, by most measures, failed where the 369th succeeded. On the first day of the assault, they moved forward up the western edge of the Argonne but were soon stalled by barbed wire entanglements, lacking the wire cutters they needed to cut through them. They had no artillery of their own to call in to cut the wire by shelling it. There were other tactical disadvantages. They'd arrived in their sector late, and their officers had no time to inspect their position or properly scout the ground across which they were to advance. It was so foggy that prior scouting may not have helped. When they came under furious shelling and machine gun fire, they took cover, with men in isolated groups, huddling in shell holes and ravines, shaking each time a shell landed near them, scared and bewildered, wondering what they were supposed to do—why didn't someone tell them? Communications had broken down within the advancing units and between the units and headquarters.

Maj. Max Elser, the white commander of the 368th's Second Battalion, found himself unable to contact Colonel Brown when the shelling worsened and did not know whether he was supposed to advance, hold his position, or withdraw and regroup. Elser himself may have been the first to panic or break down, in charge but uncertain how to stop his men from dying. When he gave the order to retreat, his men were happy to oblige. If he told them to retreat only so far but no further, some of his men chose not to hear him, and then no one knew where Elser had gone (he'd been taken to a hospital). Black officers leading companies cut off from Elser gave orders of their own to retreat. Maj. B. F. Norris of Third Battalion put another major in charge of the Second Battalion, but in short order, the battalion had broken, with its men running to the rear. Some companies retreated a few kilometers, regrouped, turned, and picked up the fight again. Others had dispersed and scattered, and regrouping wasn't possible.

The regiment was relieved, in disgrace, on the night of September 28. Both Maj. J. N. Merill, First Battalion commander, and Major Norris of the Third called their own men "rank cowards" because of their race, even though when French, British, or German soldiers panicked and ran, or when units within the U.S. Thirty-fifth Division deserted their posts, no one said it was because they were white. In the investigation that followed, the black officers felt they were being scapegoated for Major Elser's failings. One black officer testified that during the shelling, Major Norris had hidden in a ditch, even though it was not uncommon, in trench warfare, for men to do so. Division Commander Gen. Charles Ballou court-martialed all five of the black officers, who were found guilty and sentenced to death, though a later War Department investigation exonerated then. Ballou's chief of staff, Lt. Col. Allen Greer, was of the opinion that "the average Negro is naturally cowardly," and that "they have been dangerous to no one except themselves and women," a characterization that branded the entire division, despite the heroism and valor of its other regiments, the 365th, 366th, and 367th, where the First Battalion led by a Maj. Charles Appleton won the Croix de Guerre for rescuing the French Fifty-sixth Infantry.

It might have added to the conversation, had anyone asked the Germans what they thought. Negro war correspondent Ralph W. Tyler, representing the U.S. Committee on Public Information, a conference of Negro newspaper editors, and accredited by the AEF with full access to the front and camps, wrote in a letter to Emmett Scott, special assistant to Secretary of War Newton Baker,

It was a fact patent to every American officer and soldier who had had contact with German soldiers, that they had a mortal fear of colored soldiers. This fear had been occasioned by two things. First, before the American colored soldiers had been put on the battle front the Germans had encountered the fierce fighting Senegalese and Algerians, fighting with the French, who took no prisoners, and who were prone to cut off the ears and other parts of a German's anatomy before dispatching him into eternity. Then again, later, they had encountered the 372nd, 371st, 370th and 369th colored regiments, the first colored Americans to arrive in France, and who were brigaded and fought with the French. The Germans had learned that the American colored soldiers, while not brutal like the Senegalese and Algerians, were even harder, more scientific and more dangerous fighters. They were men who fought with precision—fought like trained veterans—were good in trench warfare, in raids, or in attack—any way they were ordered to fight, while the Senegalese and Algerians were best in attack—being dashing, whirlwind fighters in attacks, or as shock troops.

With only a few razor blades left to share among them, the officers of the 369th's First Battalion had to decide, on the morning of September 29, whether they wanted to shave. Some did, and some didn't. Surely it wouldn't have seemed a decision of any consequence, and, of course, it was only a coincidence that those who shaved that morning lived and walked away, while those who didn't died or were carried from the field.

Little led the attack on Sechault from a ditch at the southern edge of the town. They'd crossed Bussy Farm early in the morning with little difficulty, crawled on their bellies as they neared the village, and spread out along a half-mile line where Little commanded his men by sending runners with quickly dashed-off letters explaining his orders. Company C was working its way through the center of town, moving house to house and alley to alley, while Company D edged up the right side of town. Company B, led now by Capt. Aaron T. Bates instead of Charles Fillmore, entrenched at the west end of town to move in support of whoever needed it first. Upon their arrival, the First Battalion had not found Germans occupying Sechault in great numbers; rather, they'd chosen to defend the town with artillery and carefully placed machine guns in the town itself and in positions north of town that covered the streets from hidden placements difficult to assail.

C Company's first accomplishment was to capture a German 77 mm gun placed at the town's southern entrance. They found an ammunition dump of live shells near the gun where the Germans, before they left, had lit a bonfire, hoping to set off a kind of deadly fireworks display, but one of Capt. Seth MacClinton's men crawled in on his belly to put the fire out. D Company captured a grenade dump cashed in the middle of town. The list of casualties grew as they worked from house to house. A Second Lieutenant Hundley from Bates's unit was wounded in the arm and sent off. First Lt. D. H. Vaughn of D Company was wounded and sent to the rear as well. Lt. George Robb was working to expel a machine gun crew from a brick house at the northeast corner of town when he was shot in the left side. Robb bandaged himself with his first aid packet and continued the fight. Eventually, D Company took over the brick house that Robb had cleared and used it to fire on German machine gun nests on the plains approaching Rosier's Farm north of town. By keeping the German machine gunners pinned down, men from C and D companies were able to establish lines of defense north of Sechault. Robb was wounded a second time, taking a piece of shrapnel in his arm, but again he refused to be evacuated and stayed with his men.

Enlisted men fell as well, cut down by German machine gun snipers as they tried to cross the streets, or they died in the ditches where shells found them.

At about 5:00 P.M., a German plane strafed Arthur Little's position, coming in low enough that the men in the ditch could see the expression on the pilot's face. Little was in the midst of drafting a letter apprising Hayward of the situation—that the town was full of snipers, but they were making progress. "Cannot tell yet how soon we can go forward. Shall we halt when too dark to see?"

Then Little looked behind him and saw a large group of colored soldiers approaching, men from Company H, coming to reinforce him, led by Capt. Eric Winston, who had bad news for Little—Capt. Frederick Cobb had been killed. Cobb had been acting commander of the Second Battalion and doing a fine job, despite the fact that Hayward had declined to promote him to major. Little asked Winston what had happened.

"The battalion was being held for your support," Winston said, "as you know, upon the rear slope of that eastern spur of Bellevue Signal. We believed we were sheltered there, but suddenly they found us and opened up with heavy shell fire. Cobb got his right at the beginning. With almost a direct hit. A piece of the shell took off the entire back of his head. Of course, he never suffered. That's one thing."

One of Cobb's lieutenants was standing next to him when Cobb was hit. The lieutenant had a glazed look, a blank stare. Fish ordered him to the rear to get help. The stunned lieutenant pulled his gun and pointed it at Fish, then fainted and was carried off.

Little asked Winston the identities of the men accompanying him and was told they were what was left of the Second Battalion, about 150 troops. Capt. John Clark had taken over the Second after Cobb's death. When Clark arrived, Little gave him the task of mopping up in the town.

As evening fell, Little's First Battalion dug in on the western, northern, and eastern edges of town, making themselves comfortable occupying what had recently been German fortifications. They placed their machine guns to cover the ground in front of their trenches and the plains north of Sechault, having eighteen guns of their own, one captured German machine gun, and plenty of ammunition. They established battalion headquarters in a half-demolished stone house whose roof remained intact over a single room. They called a second stone house nearby the "Block House" to be used as a fallback position if the Germans launched a counterattack. They were accidentally reinforced by a half-platoon of men from the 372nd U.S. Infantry Regiment who'd become lost and wandered into town, led by a Capt. Frank Coleman, whose troops were folded into C Company.

Little and Clark agreed to combine their two battalions, merging companies and settling out who would lead and who would step aside. At the same time, Little received a letter from regimental headquarters. Hayward's mood was resolute—and foul. He'd been dealing with a number of replacement troops who had either deserted their posts, stayed behind when their units attacked, or in other ways disobeyed orders. His response:

> 29, Sept. 18
> 19 H. 05
>
> C.O. 1st 369th
>
> You will hold the village of Sechault tonight assisted by the 2nd Bn.
>
> 1. The high command informed of your situation and will act accordingly; also informed of possibility of counterattack and will provide for same.
> 2. The 363rd on your right and the 163rd on your left have been positively ordered to establish liaison with you tonight and to establish their lines up to your village.
> 3. Establish small outposts on enemy side of village to give warning of any attack.
> 4. Keep constant touch with 2nd Bn. Show them this order and each Bn, send into Regtl. P.C. four reliable runners under an officer or superior N.C.O.
>
> Wm. Hayward, Col.

The letter was not good news. It meant that the support on their flanks had not arrived yet; thus, they were more or less alone and extremely vulnerable to counterattack from three sides. Little dispatched scouting parties to look for the French 363rd and 163rd regiments to no avail, receiving reports that said, "No trace of troops within sight or hearing of the points where they should have been."

A second letter from Hayward, received a few hours after the first, told Little that if a counterattack came, he was to "exercise [his] own best judgment on the spot"; if a bombardment were to come, however, he might consider abandoning the town and moving forward a few hundred meters to get inside the German artillery. An officer approached and urged Little to withdraw his men, to which Little replied that he'd been ordered not to. The officer said that staying was suicidal, and Little replied that "even that extreme was covered by regulations providing for the obedience to orders."

Little's confidence, however, was a pose, masking a moment of great doubt. He found himself caving to the stress, and needing a few moments alone to pull himself together, he stepped outside his headquarters to pace, head bowed. When his adjutant pleaded for him to come back inside, saying, "Major, please—don't stay out here. They'll get you sure if you do," Little responded solemnly, in his darkest personal moment of the war, saying, "My God. I believe that's what I want." His voice suppressed a sob. He was surely suffering from a lack of sleep, exhausted, and weighed down by the responsibility of leading men in battle.

"What do I know of warfare?" he asked his young aide. "What have I done this afternoon? Lost half my battalion. Driven hundreds of innocent men to their deaths." He considered the prospect of a German shell taking his life in a blink. "It would be a relief, my boy. A relief."

❧ ❧

Horace Pippin volunteered to join a party assigned to locate and destroy a particularly nettlesome German machine gun nest, believed to be located in the wrecked shell of an old house. Sixteen men went out to get him, crawling on their bellies.

"Every heart were beating fast now," Pippin wrote, "for we were looking straight in the old house where the German with the machine gun were. We split up before we got close to the black old house and eight went one way and eight the other."

The crack in the wall of the house where they thought the gunner was hiding resembled the letter *v*.

"There were a flight of stairs that led to the cellar that were all covered up with brick and dirt and no floor in the house. The cellar were full of everything but there were no Germans to be seen. We looked all over the old house."

The German had pulled out just in time. Veteran soldiers on both sides of no-man's-land knew to keep moving. If you fired from any one place for too long, sooner or later a shell would land on your head, or you'd feel the point of a bayonet at your back.

In the night, a Sergeant Major Marshall arrived at Arthur Little's improvised headquarters in the brick house with good news: a detail out foraging had managed to uncover eighty *boules* of French bread, fat round loaves with thick crusts. The officers distributed the bread to their men, who had not eaten for eighteen hours. They ate in the darkness and felt better. Little had given instructions to his men not to fire unless the enemy were actually upon them, lest they give away their strength and position. All night, the Germans tried to coax the battalion into returning fire, sending up flares, firing in bursts, and then waiting.

Little's men showed good discipline and stayed silent, preventing an attack by not giving the Germans enough information to act on. The only real danger came when Little received a message from headquarters asking him to provide an accurate map of his trench positions in order to aid the French artillery, a feat Little could not accomplish in the dark. He had men cover the door and the single window with blankets as best he could and used his lamps as briefly as possible, but it was enough to send a German shell his way. He moved his headquarters to his fallback position in the Block House. Little sent the runner back with the map he'd drawn, hoping it was accurately rendered and would be, more to the point, accurately read and considered.

Just before daybreak, a runner arrived from the front trenches to report that activity had been observed across the open fields to the north, across which the 369th was to advance. It looked like a German counterattack would come, at what experience had taught was a predictable hour, just before dawn. Men were roused from their sleep.

A barrage of German shells smashed into the town. Cannons flashed in the distance, making the sky flicker to show the distant line of trees in silhouette, explosions blowing holes in what was left of Sechault, sending up showers of debris. The men held and did not fire back, even though many suspected the shelling was in advance of an attack, as per custom. In fact, it was just another feint. The Germans could not attack without some inkling of the size of the force opposing them. The First Battalion withheld that intelligence and, by doing so, saved itself.

In the morning, Little received a message from French division commander Lebouc with the day's orders: they were to continue their march north across Rosier's Farm with the French 162nd three hundred meters to the left and forward, the French 163rd leading the New Yorkers, and the French Division L'Ardenel, supported by the French 363rd Infantry, four hundred meters to the right. The attack was to move forward at H hour, 7:00 A.M., with "local resistance to be overwhelmed by outflanking."

The order forced Little's hand and required him, at 5:00 A.M., to withdraw the bulk of his men from the front lines and re-form, leaving only holding squads and machine gun companies. The men's movement exposed them to enemy observers. In no time, the town fell under a hail of artillery fire and became too hot to hold. Little withdrew again to the trenches south of town.

When H hour arrived, 7:00 A.M., the French 163rd was nowhere to be found, nor were the flanking elements in evidence. They were alone. They waited, while German shells tried to flatten the town, machine gun fire raking the streets from distance positions.

Almost ninety minutes late, the 163rd came up and passed their positions, then maneuvered through and around the town to cross the fields and enter the woods opposite. The First Battalion advanced behind them. Little worked his way forward until he found Captain Clark. They made an observation post and received reports from their companies: machine gun placements here, this way safe, that way not, taking casualties, then "clear sailing." They managed to locate one particularly troublesome German machine gun nest and tasked Captain Bates and B Company to take it out. Little sent a cheeky note back to headquarters:

> We are trying to get behind the M.G. nests by going far around our left (enemy right) flank. Also we are going to use one M.G. on the positions.
>
> Do try to have Boche barrage stopped while we are working.
>
> A.W.L.

Despite Little's flippant tone, all was not going well. The battalion had taken too many losses, fighting house to house. Once again, he felt a creeping sense of depression and suspected Clark was of equally diminished spirits. He knew that Clark had been married while the regiment was at Camp Whitman, with a baby boy back home who'd been born in his absence. He asked him about it. Clark took a picture from his breast pocket, studied it for a few moments, then slid it across the distance between them to show it to Little, mother and child, their cheeks pressed together. Little had a son of his own, a big one, Winslow, who was a sergeant with the 326th Tank Battalion. Winslow had in fact run away from St. Paul's School at the age of sixteen to join the French ambulance drivers' service. Arthur Little understood what it was like to miss a child.

"I'd like to see that boy sometime," Clark said.

Before Arthur Little could say anything in reply, they heard a familiar "whiz" and a thud as a shell struck midway between them, ten feet from either, and buried itself in the earth.

A dud.

By Monday, September 30, it was becoming clear that the Allies were winning unexpected victories from Verdun to the North Sea. In the Balkans, Bulgaria became the first member of the Central powers to surrender. The day before, Allied troops had crossed the previously impenetrable Hindenburg Line. Veteran French and British soldiers had heard the phrase "the tide is turning" too many times to use it anymore, and yet now that they had successfully pushed the Germans back, the Germans were staying pushed. They were still fighting, sometimes as ferociously as ever, but moving backwards.

Horace Pippin had one last fight in him and wrote in his journal of the attack that left him wounded and took him out of the action. He seldom dated his journal entries, and when he did, he sometimes got the date wrong, having said in other journal entries that the men often did not know what day it was. His statement that he hadn't eaten in three days suggests he was shot sometime on September 29 or 30, three days after the autumn offensive began.

Horace Pippin recalled a night brightly lit with stars, then German shells bursting like lightning to show the way, the show commencing around 1:00 A.M. Then a fog rolled in, limiting visibility to about one hundred feet, at which point the artillery lifted and the troops went over the top. Pippin fought an uphill battle all morning, losing half his platoon. He found himself in a pit with four others, and then they ran, taking withering cross fire. At one point, one of Pippin's friends took a hit directly behind him, said only, "I'm done up," and died. Pippin's journal entry reads,

> I crept away. Then the bullets were hitting in front of me and would throw dirt in my face. I knew that if I stayed there I would get it so I said to my buddy when I say go, be ready and make it for the little bridge and cross the swamp if we can. So I said go, and we made the bridge. The Germans were shelling the swamp with gas and shrapnel. The mud were so thick that I stuck and could not make time like I wanted to. But we made it across all right and were at the bottom of the hill the same hill the German were and he were still at work.
>
>   I did not see him but I knew I were close at hand. He were the one I wanted to get for he were in a good place and no one could get away from him and he cleaned out the first platoon I knew it so my buddy and I made our way to him keeping well down under the hill. I did not go many feet when I seen him. That were all I wanted to do. I'm a good shot and I seen him leave the gun. Then the swamp were safe to cross.

Pippin saw German prisoners being marched at gunpoint to the rear, and they looked happy to be out of the battle, to know one day they would go home again. Pippin took out another German machine gun nest, then, with a buddy, went after a third positioned behind a large rock. Pippin and his buddy decided to split up. It would be Horace Pippin's last act as a soldier.

> Both of us left the shell hole at the same time. I got near the shell hole that I had picked out when he let me have it. I went down in the shell hole. He clipped my neck and got

me through the shoulder and right arm. I only had a little water in my canteen. I began to plug my wounds when my buddy came to me and did what he could for me. Then he told me that he got the German and the gun. I were lying on my back. I thought I could get up but I could not do so. I shook hands with him and I never seen him again.

Now the shells were coming close to me. Pieces of shell would come near me some times. Then the German sniper kept after me all day. His bullets would clip the shell hole that held me. . . . Some time that afternoon some French snipers came by. They looked for Germans that is left back so he sees me lying there when he did so he stopped to say something to me but he never got it out for just then a bullet passed through his head and he sank on me. I seen him coming but I could not move. I were just that weak, so I had to take him. I were glad to get his water and also bread. I took my left hand and I got some coffee after some hard time getting it from him.

After that I felt good and I tried to get up again but I were too weak to do so. Night were coming on and it began to rain. Then I tried to get the blanket from my dear comrade. That I could not do and I could not get him off me. The rain came more and more until I were in water. Yet I were growing weaker and weaker all the time and I went to sleep. I can't say how long.

Two boys came and I woke up. They took the French man off of me and then took me out of the shell hole for some distance where there were more wounded ones. I were left there the rest of the night. . . .

When I woke up it were day. Then I were carried out of the dugout. . . . I were shoved in the ambulance with five others made six all and shells followed us until we got to the field hospital. . . . I knew no more until I were taken

to the table to see what were wrong with me. They gave me
some dope and that did put me away for good. I can't say
how long I were in it.

    After I came out of it I were not there long. They took
me to another hospital base in Lyon.

Arthur Little, carrying the attack to the Germans in the hope of
reaching Rosier's Farm, had found himself stymied and frustrated by
German machine gun nests in the woods beyond the open field before him. He'd sent Companies B, C, and D in to try to clear them
out but with little success. Finally, at 2:55 A.M. on September 30, he
gave up and sent runners to call his companies in, advising them that
he was going to have to call in artillery to clean out the woods. The
French advance on the left by the 162nd had stopped at the river
Avègres, which had overflowed its banks in the recent rains.

    Little sent Hayward a letter:

Cannot get through woods without artillery. About a dozen
M.G. nests reported. Shrubs not high enough to provide
cover for surrounding. I am withdrawing men to 300 meters
in front of woods. Entire section mapped should be heavily shelled.

    A.W.L.

At the same time, First Lieutenant Robb was doing his part to
protect his men by absorbing a company's worth of injuries all by
himself, or so it seemed. He'd been at the command post for Company D, which was nothing more than a large shell hole, when an
enemy plane spotted him, and a few minutes later, a German artillery
shell scored a bull's-eye, landing in the hole and killing 1st Lt.
George F. Seibel, Lt. Ernest McNish, and a number of enlisted men.
Robb was wounded for the third time in twenty-four hours. After

the first two times he'd been shot, he'd dressed his own wounds and refused to leave his men; after the third time, he finally decided that perhaps he was pressing his luck. He'd also had his pistol grip shot off and discovered, upon closer examination, that another bullet had pierced his helmet but somehow missed him.

It was plain to all that the regiment was taking a serious beating. Many men had been lost, killed, wounded, evacuated, or transferred. Europe was in Paris. Sissle was attending an officer training program south of Paris. Needham Roberts had not yet recovered from his injuries. Henry Johnson had a steel rod in his leg but was unable to fight and had been attached to Headquarters Company, where he served as what one officer described as a kind of regimental mascot. Pippin was hospitalized. Charles Fillmore, Napoleon Marshall, George Lacy, and Lincoln Reid were gone. Turpin was dead. Spots Poles, Kid Cotton, Elmer McCowan, and William Butler were alive but tired. So many had been lost.

Little received a mixed message of good and bad news at 4:00 P.M. The good news was that Capt. David L'Esperance, who'd taken over the Third Battalion after Lorillard Spencer was wounded, was bringing up all of his men to support Little in his advance. The bad news was that L'Esperance's battalion had been shot to pieces even more than Clark's the night before; he was bringing a mere 137 men and 7 officers to support what remained of the 369th.

For the first time, all three battalions were in the same fight at the same time. When Little, L'Esperance, and Clark assessed their troops' fighting capacities, they reached the same conclusion: the men were still full of spit and in magnificent fighting, "Goddamn, let's go!" spirit—perhaps more so than their leaders—but physically they had given their last measure and were spent.

Little sent Captain Clark to report the news to Hayward in person. The men would not quit, they would fight to the end, but these were not the men who should fight this battle, because they were too few, too tired, too hungry, too hurt, and too proud to give up unless somebody ordered them to. Little sent Clark because in civilian life, Clark had worked for Hayward as his secretary, knew him well, and might base his appeal upon their friendship. Clark was happy to bear the message in person but advised Arthur Little that something in writing would be more persuasive.

Little, a magazine publisher and writer of no small talent, obliged him with a note of considerable economy and cogency. He addressed it to Harold London, Hayward's aide:

> Dear Harold,
>
> Please say to the Col. for me that in my opinion no attempt further should be made to go through those woods without either tanks or full demolition of concrete pill boxes by heavy artillery.
>
> The 2nd Batt. has about 100 men and 3 officers.
>
> The 1st Batt. has about 300 men and 9 or 10 officers.
>
> The 3rd Batt. has about 137 men and 7 officers.
>
> I believe every man will obey orders to go into those woods if orders are given; but, under present conditions, they will all stay there—and the 15th N.Y. will be a memory.
>
> Our men are wonderful. Without 5% of normal food or sleep they are standing by; but great weakness is upon us all.
>
> I hope that a relief can be made.
>
> Also, that no unsupported advance by any soldiers be made through those woods.
>
> A.W. Little,
> Major

Hayward wrote back:

Sept. 30/18
16:15 o'clock

Major Little—

The artillery fire you asked for will be given. After its completion, continue your advance as before.

Colonel Hayward
Lt. Col. W. A. Pickering

In fact only a very small portion of the artillery fire Little asked
for was given, no more than a half-dozen shots. Little knew the
shelling had accomplished nothing and that the German machine
guns that had been killing his men all day were still in place and
waiting for him. Yet, he had no choice but to follow orders—
suicidal orders were still orders.

He gave the command to his men to fall out for "Custer's last
stand," as some men were calling it, and took care that the written
orders were on his person so that when his body was found, as he
hoped it would be, blame could be accurately assigned. He sent out
advance scouts. Earlier, he had thought of suicide, but it had been
only a personal notion, not a decision he wanted to make for his
men. Did they know what was about to happen?

His orders said to attack after the artillery barrage ceased. They
did not state how long he was to wait. He waited to make certain his
"support" artillery had ceased, and perhaps he waited a moment or
two longer to let his men finish their prayers, or to finish his own.

Then, miraculously, a second message arrived by runner, the
man panting, out of breath. The runner conveyed a communication
from Hayward: they were to be relieved by the 363rd French Infantry. Sit tight.

The 363rd came to relieve them at 1:00 A.M. on Tuesday, October 1. At 6:00 A.M., the true shelling Arthur Little had asked for fell

on the woods in front of them. Food arrived at 7:00 A.M., and they ate after thirty hours of involuntary fasting, listening to the shelling. At 8:00 A.M., the French attacked the Germans and left the 369th behind.

Later that morning, a German shell hit the emergency hospital set up by the regiment's surgeon, Dr. Keenan, where two hundred wounded waited to be taken out on stretchers. It was a gas shell. Among the men affected was 1st Lt. George S. Robb, wounded for the fourth time.

❧ ☙

With only 725 men left, the French pulled the soldiers of the 369th from the front lines and assigned them to lighter duties. They moved back to Maffrecourt and rested. They'd done their part. The dead and wounded would not be replaced this time.

On October 8, they were loaded into camions and driven south to Arrigny, billeted by battalion in nearby villages. On October 13, they hiked to Chavanges and boarded a train. They traveled through the night and all day on October 14. At 10:00 A.M. on October 15, they reached the town of Belfort, famous as the home of Frédéric-Auguste Bartholdi, creator of the Statue of Liberty, then on to Vauthiermont, where they detrained and hiked ten kilometers in the rain to the town of Roppe. On October 16, they moved by camion again into the Vosges Mountains and the Valley of the Thur in Alsace. The trucks they rode in strained as they climbed roads high into the Alps, reaching an elevation of six thousand feet. Looking down, the men from New York saw the valley and the Rhine. Reaching the Rhine was the prize, the honor sought by virtually every American soldier in France, including a pair of young AEF officers named George Patton and Douglas MacArthur, who would have been chagrined to learn that black troops had reached it ahead of them.

The fighting that remained was nothing like that they'd experienced before. The German shelling came twice a day, once at dawn and once at sundown, and became routine. The regiment took perhaps its final losses, three men killed and eight wounded, during a ten-minute bombardment on the morning of October 28.

Jim Europe returned from Paris with his band in tow and rejoined the regiment in mid-October. He had been refining his postwar plans. He still wanted to start a music school in Harlem. He wanted to restore the black musical theater to reflect a more authentic African American experience—no more minstrel shows for white consumption. He wanted to create the greatest black orchestra in history and play again at Carnegie Hall. And the band—there was no reason why the band should break up once the regiment demobilized. They had a good thing going. Irving Berlin was getting all kinds of attention for songs like "Over There" and "Oh How I Hate to Get Up in the Morning." Europe had been writing war songs too. The band could probably do a national tour.

He had another performance to give on November 11. The armistice went into effect at 11 A.M. The day found them in the town of Bitschwiller, about thirty kilometers north-northeast of Belfort, too far to hear the bells of St. Christopher's ring out the news that peace had come, but perhaps they heard the cannon from the citadel fire a twenty-one-gun salute. French citizens kissed each other in the streets, and boys threw their arms around girls they barely knew—but the girls didn't mind. Their happiness was overwhelming. They had joy again, and they had hope again, hope that triumphed over death, a feeling rising up in them that they were free, favored, and forgiven by God. The desire to make new lives for themselves awakened.

The music Europe's band made added to the joy in Bitschwiller. Pvt. Marvin Miller recalled,

> As we marched in to this particular town, I don't quite remember the name, I think it was Bittsvilla—the colonel before we marched in gave us the command to get into formation and we straightened up and struck up the band, the

flag of New York State was flying for the 15th New York Infantry, our colors flying, and as we approached the town, at the outskirts of the town . . . you could see the German troops leaving. They were marching out of the town and we come in with the band playing "The Army Blues." And Jim Europe and—Noble Sissle was not our bandmaster, drum major, at the time—it was a fellow named Thompson, since passed. And we marched into that town and the people on both sides were waving; they didn't know whether we were coming as conquerors or liberators, but they were playing safe and cheering—whether they were cheering and happy out of fear, to win us over, or because they were happy, I have no way of telling. But that day the sun was shining and we were marching and the band was playing and everybody's head high and we were all proud to be Americans, proud to be black, and proud to be the 15th New York Infantry. We had a ball.

It bears repetition: "We were all proud to be Americans, proud to be black."

That statement contains no sense of "two-ness"; rather, it reflects a sense of unity and completed purpose, though how long it would last remained to be seen.

Who Won
the War?

The war is over
The whole wide world is a-wreathed in clover
Then hand in hand we'll stroll through life
Just think how happy we will be
I mean we three
We'll pick a bungalow among the flagrant boughs
When I come back to you with the blooming flowers
All of No Man's Land is ours
—JAMES REESE EUROPE, "ALL OF
NO MAN'S LAND IS OURS," 1918

The armistice came at 11:00 A.M. on the eleventh day of the eleventh month in 1918. The war was over, but the work was not. There were prisoners to transfer, trenches and fortifications to disassemble and clear, and refugees to tend to, men and women without adequate clothing against the November cold, most of them hungry. The regiment, what was left of it, fed them what they had and helped where they could. Of the 369th Regiment's original two thousand men, over thirteen hundred had died or been wounded by the time the Battle of Meuse-Argonne was over, including fifty-five officers. It was the highest casualty rate of any American regiment. Unlike other American regiments, the 369th never gave an inch of ground or had a single man taken prisoner. Other colored regiments had performed nobly, but none had received the acclaim of the men from Harlem.

On November 17, they were roused from their sleep and marched to the town of Wattwiller, then south to Uffholtz and Cernay, and through a number of small towns to Wittelsheim. On November 18, they marched again to Pulversheim, then six kilometers to Ensisheim, where they saw flags and girls in native Alsatian dress. The girls threw flowers in the streets for the men to walk on and kissed the black soldiers right on the lips.

On November 20, the soldiers of the 369th reached the town of Blodelsheim, where Arthur Little and Seth MacClinton, on horseback, led a patrol to Nambsheim, and saw the last ferryboat containing evacuating German troops sailing across the Rhine. When they arrived at the shore, they bent down and dipped their fingers in the water, making the 369th the first American regiment to reach the river.

On Thanksgiving, Jim Europe wrote to his sister Mary:

I think I have told you that we are now guarding the Rhine. I have so much to give thanks for this time for I have been through the valley and shadow of death so often and still I am unscathed. Now dear little loved one, have a merry cherry time but remain away from large gatherings until that terrible epidemic of influenza has passed over. I am so tired of army life now that I do not know what to do. I want to get home and get to work and make some money. It costs all we earn over here to live and clothe ourselves. Now I must close. I've so many things to do.

On December 13, a surprisingly warm Friday afternoon, General Lebouc summoned the unit to the parade grounds on the Plains of Munchausen, and there they received their commendations. General Lebouc had written to Col. William Hayward how proud he was "to have under my command an American regiment which, with little previous training, has fought with extreme bravery, and . . . has applied itself to such regular and steady work that as far as attitude and military discipline are concerned, the American Regiment can compare with any of my French regiments. . . . I shall take great joy in decorating your flag and in kissing you in front of your Regiment. And that day we shall not only drink water from the Rhine, we shall drink Champagne, and it will be a beautiful day."

Within the regiment, 170 individual citations for the Croix de Guerre were awarded, as was a unit citation.

The men were released from French command on December 17. They wanted to go home, lie in their own beds, break bread with the people who'd known them their whole lives, and close their eyes in a place they knew. It was winter in the French Alps, but they were not inclined to appreciate the natural beauty of their surroundings. They would have traded it in a heartbeat for the Manhattan skyline.

On December 18, in a driving snowstorm, they marched twenty-two kilometers to the town of Roderen, where they found the rooms they were supposed to occupy already taken by Moroccan troops who "had neither orders nor inclination to move." They hiked instead to Bourbach-le-Haut. Officers let tired enlisted men ride their horses. The strong carried the packs for those who were weak. At Bourbach-le-Haut, they found accommodations for half the regiment, but another three hundred men were left out in the storm, wet and cold and tired. Arthur Little asked a priest to lend them the use of his chapel, and when the priest refused, Little ordered his men into the sanctuary anyway, certain that God would understand.

They made Belfort by December 20 and billeted in nearby villages, finding quarters in Banvillars, Urceray, Buc, Argesians, Dorans, and Bavillers, but they managed all to get together on Christmas Day at a farm at the edge of Belfort, where company funds were used to buy turkeys and potatoes and the traditional things Americans ate at Christmas. The Red Cross station supplied gift items, cigarettes, gum, candy, sewing kits, toothpaste, shaving soap, cookies, bouillon cubes, and cigars, and some men even received packages from home.

"All hands shouted 'Merry Christmas' back and forth," Little recalled, "and cracked our faces into smiles. At about three o'clock in the afternoon, just after we'd gone through that regular Christmas dinner function of letting out the belt three holes, came the sound of martial music. In an instant our banquet table was deserted. Down the rickety stairs we rushed, out through the shed into the open, and there in our barnyard facing us . . . was Jim Europe and his band. . . . We had a happy hour—all the men of our town and the civilian population too, crowded into that barnyard, to listen to the best music of the American army."

The Third Battalion marched to Marvillars and entrained for Le Mans on New Year's Eve. The First and Second battalions marched to Héricourt two days later for the long 635-kilometer ride west. At every stop and station where they saw other troops from other branches of the service, a good-natured call went up, men hooting and crying out, "Who won the war?" And if they were talking to bakers, they'd answer their own question, "The Bakers won the war!" "Who won the war?" The stevedores, the quartermasters, the Red Cross, even the MPs (though as a general rule the MPs were not well liked). At some stations, if the stopover was long enough, Jim Europe would tell the band to get their instruments out and assemble on the platform—to play for the other soldiers there and to play for the joy of playing. They all felt a sense of joy that increased the closer they drew to home, as well as a sense that they were leaving their service with the French behind and becoming more and more American with every mile.

At the forwarding camp in Le Mans, they joined the other regiments of the Ninety-third Division, side-by-side for the first time.

Noble Sissle found Jim Europe and the other members of his former regiment, with whom he still identified despite his transfer.

"Who won the war?"

"The 370th won the war!"

"Who won the war?"

"The 371st won the war!"

"Who won the war?"

"The 372nd won the war!"

"Who won the war?"

"The 369th won the war!"

"What a glorious meeting," Sissle wrote. "Amongst those four
regiments could be found all the active personnel of the 369th. It
was the same as a family reunion—smiles and tears! Smiles and
laughs and happiness that we were present, spared; tears of sorrow
for those whom we left behind, beneath the poppy fields of France."

The significance of their service was not lost on Arthur Little,
who, though oblivious to a significant portion of the African American experience, appreciated the war they'd fought on two fronts, the
one against the Germans and the more unbending battle they were
"bound to suffer for a long time still to come" against "the prejudices in the hearts of white men, the cumulative prejudices of hundreds of years."

"Recruited as fighting men, in ridicule," Little wrote, "trained
and mustered into Federal service, in more ridicule; sent to France as
a safe political solution of a volcanic political problem; loaned to the
French army as another easy way out—these men had carried on. In
patience and fortitude, these men had served."

They stayed a week in Le Mans, where the winter weather was
miserable, with more rain, more mud. The U.S. Army, in its wisdom, determined that now that the war had been over for nearly two
months, the men of the 369th, who had spent 191 days at the front,
needed rifle instruction. It sent them a young officer who had himself spent the war in training schools and had only an approximate
idea of which end of the rifle to point toward the enemy. He was the

first such instructor the American army had provided for the 369th, and the men listened to him with great interest.

But the mood at Le Mans was one of cheerfulness.

They were going home.

On January 10, they boarded a train for Brest.

"Who won the war?"

"The train conductors won the war!"

It is said that soldiers do not fight for their country—they fight for each other. Men who do not know how a war started or why it is being fought battle to save the lives of their friends because their friends would do the same for them. Thus the brotherhood of warriors is formed, an alliance based on love and gratitude, as well as on a shared understanding incomprehensible to civilians who have never seen combat. In any war, men see things that no human ought to see, things they can never forget and often never describe, things they don't fully understand themselves, but the brotherhood of warriors understands—we are the men who have seen things we can't understand.

When Sgt. John Jamieson felt the blood of James Turpin slosh over him, his life was changed in an instant and would never be the same. He had been given information impossible to assimilate, information that would imprison him, in a sense. The experience was unique to him but common among soldiers. Only in the presence of other men who'd also seen their friends blown to bits and pulped before their eyes, in the company of warriors, could men like John Jamieson feel released from their prisons. Warriors understood each other, even if they didn't understand what they themselves had been through, or why the same God they prayed to when they were children would give them so much to cope with as adults. Soldiers felt a bond, even with men who were not from their units but who had simply served in the same war.

On the train to Brest, where they would be united with their fellow American soldiers, the men of the Ninety-third Division and of the 369th Regiment, formerly the Fifteenth New York National Guard, felt a sense of completion, a sense, when they looked out the window at the train station in Brest and saw the faces of all the white doughboys waiting to go home, that they knew the real answer to the question, Who won the war?

"We won the war!"

That "we" included all the soldiers who'd fought.

The train stopped, and they disembarked, "four thousand hearts singing."

It was confusing—there were so many people.

One private needed to use the latrine. He found it but when he was finished, he couldn't locate his company.

He found an MP and asked him if he knew where his company was.

The MP, a white man, turned, raised his baton over his head, brought it down, and cracked the private's skull open.

Captain MacClinton was on the scene to disperse the crowd before there was further trouble. The private was placed under arrest and carried off. MacClinton was going jaw to jaw with an MP captain when Arthur Little arrived, demanding an explanation. The MP captain showed Little the same insolence he'd shown MacClinton. Little ordered him to stand at attention in the presence of a superior officer. The MP said he answered to the major general commanding. Little told him he answered to the commander in chief and to stand at attention.

More respectfully, the MP captain explained, as if confiding white man to white man and therefore able to speak freely, that he'd been told, "The Niggers were feeling their oats a bit," and he'd been instructed to "take it out of them quickly, just as soon as they arrived, so as not to have any trouble later on."

The private who'd used the latrine was returned to the regiment the following morning with his head bandaged—and with the message that the charges against him had been dropped, whatever they could have been.

The leadership's worst fears about the black soldiers had come true: their treatment by the French had indeed "spoiled them," to the extent that some of them seemed to have been temporarily blinded by a sense of solidarity with their fellow soldiers. They had forgotten what sort of treatment they'd left behind—and were returning to.

The men of the 369th sailed from Brest on January 31, 1919, and arrived home in New York on February 12, the birthday of Abraham Lincoln.

The band played "Goodbye France, Hello Broadway" on the pier as they boarded their ships for home, reversing the lyrics to a popular song, "Goodbye Broadway, Hello France":

> *Hello Broadway, Goodbye France,*
> *We're ten million strong,*
> *Hello sweethearts, wives and mothers,*
> *It didn't take us long,*
> *Don't you worry while we're here*
> *It's for you we're fighting too,*
> *So Hello Broadway, Good-bye France,*
> *We squared our debt to you.*
> *Hello Broadway, Good-bye France!*

nine

The Last
Parade

*We are cowards and jackasses if now that the war is over, we do not
marshal every ounce of our brain and brawn to fight a sterner, longer,
more unbending battle against the forces of hell in our own land.
We return. We return from fighting. We return fighting. Make way for
Democracy! We saved it in France, and by Great Jehovah, we will save it
in the United States of America, or know the reason why.*
—W. E. B. DuBois, *Crisis* MAGAZINE

William Hayward had promised his men a parade and would
not be denied, not this time, not after what they'd been
through. He'd crowed about his regiment's achievements in an interview to the *New York Tribune* on February 14, 1919, the reporter
writing, no one ever "filled with greater pride than swelled in
Colonel Hayward as he talked of his men, the best regiment, he said,
with pardonable emphasis, 'of all engaged in the great war.'"

The men had cheered when they saw the Statue of Liberty. Hayward wanted somebody to cheer for them. It would not be his
parade—it would be theirs—and if a little glory got thrown his way
in the process, his ego was big enough to handle it. There were,
across America, in towns large and small, "Welcome Home" parades,

with bands, banners, flags, and crowds turned out to welcome back their boys. In one small town in Missouri, the black veterans who saw action in France were even allowed to march in the town's victory parade with the white troops, but only at the very end, behind all the white troops and the members of the local Red Cross.

Recognition from the American army was perfunctory. Gen. John "Black Jack" Pershing, contributing to Emmett J. Scott's official history, *The American Negro in the World War*, wrote,

> The stories, probably invented by German agents, that colored soldiers in France are always placed in the most dangerous positions and sacrificed to save white soldiers, that when wounded they are left on the ground to die without medical attention, etc., are absolutely false.
>
> A tour of inspection among American Negro troops by officers of these headquarters shows the comparatively high degree of training and efficiency among these troops. Their training is identical with that of other American troops serving with the French Army, the effort being to lead all American troops gradually to heavy combat duty by a preliminary service in trenches in quiet sectors.
>
> Colored troops in trenches have been particularly fortunate as one regiment had been there a month before any losses were suffered. This was almost unheard of on the western front.
>
> The exploits of two colored infantrymen in repelling a much larger German patrol, killing and wounding several Germans and winning the Croix de Guerre by their gallantry, has aroused a fine spirit of emulation throughout the colored troops, all of whom are looking forward to more active service.
>
> The only regret expressed by colored troops is that they are not given more dangerous work to do. I cannot com-

mend too highly the spirit shown among the colored combat troops, who exhibit fine capacity for quick training and eagerness for the most dangerous work.

Pershing alluded to the exploits of Henry Johnson and Needham Roberts but declined to mention them by name. The colored troops who had asked for more dangerous work were those he kept in the Service of Supply. His mention of a "particularly fortunate" regiment sounds begrudging, implying that they weren't pulling their weight and were just lucky. Finally, in denying that colored troops were used as "sacrifice troops," he suggests they were not put in very dangerous positions at all and were merely "comparatively efficient." In truth, the 369th lost a higher percentage of its original contingent than any other regiment: thirteen hundred men out of two thousand. That would suggest that they were indeed in dangerous positions. It would actually have made a great deal of sense for a general to put his best troops, rather than his worst, in the most dangerous positions, particularly when his army was fighting in a long line that he didn't want the enemy to break through.

In the same text, Scott cites Rev. D. Leroy Ferguson, a U.S. Army chaplain who, after witnessing the bravery of the colored troops firsthand in France, said,

> When the history of the war is written our soldiers will have their names written large with honors, and though here in France for victory, they all want to and expect to return to the good old U. S. A. With all her faults we love her still— our wives, our sweethearts, families and our homes. I am proud to be able to contribute something to the war.

Pershing distributed a number of Distinguished Service Crosses among the Ninety-third and Ninety-second divisions, but from the 369th, only Lt. George Robb, injured four times at Sechault, received the Congressional Medal of Honor, one of seventy-eight Americans so cited. Some felt Henry Johnson was at least as deserving. It seemed clear to the survivors of the 369th RIUS that if their names were to be written large, they would have to write them themselves.

Had the men been denied their parade, Hayward would not have had to arm them—they would have armed themselves. They talked about it on a daily basis. The threat of not being allowed to march in the parade was enough to make the rowdiest "scapegrace" toe the line. Hayward had seen a photograph of one of their earlier recruiting parades down the streets of Harlem, before the war, depicting men carrying broomsticks in "a stringy column of irregularity . . . a 'Column of Bunches,'" and he'd been embarrassed. They had come a long way from those days, literally and metaphorically, and he wanted New York to know it.

At daybreak on February 17, they boarded a train at Camp Upton in Yaphank, Long Island, bound for Long Island City, then crossed the East River on ferryboats. Of all the rivers they'd crossed in the last year, this one was by far the sweetest. They marched six blocks west on Twenty-fifth Street to Madison Avenue, then turned down Madison until the head of the column reached Twenty-third.

The band tuned their instruments, cleared their spit valves, tightened their mouthpieces, and cleaned and wetted their reeds. In attendance were sixty pieces of brass, thirty trumpets (according to Arthur Little, Jim Europe's band consisted of forty-four members in France), with the percussion twins, Steven and Herbert Wright from the Jenkins Orphanage, playing drums. Jim Europe had given them all their music. He knew that a parade's soul is its band, and he always ran a tight ship. Before the parade he may have even privately chastised Herbert Wright, who had been acting somewhat erratically lately, showboating a bit, getting up and leaving the stage in the middle of a tune when his part was over.

Men adjusted their belts, wiped their helmets clean, and rubbed the toes of their boots on the backs of their legs to make their boots shine. As they got ready, they wondered if anybody was going to show up to watch.

Noble Sissle waxed as lyrical as he knew how: "Alexander the Great conquered the world, Napoleon and his mighty army still furnish startling material for writers and poets, Charlemagne and William the Conqueror are men of valiant character, heroes that had marched at the head of victorious armies, but there was never a soldier that sat in Elysium as he led the march of a victorious army any more happy or felt more honored, than did Colonel Hayward."

The next day, February 18, 1919, the *New York World* gave a more measured, if equally exuberant, account. The newspaper's description of the parade captures both the joy and the solemnity of the occasion:

> The town that's always ready to take off its hat and give a whoop for a man who's done something—"no matter who or what he was before," as the old Tommy Atkins song has it—turned itself loose yesterday in welcoming home a regiment of its own fighting sons that not only did something, but did a whole lot in winning democracy's war.

Tommy Atkins was a generic Britishism, usually shortened to just "Tommy," referring to British soldiers in the First World War.

> In official records, and in the histories that youngsters will study in generations to come, this regiment will probably always be known as the 369th Infantry, U.S.A.
>
> But in the hearts of a quarter million or more who lined the streets yesterday to greet it, it was no such thing. It was the old Fifteenth New York. And so it will be in this city's memory, archives and in the folk lore of the

descendants of the men who made up its straight, smartly stepping ranks.

New York is not race-proud nor race-prejudiced. That this 369th Regiment, with the exception of its eighty-nine white officers, was composed entirely of Negroes, made no difference in the shouts and flag waving and handshakes that were bestowed upon it. New York gave its Old Fifteenth the fullest welcome of its heart.

Through scores of thousands of cheering white citizens, and then through a greater multitude of its own color, the regiment, the first actual fighting unit to parade as a unit here, marched in midday up Fifth Avenue and through Harlem, there to be almost assailed by the colored folks left behind when it went away to glory.

Later it was feasted and entertained, and this time very nearly smothered with hugs and kisses by kin and friends, at the 71st Regiment Armory. Still later, perfectly behaved and perfectly ecstatic over its reception, the regiment returned to Camp Upton to await its mustering out.

Some men, after hugs and kisses from long-missed wives and girl-friends, did not return immediately to Camp Upton, nor did they wait patiently to muster out. Henry Johnson went AWOL immediately after the parade to celebrate with a few new friends and admirers and didn't return for three days.

You knew these dark lads a year and a half ago, maybe, as persons to be slipped a dime as a tip and scarcely glanced at. They were your elevator boys, your waiters, the Pullman porters who made up your berths (though of course you'd never dare to slip a Pullman porter a dime). But, if you were like many a prosperous white citizen yesterday you were mighty proud to grasp Jim or Henry or Sam by the hand and then boast among your friends that you possessed his acquaintance.

When a regiment has the medal honors of France upon its flags and it has put the fear of God into Germany time after time, and its members wear two gold stripes, signifying a year's fighting service, on one arm, and other stripes, signifying wounds, on the other, it's a whole lot different outfit from what it was when it went away. And that's the old Fifteenth N.Y. And the men are different—and that's Jim and Henry and Sam.

Col. William Hayward, the distinguished white lawyer and one time Public Service Commissioner, who is proud to head these fighters, was watching them line up for their departure shortly after 6 o'clock last evening, when someone asked him what he thought of the day.

"It has been wonderful!" he said, and he gazed with unconcealed tenderness at his men. "It's been far beyond my expectations. But these boys deserve it. There's only one thing missing. I wish some of Gen. Gouraud's French boys, whom we fought beside, could be here to see it."

Gen. Henri Gouraud returned to the Middle East after the Great War. He presided over the creation of the state of Lebanon in 1920 but returned to Paris in 1923 to serve as its military governor. He came to America in 1923 and on Bastille Day, July 14, gave a speech in Indianapolis to the Rainbow Division, where he called the 369th "one of the greatest regiments that ever fought under his command." On August 13, 1923, Arthur Little hosted a reception for General Gouraud at the regiment armory at Sixty-seventh and Park, where the band played "Sambre et Meuse" and a medley of field marches. Noble Sissle sang "Joan of Arc" one more time, and a young dancer named Bill "Bojangles" Robinson performed. They wanted the general to know, according to the program printed for the event, that "his treatment of our colored soldiers has written his name in the hearts of every man, woman and child of the colored race."

Noble Sissle got a letter from General Gouraud's secretary, dated April 26, 1927, saying, "Dear Mr. Sissle, General Gouraud has received your letter in which you stated that you are writing a book of the life of Jim Europe. Though the General is much occupied by his duties, he asks me to write to you that he well remembers Jim Europe . . . [and] cannot forget the excellent orchestra that Jim Europe led on the days when he had the pleasure to hear him, especially at the American Cantine at Chalons on Independence Day of 1918, and he is confident that a military orchestra like this one is able to prevent anyone from becoming blue." Gouraud retired in 1937 and died in Paris in 1946.

The newspaper account continues:

> The Colonel slapped his hand affectionately upon the shoulder of his dark-skinned orderly.
>
> "How about that, Hamilton, old boy?" he inquired.
>
> "That's right, Colonel, sir; Gen. Gouraud's boys sure would have enjoyed this day!" the orderly responded as he looked proudly at the Colonel.
>
> There's that sort of paternal feeling of the white officers toward their men, and that filial devotion of the men to their officers, such as exists in the French Army.
>
> Much as the white population of the town demonstrated their welcome to the Regiment, it was, after all, those of their own color to whom the occasion belonged. And they did themselves proud in making it an occasion to recall for years in Harlem, San Juan Hill and Brooklyn, where most of the fighters were recruited.
>
> At the official reviewing stand at 60th street, the kinsfolk and admirers of the regimental lads began to arrive as

beforehandedly as 9 o'clock. They had tickets, and their seats were reserved for them. The official committee had seen to that—and nine-tenths of the yellow wooden benches were properly held for those good Americans of New York whom birth by chance had made dark-skinned instead of fair. BUT this was their Day of Days, and they had determined (using their own accentuation) to BE there and to be there EARLY.

The first-comers plodded across 59th Street from the San Juan Hill district, and it was fine to see them. There seemed to be a little military swank even to the youngsters, as platoons of them stepped along with faces that had been scrubbed until they shone. Had a woman a bit of fur, she wore it. Had a man a top hat—origin or vintage-date immaterial—he displayed that. All heads were up, high; eyes alight. Beaming smiles everywhere. No not quite everywhere. Occasionally there was to be seen on a left sleeve a black band with a gold star, which told the world that one of the Old Fifteenth would never see the region west of Columbus Circle, because he had closed his eyes in France. And the faces of the wearers of these were unlaughing, but they held themselves just as proudly as the rest.

Soldiers marching saw the gold stars on the armbands of onlookers and wondered if they knew what they signified. They remembered the ones they'd saved and the ones they couldn't save, the ones they'd watched die and the ones who after a raid or a battle just didn't show up again. John Jamieson remembered James Turpin, the boy who really believed in all the things the preachers had said they were fighting for. "Are you afraid, Jimmie?" he'd asked. He never complained. Turpin would have loved this. Herbert White could still hear his comrades lying on the ground crying, "Help me boys"; he still remembered the wounded he'd carried and the platoon he'd seen obliterated in front of him.

Wars end but the memories they create don't. Soldiers are given large abstractions, words like "glory," "honor," and "patriotism." Even soldiers who believe wholeheartedly in such abstractions have trouble reconciling them with the concrete images they take away from the battlefield; they have trouble sorting the things they must remember from the things they can't bear to, things no human being should have to know.

For some, the parade would have a therapeutic effect, becoming a larger memory to absorb or blot out the others. This was what "glory" and "honor" and "patriotism" looked like, sounded like, smelled like, felt like. It was hard to grasp an abstraction but easy to remember a parade—particularly one like this.

Few of the welcomers went flagless. No matter whether a man or woman wore a jewel or a pair of patent leather boots as a sign of "class," or tramped afoot to the stand or arrived in a limousine, nearly every dark hand held the nation's emblem.

Nearly every one wore white badges bearing the letters: "Welcome, Fighting 15th," or had pennants upon which stood out the regimental insignia—a coiled rattlesnake of white on a black field.

Those colored folk who could afford it journeyed to the stand in closed automobiles. Gorgeously gowned women alighted with great dignity beneath the admiring gaze of their humbler brethren. Taxies brought up those whose fortunes, perhaps, were not of such amplitude. Hansoms and hacks conveyed still others, and one party came in a plumber's wagon, its women members all bundled up in shawls and blankets against the cold, but grinning delightedly as the whole stand applauded.

Children by the thousands lined the east side of the avenue—Boy Scouts and uniformed kids and little girls with their school books under their arms, and they sang to the great delight of the crowd.

Just why it was that when Governor Smith and former Governor Whitman and Acting Mayor Moran and the other reviewers appeared behind a cavalcade of mounted policemen, the youngsters struck up that army classic, "Oh, How I Hate to Get Up in the Morning," no one could tell, but it gave the reviewers and the crowd a laugh.

The other day I chanced to meet a soldier friend of mine,
He'd been in camp for sev'ral weeks and he was looking fine;
His muscles had developed and his cheeks were rosy red,
I asked him how he liked the life, and this is what he said:
"Oh! how I hate to get up in the morning, Oh! how I'd love to remain in bed."

With the state and city officials were the members of the Board of Aldermen, the Board of Estimate, Major Gen. Thomas J. Barry, Vice Admiral Albert Gleaves, Secretary of State Francis Hugo, Rodman Wannamaker and—in a green hat and big fur coat—William Randolph Hearst. Secretary Baker of the War Department was unable to attend, but he did the next best thing and sent his colored assistant, Emmett J. Scott.

The reviewers arrived at 11:30 and had a good long wait, for at that time the paraders had not yet left 23rd Street. But what with the singing, and the general atmosphere of joyousness about the stand, there was enough to occupy everyone's time.

There was one feature which took the eye pleasingly—the number of babies which proud mothers held aloft, fat pickaninnies, mostly in white, and surrounded by adoring relatives. These were to see (and be seen by) their daddies for the first time. Laughingly, the other day, Col. Bill Hayward spoke of "our boys' posthumous children," and said he thought there were quite a few of them.

Upon returning home, Jim Europe resumed his marriage to Willie Angrom Europe. He also paid a visit to twenty-eight-year-old Bessie Simms and their son, James Reese Europe Jr., born February 2, 1917. Willie was aware of her husband's other family. Europe promised Bessie Simms that he would continue to support their son financially, and said he'd like to make enough money to send James Jr. and his half-sister Madeline to school in France. He brought his son two souvenirs from the war, his helmet and his gas mask. James Jr. grew up unaware that there was anything unusual about his paternity. When his mother died in 1931, he raised himself, mopping floors at Radio City Music Hall and occasionally sleeping on the subways. He became a merchant marine, a policeman, and a fireman. Years later, when James Reese Europe Jr. traveled to Washington, D.C., to meet his grandmother Lorraine, after he'd found her name in the phonebook, she would slam the door in his face.

"Some of our boys had to go away pretty quickly," he reminisced. "Some of them were only married about twenty minutes or so."

"O Colonel!" said the modest Major Little on that occasion.

"Well, maybe it was a trifle longer than twenty minutes," admitted Bill. But anyhow, there was the regiment's posthumous children in the stand.

Before the war, Arthur Little had been the publisher of *Pearson's Magazine*, which featured writers like Upton Sinclair and George Bernard Shaw and had serialized H. G. Wells's *War of the Worlds*, set in England but later adapted for radio by Orson Welles. Little had heard Jim Europe's music at society parties before the war. After the war, he ran Knickerbocker Press in Yonkers and helped Alfred Knopf get started with his publishing house. He lived in Long Island but bought land in Cody, Wyoming, and became involved in creating a monument to Buffalo Bill Cody. In 1921, he gave the commencement speech at Lincoln College in Chester, Pennsylvania, a school funded to produce colored Christian leaders. Before retiring at the rank of brigadier general, he traveled to France in the 1920s on behalf of federal and New York State authorities to bestow honors on General Gouraud, General Lebouc, and other French officials who'd commanded attached American forces. He was made honorary mayor of Harlem, became a republican activist, and in 1936 spoke at the Republican convention in Cleveland, where he was bruited as a possible vice presidential candidate in Alf Landon's futile run against Franklin Roosevelt. He married five times. His fifth wife, Harriet Little, died in Palm Beach in 1994.

It was 11:26 when the old 15th stepped away from 23rd Street and Fifth Avenue. They looked the part of the fighting men they were. At an exact angle over their right shoulders were their long-bayonetted rifles. Around their waists were belts of cartridges. On their heads were their "tin hats," the steel helmets that saved many a life, as was attested by the dents and scars in some of them. Their eyes were straight forward and their chins, held high naturally, seemed higher than ever because of the leather straps that circled them. The fighters wore spiral puttees and their heavy hobbed hiking shoes, which caused a metallic clash as they scraped over the asphalt.

At the head of the line rode four platoons of mounted police, twelve abreast, and then, afoot and alone, Col. Hayward, who organized the Fifteenth, drilled them when they had nothing but broomsticks to drill with, fathered them and loved them, and turned them into the fightingest military organization any man's army could want.

The French called them "Hell Fighters." The Germans after a few mix-ups named them "Blutlustige Schwarzmänner" (blood-thirsty black men). But Col. Bill, when he speaks of them uses the words "those scrapping babies of mine," and they like that best of all. Incidentally (when out of his hearing) they refer tenderly to him as "Old Bill, that fightin' white man." So it's fifty-fifty.

The Colonel had broken a leg in the war, so there were those who looked for him to limp as he strode out to face the hedge of spectators that must have numbered a quarter of a million. But nary a limp. With his full six feet drawn up erectly and his strong face smiling under his tin hat, he looked every bit the fighting man as he marched up the centre of the avenue, hailed every few feet by enthusiasts who knew him socially or in the law courts or in the business of the Public Service Commission.

"Didn't your leg hurt you, Bill?" his friends asked him later.

"Sure it hurt me," he said, "but I wasn't going to peg along on the proudest day of my life!" Which this day was.

William Hayward resigned once the regiment was taken from federal service and made into a National Guard unit again. Arthur Little replaced him but also resigned, both men believing the Fifteenth should be commanded by an African American. Hayward surprised New York society by marrying thirty-six-year-old Mary Cadwell Manwaring Plant, the widow of a well-known financier, the wedding kept secret and out of the society papers. He became a district attorney in New York City. His son Leland became a Hollywood talent agent who handled Fred Astaire and Ginger Rogers (portrayers of Vernon and Irene Castle in a 1939 movie), as well as Jimmy

Stewart, Judy Garland, Henry Fonda, Greta Garbo, and Katharine Hepburn, whom he was said to have dated. On Broadway, Leland "Haywire" Hayward produced *South Pacific* and *The Sound of Music*. Col. William Hayward died in 1946 and was buried in the Cedar Grove Cemetery in New London, Connecticut.

Behind the Colonel marched his staff, Lieut. Col. W.A. Pickering, Capt. Adjutant Robert Ferguson, Major E.A. Whittemore, Regimental Sergt. Majors C.A. Connick and B.W. Cheeseman, Regimental Sergts. L.S. Payne, H.W. Dickerson and W.W. Chisum, and Sergts. R.C. Craig, D.E. Norman and Kenneth Bellups.

The regiment of Sambre and Meuse
Always went to the cry of "Freedom,"
Seeking the glorious road
Who led to immortality.

The Police Band was at the front of the line of march, but it was a more famous band that provided the music to which the Black Buddies stepped northward and under the Arch of Victory—the wonderful jazz organization of Lieut. Jimmie Europe, the one colored commissioned officer of the regiment. But it wasn't jazz that started them off. It was the historic Marche du Regiment de Sambre et Meuse, which has been France's most popular parade piece since Napoleon's day. As rendered now it had all the crash of bugle fanfares which is its dominant feature, but an additional undercurrent of saxophones and basses that put a new and more peppery tang into it.

All these proud children of Gaule
Went without truce and rest,
With their rifles on the shoulder.

Courage in the heart and back bag,
Glory was their food.

One hundred strong, and the proudest band of blowers and
pounders that ever reeled off marching melody—Lieut. Jimmie's boys lived fully up to their reputation. Their music was
as sparkling as the sun that tempered the chill day.

Four of their drums were instruments which they had
captured from the enemy in Alsace, and ma-an, what a beating was imposed upon those sheepskins! "I'd very much
admire to have them bush Germans a-watchin' me today!"
said the drummer before the march started. The Old 15th
doesn't say "Boche" when it refers to the foe it beat. "Bush"
is the word it uses, and it throws in "German" for good
measure. Twenty abreast the heroes marched through a din
that never ceased. They were as soldierly a lot as this town,
now used to soldierly outfits, has ever seen.

Hayward had organized his men in the French phalanx formation.
They stood in companies of sixteen squads each, four platoons of
four squads in close line, a solid mass of men thirty-five feet square
moving in synchrony, with the sergeants marching two paces in front
of their platoons, lieutenants three paces in front of their sergeants,
and captains five paces in front of their lieutenants.

They had that peculiar sort of half careless, yet wholly perfect, step that the French display. Their lines were straight,
their rifles at an even angle, and they moved along with the
jaunty ease and lack of stiffness which comes only to men
who have hiked far and frequently.

The colored folks on the official stand cut loose with a
wild, swelling shriek of joy as the Police Band fell out at 60th
Street and remained there to play the lads along when nec-

essary and when—now entirely itself—the khaki-clad regiment filling the street from curb to curb, stepped by.

George Cotton had two more fights, losing to "Big Bill" Tate in a first-round knockout in Philadelphia and soon after getting knocked out in a seven-round fight by a man named John Lester Johnson. Spots Poles earned five battle stars and a purple heart in France. Black actor and singer Paul Robeson ranked Poles as one of the four greatest black athletes of all time, with Jack Johnson, Jesse Owens, and Joe Louis. He resumed his baseball career after the war, batted .310 in 1919, and was believed to have a lifetime batting average of over .400. He tired of the endless travel Negro league teams had to endure and retired in 1923, after which he drove a cab in his hometown of Harrisburg, Pennsylvania. He died on September 12, 1962, in a Veterans' Administration (VA) hospital in Lebanon, Pennsylvania, and is buried in section forty-two of Arlington National Cemetery.

> Colonel Hayward, with his hand at salute, turned and smiled happily as he saw his best friend, former Governor Whitman, standing with his other good friend, Governor Al Smith, with their silk ties raised high over their heads. It was the Governor's first review in New York and the first time he and Mr. Whitman had got together since Inauguration Day. They were of different parties, but they were united in greeting Colonel Bill and his Babies.

Hamilton Fish was elected congressman from New York in 1920 and served until 1945. He helped organize the inaugural caucus of the American Legion that opened in St. Louis on May 8, 1919, where he urged the members to admit colored veterans, but by the time the convention adjourned, two days later, the question of integrating the American Legion was left for the local chapters to decide, which meant that chapters in the South (and the North) were free to exclude blacks. Ostensibly a veterans' organization advocating for veterans' rights—soldiers had only been paid a dollar a day for their services and sacrifices, with a $60 bonus at the end—the patriotic American Legion soon turned its attention to attacking Bolsheviks, Industrial Workers of the World workers (believed to be recruiting colored workers to their labor unions and un-American causes), and strikebreakers. Fish became both a ferocious anti-Communist whose Fish Committee in the 1930s prefigured the McCarthy-era hearings and a sworn enemy to his former friend Franklin Roosevelt, to whom he'd written during the war. He opposed America's entry into World War II but supported a Palestinian homeland for the Jews and sponsored legislation to help Germany's Jewish population.

He also became one of Congress's leading representatives for racial equality and against Jim Crow. He advocated in Congress for a federal antilynching law. Congressman Fish told the House of Representatives on January 8, 1940, "Every time a colored man or woman is lynched or burned at the stake in America it means the Emancipation Proclamation has been suspended and that their civil and equal rights have been destroyed under the law and Constitution. I would be derelict to those colored soldiers who served under my command and who paid the supreme sacrifice on the battlefields of France fighting to make the world safe for Democracy if I did not raise my voice and do everything in my power to help pass a Federal anti-lynching bill in order to make America safe for their own people, their families and sons. . . . Lynching is an outrageous, un-American, bestial and barbaric practice. It is the worst crime in America. A nation that does not protect its own citizens is not worthy of the name. A nation that sits supinely by and permits its own citizens to be destroyed by mob violence is in no position to protest racial injustices and persecution in foreign lands."

No federal antilynching law was ever passed, but the crusade to enact such a law publicized a crime to the extent that its perpetrators were more often punished under extant murder statutes. Lynchings died out in the 1950s.

In 1954, Fish, twice an all-American, was inducted into the College Football Hall of Fame. He died in 1991 at the age of 102. His son, Hamilton Fish IV, was a U.S. congressman from New York from 1969 to 1995. His grandson, who ran unsuccessfully for Congress in 1994, was known at various times as Hamilton Fish III, Hamilton Fish Jr., and Hamilton Fish V.

From the stand, from the Knickerbocker Club across the street, from the nearby residences and from the curbing sounded shouts of individual greetings for the commander and his staff. But these were quickly drowned as a roar went up for Lieutenant Europe's band, with its commander at the head—not swinging a baton like a common ordinary drummajor, but walking along with the uniform and side-arms of an officer.

"The Salute to the 85th," which they learned from their comrade regiment of the French Army of General Gouraud, was what they were playing, a stirring thing full of bugle calls and drum rolls, which Europe says is the best march he ever heard.

So swiftly did the platoons sweep by that it took a quick eye to recognize a brother or a son or a lover or a husband; but the eyes in the stand were quick, and there were shouts of "Oh, Bill!" "Hey, boy, here's your mammy!" "Oliver, look at your baby!" (It wasn't learned whether this referred to a feminine person or one of those posthumous children Colonel Hayward spoke about.) "Hallelujah, Sam! There you are, back home again!"

Half way down the ranks of the 2,992 paraders appeared the colors, and all hats came off with double reverence, for the Stars and Stripes and the blue regimental standard that two husky ebony lads held proudly aloft had been carried from here to France, from France to Germany and back again, and each bore the bronze token with its green and red ribbon that is called the Croix de Guerre. Keen eyes could see these little medals swinging from the silk of the flags, high toward the top of the poles.

At the end of the lines which filled the avenue came a single automobile, first, with a round-faced smiling white officer sitting in it and gazing happily from side to side. This was Major Lorillard Spencer, who was so badly wounded that he came back in advance of the outfit some weeks ago. There was a special racket of cheers for him, and then another for Major David L'Esperance, also wounded and riding.

Charles W. Fillmore went to work for the New York State tax bureau after the war. In 1929, he was chosen by a coalition of politicians and clergy to replace Abraham Grenthal as district leader of the Republican Party in Harlem, a position that had until then been held by white men, even though whites were no longer the majority in Harlem. Fillmore had patched up his differences with Arthur Little when the regiments comprising the Ninety-third Division were united at the forwarding camp in Le Mans before shipping stateside. There Fillmore sought Little out to ask if he'd been the one to recommend him for the Croix de Guerre. When Little admitted he had, citing Fillmore's courage leading his men through the gassed swamps on the Marson Road, Fillmore extended his hand, and the two men shook.

After transferring to the 365th Regiment, Capt. Napoleon B. Marshall had been seriously injured at a place called Xon Hill, with shrapnel wounds to his spine, ribs, and lungs, and came home with his upper body trussed in a steel corset.

"Do you remember when I used to have to go around talking on the corners to find recruits for Col. Bill Hayward's 15th Regiment?" he asked an interviewer. "But we got them, and they fought some fight. The French wanted us to stay with them the whole time. On the night of Oct. 21st, we were ordered to make a raid . . . preparatory to a raid on Metz. I took thirty-one men along. We crawled into No Man's Land and blundered into a German patrol party. The enemy sent up a rocket signal and the next thing, the Germans showered us with an artillery deluge, shrapnel and high explosives and a few bullets for good measure. We were far from our own lines. We were up against it bad. There was one thing to do. We advanced towards the enemy lines and thereby got under their range. Then we detoured and in three hours got back to our own lines."

After the war, he resumed his law practice and became active in the Democratic Party. In 1922, he became a military liaison to Haiti, an independent black nation that had been occupied by the U.S. military since 1915 and governed by a high commission of whites, who did not welcome Marshall's appointment. In Haiti, he worked with the poor and fought an ongoing battle with the high commission, coming home in 1929. He worked again as a lawyer, presided over banquets at the Harvard Club, and continued to advocate for the people of Haiti. He was one of the founders of the National Negro Music Center, as well as a college professor at Howard University. He died on June 5, 1933.

Then a far different figure, but one of the most famous of the whole war. Henry Johnson! That Henry, once a mild-mannered chauffeur, who to protect his comrade, Needham Roberts, waded into a whole patrol of "bush Germans" with a lot of hand grenades, his rifle and his trusty "steel" in the shape of a bolo knife, and waded into them so energetically that when the casualties were counted there were four dead foemen in front of him, thirty-four others done up so badly they couldn't even crawl away, and heaven knows how many more had been put to flight.

And now Henry, in commemoration of this exploit, was riding alone in an open machine. In his left hand he held his tin hat. In his right he held high over his head a bunch of red and white lilies which some admirer had pressed upon him. And from side to side Henry—about as black as any man in the outfit if not a trifle blacker—bowed from the waist down with all the grace of a French dancing master. Yes, he bowed, and he grinned from ear to ear and he waved his lilies, and he didn't overlook a bet in the way of taking (and liking) all the tributes that were offered to him.

A fleet of motor ambulances, back of Henry, carried the wounded men who were unable to walk, nearly 200 of them. But though they couldn't walk, they could laugh and wave and shout thanks for the cheers, all of which they did.

Needham Roberts came home to Trenton a celebrated hero, given his own parade down Clinton Avenue and feted at a reception by the mayor. He'd been promoted to sergeant on November 6, a week before the armistice. At nineteen years of age, he was a war hero, with a big article about him in the *Saturday Evening Post*. That summer, the YMCA sponsored him on a speaking tour in Ohio, where he talked of his "thrilling adventures" and how he and Henry Johnson had killed four Huns. He married and had a daughter, Juanita. He was still suffering from his wounds, however, with an artificial elbow and a hole in his side where the German bayonet had pierced. His injuries made it difficult to work in a town where black men had few options for gainful employment to begin with. The war had given him an identity, and he could neither find another identity to replace it nor hold on to the one he had. In 1924, he was arrested for wearing his military uniform, considerably beyond the three-month legal limit. He was arrested again in 1928 for "sexual abuse" and went to jail. He and his wife and daughter moved to Newark. He was arrested again in 1949 when a girl in a theater complained that Roberts was "bothering her." He was released on bail, but that evening, Roberts and his wife hanged themselves in their bathroom. His wife had written a note that said, "This is a very hard letter to write. Needham and I are going together. It is the best way. He is innocent of any charge against him." His daughter continued to think of him as a great man.

William Butler received a similar hero's welcome upon his return to Salisbury, Maryland, a small town on the Delmarva Peninsula. The *New York Tribune*, on April 28, 1919, wrote,

> Bill Butler, a slight, good-natured colored youth, who until two years ago was a jack-of-all-trades in a little Maryland town, yesterday came into his own as a hero among heroes. More than 5,000 men and women arose to their feet in City College stadium and cheered themselves hoarse while representatives of two Governments pinned their highest medals upon the breast of the nervous youth. Sergeant Butler was one of a list of twenty-three members of the famous 15th Regiment upon whom both France and the United States conferred medals of honor because of extraordinary heroism on European battlefields. But by common consent his name comes first on the list, a list that was made up only after a careful comparison of the deeds of gallantry that finally resulted in the breaking of the Hun lines.

Most feted of all was Henry Johnson, the black Sergeant York, renowned among both black and white Americans and an accidental spokesman for his race, a role he embraced. Theodore Roosevelt himself was an admirer and called him "one of the five bravest" soldiers to take part in the Great War. He gave interviews to reporters from national magazines and white newspapers, sometimes side by side with Colonel Hayward himself. As with Needham Roberts, his actions had conferred upon him not just an identity but, if he played his cards right, a livelihood—or at least a card to play for as long as he could. His injuries left him in pain, the bones in one leg replaced with a steel rod that made him walk "slap-footed." His work before the war as a redcap at the train station had not trained him to do anything else.

He went home to Albany to see his wife, Edna, and two-year-old son, Herman, and there New York governor Al Smith toasted him at an official dinner, even promising to name a street after him. Another wealthy benefactor promised to build him a house. In March 1919, he was invited to address the state legislature to talk about veterans' benefits. Soon after that, Colonel Hayward invited him to participate on a speaking tour on behalf of Liberty Loans. Posters asked, "Henry Johnson Licked Twenty Germans—How Many War Bond Stamps Can You Lick?" He was also invited, in March 1919, to speak in St. Louis as part of a program commemorating black soldiers.

Almost before the happy colored folk could realize at the official stand that here were their lads back home again, the last of the parade rolled along and it was over. With that formation and the step that was inspired by Lieutenant Europe's band—and by the Police Band which stood at 60th Street and kept playing after the music of the other died away—it required only seventeen minutes for the regiment to pass.

From this point north the welcome heightened in intensity. Along the park wall the colored people were banked deeply, everyone giving them the first ranks nearest the curb. Wives, sweethearts and mothers began to dash into the ranks and press flowers upon their men and march alongside with them, arm-in-arm. But this couldn't be, and Colonel Hayward had to stop the procession for a time and order the police to put the relatives back on the sidewalks. But that couldn't stop their noise.

The residents of the avenue paid fine tribute to the dusky marchers. It seemed inspiring, at 65th Street, to see Mrs. Vincent Astor standing in a window of her home, a great flag about her shoulders and a smaller one in her left hand, waving salutes. And Henry Frick, at an open window of his home at 73d Street, waving a flag and cheering at the top of his voice.

At the corner of 86th Street was a wounded colored soldier wearing the Croix de Guerre and the Victoria Cross as well. Colonel Hayward pressed to his side with a hearty handshake, exclaiming: "Why, I thought you were dead!" It was one of his boys long ago invalided home.

"No, sir, Colonel, not me. I ain't dead by a long ways yet, Colonel, sir," said the lad.

"How's it going, Colonel?" asked a spectator.

"Fine," said the Commander. "All I'm worrying about is whether my boys are keeping step." He needn't have worried.

The real height of the enthusiasm was reached when, after passing through 110th Street and northward along Lenox Avenue, the heroes arrived in the real Black Belt of Harlem. This was the Home, Sweet Home for hundreds of them, the neighborhood they'd been born in and had grown up in, and from 129th Street north the windows and roofs and fire-escapes of the five and six story apartment houses were filled to overflowing with their nearest and dearest.

Noble Sissle described Colonel Hayward as nearly falling off his horse, the crowds shrieking with laughter, "when Jim Europe caused the soldiers to lose their dignified expressions on their faces by commanding his band to play, 'Who's Been Here Since I've Been Gone' (*'Who's been here since I've been gone/A great big man with a derby on'*), for had he played something of military sentiment, between the mothers and the sisters and brothers of those who had been left beneath the fields of France, and those who were scattered over this country and abroad in the different hospitals; of those who were among the absent in our line, it would have been a very depressing and serious atmosphere for our boys to have paraded through; but for the tune that had always been a source of amusement to the men while abroad to sing brought a spirit of revelry over the gathered multitude and turned the home-coming into one of happiness, at the same time not losing any patriotic spirit."

Noble Sissle remained a sweet man, a bit square, and "never on time for anything," according to Eubie Blake, with whom Sissle formed a historic partnership, a vaudeville act called "The Dixie Duo." In 1921, Sissle, Blake, and former James Europe collaborators Forney Miller and Aubrey Lyles wrote a musical they called *Shuffle Along*, which opened at the Sixty-third Street Theater, the first all-black-produced and -performed show on Broadway. *Shuffle Along*, with songs like "I'm Just Wild about Harry" and "Love Will Find a Way," became a nationwide hit, toured the Erlanger and Schubert Circuit, and opened the door for other black musicals, as well as clearing the way for black actors like Paul Robeson and Bill "Bojangles" Robinson to appear beside white actors in other productions. Sissle and Blake played London in 1925, then the Ambassadors Restaurant in Paris in a show Cole Porter wrote for them. In 1941, Sissle sat on the board of governors for the United Service Organizations, worked for the Warwick New York School for Boys, founded an organization to help gifted young black musicians, and sang on Sundays at St. Mark's United Methodist Church in Harlem.

In 1952, he became the first black disk jockey to air at a major station, WMGM out of New York. W. C. Handy and Eubie Blake were guests on his show, and Sissle was credited with launching the career of Lena Horne. He founded the Negro Actors Guild of America and was a member of the American Society of Composers, Authors and Publishers, the Screen Actor's Guild, and a number of other organizations. He died with a smile on his face at the age of eighty-six in December 1975. Honorary pallbearers at his funeral included Cab Calloway, Duke Ellington, John Hammond, Earl "Father" Hines, Billy Taylor, and Roy Wilkins.

The noise drowned the melody of Lieut. Europe's band. Flowers fell in showers from above. Men, women and children from the sidewalks overran the police and threw their arms about the paraders. There was a swirling maelstrom of dark humanity in the avenue. In the midst of all the racket there could be caught the personal salutations: "Oh, honey!" "Oh, Jim!" "Oh, you Charlie!" "There's my boy!" "There's daddie!" "How soon you coming home, son?" It took all the ability of scores of reserve policemen between 129th Street and 135th Street, where the uptown reviewing stand was, to pry those colored enthusiasts away from their soldiermen.

There was one particular cry which was taken up for blocks along this district: "O-oh, you wick-ed Hen-nery Johnson! You wick-ed ma-an!" and Henry the Boche Killer still bowed and grinned more widely than ever, if possible.

"Looks like a funeral, Henry, them lilies!" called one admirer.

"Funeral for them bush Germans, boy! Sure a funeral for them bushes," shouted Henry.

Henry Johnson was surely enjoying himself at this parade, virtually its guest of honor. Yet, he may have already been aware of a kind of deceit being perpetrated. His featured act as war hero assigned him a role that in many ways restricted him. The parade was a celebration of everything positive about his own personal achievements and those of his fellow soldiers. The papers were full of what black soldiers were supposed to be like.

"Under his smile and ready laugh or grin," wrote the *Brooklyn Standard Union*, "the colored man has the qualities of a fighter—coolness, patience, steadfastness, optimism, pluck and, of course, courage. . . . Easy to mold to the requirements of discipline, happy under any and all circumstances, he is an exemplary soldier. On the charge he sees red, as the fighter should, and in rest billets or even in the trench he seldom loses his cheerful outlook upon life."

Henry Johnson was expected, after the parade was over, to grin, laugh, show good cheer, and talk about what he'd done that night in

May as if it had afforded him the thrill of a lifetime. In truth, his life had been suddenly and irreversibly transformed in an instant by an act of extreme violence in which he'd killed a man, disemboweling him with a knife. Certainly it was kill or be killed, just as surely as he'd saved Needham Roberts's life by his actions, but it was a horrible experience, and now everybody was patting him on the back and asking him to talk about it.

In Ernest Hemingway's short story "A Soldier's Home," Harold Krebs comes home from France utterly unwilling to lie about what he's seen and done there, having suffered from the lies his country sold him—that war would be a great adventure, when it was just senseless carnage. Hemingway's hero refuses to play the hero and won't accept the deceptions about "the romance of the war" he feels forced upon him at every turn. Henry Johnson may have felt a similar unwillingness to tolerate duplicity. He'd become, to his own race, a symbol of black manhood, but to whites, he was expected to be a voice for racial harmony, when his experiences at Spartanburg and St. Nazaire and in Brest at the war's end had taught him otherwise. Arthur Little wrote that as the regiment demobilized, Johnson purportedly told him, "You made a man out of me." By March 1919, it seemed clear that Henry Johnson was not giving whites credit for making him anything other than angry.

At the celebration for Negro soldiers at the Coliseum in St. Louis, Henry Johnson was no longer willing to put up with the lies. The speakers who preceded him at the podium spoke of how blacks and whites worked together to defeat the Hun, claiming that a new age was dawning. Henry Johnson stepped up, received a loud ovation, then delivered a speech excoriating everything the speakers before him had said. He said that white soldiers refused to fight beside blacks because they were cowards and that blacks were the real fighters. He said that white officers tried to get their black soldiers killed and that he'd heard a white officer say, "Send the niggers to the front and there won't be so many around New York." He said that black soldiers had not been properly credited for their roles, adding, "If I was a white man I would be the next governor of New York. . . . I have seen so many dead bodies piled up that when I saw a live one I didn't think it was natural." Another speaker from the Ninety-second Division said white soldiers were shooting black soldiers in the back. The crowd approved of Henry Johnson's message and practically carried him out of the Coliseum on their shoulders.

The War Department, however, did not approve of his speech and promptly withdrew its support for his touring activities. That night, a half dozen angry white marines (acting on their own, not in an official capacity) knocked on Johnson's hotel room door but apparently failed to recognize him, leaving after Henry answered the door in his bathrobe and said, "Sergeant Johnson is out."

Without further speaking engagements, he returned home to Albany but couldn't find work. He grew despondent, began to drink heavily, and was thought to be using drugs. His wife divorced him in 1923. He moved in and out of Edna's and his son Herman's lives for a while, then eventually disappeared. He died alone in 1929 in a VA hospital in Albany and was buried in Arlington National Cemetery, though for some reason, the army didn't notify his family, who thought he'd been buried in an unmarked pauper's grave somewhere and did not locate his final resting place until 2001. The only American award he received was a posthumous Purple Heart from President Bill Clinton in 1996. Congressional Medal of Honor winner George Robb (who became an auditor for the state of Kansas and a Republican politician) said on numerous occasions that he didn't deserve his medal and that because of the politics of the times, deserving black soldiers never got their due. Henry Johnson's son, Herman Johnson, served with the 332nd Fighter Group, known as the "Tuskegee Airmen," during World War II.

The official reviewing party, after the parade had passed 60th Street, had hurried uptown, and so had the Police Band,

and so there were some doings as the old 15th breezed past 135th Street. But no one up there cared for Governors or ex-Governors or dignitaries. Every eye was on the Black Buddies and every throat was opened wide for them.

At 145th Street the halt was called. Again there was a tremendous rush of men and women with outstretched arms; the military discipline had to prevail, and the soldiers were not allowed to break ranks, nor were the civilians (save the quickest of them) able to give the hugs and kisses they were overflowing with.

As rapidly as possible the fighters were sent down into the subway station and loaded aboard trains which took them down to the 71st Regiment Armory at 34th Street and Fourth Avenue. Here the galleries were filled with as many dusky citizens as could find places (maybe 2,500 or 3,000) and so great was the crowd in the neighborhood that the police had to block off 34th Street almost to Fifth Avenue on the west and Third on the east.

As each company came up from the subway the friends and relatives were allowed to go through the lines, and, while the boys stood still in ranks, but at ease, their kinsfolk were allowed to take them in their arms and tell them really and truly, in close-up fashion, what they thought about having them back.

Cpl. Horace Pippin recovered from his injuries in time to march in the great parade of February 17, but he had permanently lost the use of his right arm. In 1920, he married a widow named Jennie Featherstone Wade Giles, four years his senior and mother to a six-year-old boy. For a while, Pippin supplemented his disability pension of $22.50 per month by working as an iron molder, then a hotel porter, then a junk dealer. One day, he realized he could draw by using his left hand to support his right. He executed a series of drawings from memory, depicting his wartime experiences.

If art came the hard way, a career in art came more easily, the result of both talent and good fortune. Pippin's drawings were discovered by painter N. C. Wyeth and West Chester art critic Dr. Christian Brinton, who spotted them in the window of a shoe-repair store as they were walking down the street. They inquired within and were directed to Pippin's house just down the block. Championed by Brinton, who later became his patron, Pippin moved from drawing to painting, becoming, as one Philadelphia art collector called him, "the most important Negro painter to appear in America." He was a self-taught "primitive" in the tradition of Henri Rousseau, with the flattened picture plane of Grandma Moses and a dark palette. Four of his canvases were included in a 1938 show entitled "Masters of Popular Painting" at New York's Museum of Modern Art. A *New Yorker* reviewer said, "I imagine there are not many painters . . . who can fail to admire the dexterity and daring he displays." He was picked up by a gallery in Philadelphia and made a living selling paintings until his death in 1946.

The *New York Tribune* concluded its review of the Great Parade:

When the entire regiment was in the Armory, the civilians in the gallery broke all bounds. They weren't going to stay up there while their heroes were down below on the drill-floor! Not they! They swarmed past the police and depot battalion and so jammed the floor that it was impossible for the tired Black Buddy even to sit down. Most of the boys had to take their chicken dinner—served by colored girls, and the chow, incidentally, from Delmonico's—standing up with arms about them and kisses punctuating assaults upon the plates.

"Some chow, hey Buddy?" would be heard.

"Pretty bon." You'd get the answer. "I'd like to have beaucoup more of this chicken." There was noticeable a sprinkling of French words in the conversation of the Old 15th, and, indeed, some of them spoke it fluently.

"Sam told me," one girl was heard to say, "that he killed nineteen of them Germans all his own self, but nobody saw him and so he didn't get that Cross doo Gare."

Horace Pippin's memories ranged from the suffering to the sunsets. For other soldiers, it was difficult or impossible to strike that balance. Pvt. John Graham recalled how, when his company went into the trenches for the first time, he felt "happy, but shaky. After engaging in many . . . patrols, raids, and in the September drive, I was taken and sent to the hospital in the town of Marns, where I received much needed treatment. I was restored to my former health through the careful nursing of the girls who treated everybody there and under the watchful influence of officers who felt that we were all created equal and men who lived up to the spirit of the U.S. Army. With all the hardships we went through [and] the abuse we received, we are still true Americans and love our country and were another war to break out tomorrow, we would again be ready to defend our country."

Graham doesn't specify his injuries or his treatment, but the tone of his statement, that he attributes his recovery more to the careful nursing of girls than to the watchful doctors, suggests his injuries may have been psychological or emotional.

Such injuries don't always show up right away. James Henry Jackson, from Huntington, Long Island, had served as a private in Company G. He came home, went about his business, and never said much to his daughter Florence about his experiences, only telling her they were "horrible" and sharing an anecdote about having to eat rats. After the war, he worked as a laborer and on the railroads. He played amateur baseball Sunday afternoons with a group on Long Island, his wife and her sisters gathering at the house, until the Great Depression hit and he couldn't take care of his family. He was devastated. Unable to find work, he grew despondent. His family and his cousins worried about him, kept tabs on him, checked in to see how he was doing. It was a cousin who found him when he tried to hang himself. He was taken to a VA hospital in Northport, Long Island, where he was treated for depression. The doctors there believed his condition was compounded by the gassing he'd taken in France. It was "all that horror," his daughter would say. "This was his country, his land. He knew nothing else."

The contemporary term for James Henry Jackson's condition is post-traumatic stress disorder (PTSD). After the war, it was called simply shell shock. PTSD is essentially a psychic injury that results when neither of the body's natural fight or flight defense mechanisms is applicable and the victim is trapped in an unendurable situation that he must, nevertheless, endure. It would be difficult to design an environment more conducive to post-traumatic stress disorders than the trenches of World War I. In the British army, shell shock accounted for about a seventh of all disability discharges.

In a talk entitled "The Repression of War," delivered to the Royal Society of Medicine on December 4, 1917, by a Dr. W. H. R. Rivers, medical officer at Craiglockhart War Hospital, Dr. Rivers described shell shock as "repression for the active or voluntary process by which it is attempted to remove some part of the mental content out of the field of attention with the aim of making it inaccessible to memory."

He noted, "The training of a soldier is designed to adapt him to act calmly and methodically in the presence of events naturally calculated to arouse disturbing emotions," but the events of actual war cannot be overcome by such training. Absent the ability to flee or to fight against a barrage of shells or a cloud of gas, the soldier can only absorb the experience, then seek to shed the memories or repress them. "This natural tendency to banish the distressing or the horrible," Rivers noted, "is especially pronounced in those whose powers of resistance have been lowered by the long-continued strains of trench-life, the shock of shell-explosion, or other catastrophes of war."

Traumatized soldiers not only were trained to suppress their feelings, but were also drilled to stick a manikin over and over again with a bayonet until, in actual combat, they wouldn't feel anything.

If they couldn't suppress their emotions, they were called cowards or even court-martialed as malingerers. Some punished themselves for the feelings they were ashamed of, feelings soldiers weren't, by a firm but unwritten code, allowed to have. Traumatized soldiers came home and experienced a wide range of symptoms: loss of sleep, loss of appetite, headaches, phobias, rages, anxiety, and frequent disturbing dreams in which dead friends returned to them, friends they couldn't save. They struggled to push the memories from their thoughts, but like a Chinese finger puzzle made of straw, the harder they struggled, the more the memories entangled them. Panicked reactions could be triggered involuntarily by innocent stimuli: the click of a dog's toenail on the kitchen linoleum floor sounds just like a pair of wire cutters clipping barbed wire, and a veteran sits up in his bed, thinking, Someone's coming! Some couldn't bear darkness or loud noises, thunderstorms. Those who'd completely disassociated would feel fine, then suddenly and for no apparent reason become depressed, anxious, or alert for danger.

Psychotherapy, as a medical practice, was still in its infancy. Treatment for those who sought it or who were so far gone as to be remanded to it was often the psychological equivalent of the old joke where the patient says, "Doctor, my arm hurts when I do this," and the doctor replies, "Then don't do that." Sufferers were told to "try not to think about it." Talking about war was forbidden, and they were instructed to think happy thoughts or to paint bright, colorful pictures of beautiful scenery. Occasionally doctors used hypnosis. Horace Pippin came out the other side because in his journals and in his art, he directed his attention exactly and courageously toward the suffering, and in doing so he noticed the sunsets too. Sometimes convalescent facilities would be full of soldiers who had all gone through the same thing but were forbidden to talk about it.

Today, in addition to all the various medications available, talk therapy is still found effective in treating PTSD: rather than being discouraged from talking about their trauma, soldiers are directed to do just that, to push through the experience to get to the other side, to talk about it until it becomes a narrative the soldier can own, his story to tell, or not tell, at the time and place of his own choosing. Repressed memories become, if not released memories, then contained ones, or controlled ones.

After World War I, men did not talk of these things. If they did, perhaps it was in confession with their priest or pastor, or maybe they talked to each other, but there were no organizations for black veterans, no American Legion posts or VA hospitals (the VA system would not be established until July 21, 1930) or other structured facilities where they could get together to talk. Veterans' benefits were so inadequate and minimal that in 1932, seventeen thousand World War I veterans, called "The Bonus Army," marched on Washington to demand immediate payment in full of promised bonuses. Their peaceful demonstration turned into a violent riot when U.S. Army troops, commanded by Maj. George S. Patton and Gen. Douglas A. MacArthur, arrived to disperse the protestors. They used tear gas, which surely bore more than a whiff of familiarity to some of the doughboys in the melee. The GI Bill of Rights was passed in 1944 as a result of the Bonus Army's efforts—but where, in 1919 or the ten years following the end of the First World War, could a black veteran suffering from shell shock or psychological injuries go for help? They certainly could not tell their families what they'd seen, because then the people they loved would know what they knew, and they didn't want to inflict their suffering on others.

James Henry Jackson could tell his daughter Florence only that it was "horrible" and that he ate rats. Henry Johnson could not tell the press or the crowds he addressed the entirety of his story; perhaps he couldn't even tell himself. Needham Roberts could not tell his family what he'd seen. Herbert Wright, the drummer in Jim Europe's band, may have been another man whose mind suffered due to the war.

The irony was that Jim Europe's music had helped so many men feel better. Virtually miraculous healing powers were ascribed to the music Jim Europe played for the troops in France. Noble Sissle, for whom hyperbole was a favored conceit, would tell W. C. Handy about a time when the band entertained U.S. troops on leave in Paris, along with a French band, and when the French band hacked their way through "The Star Spangled Banner," the American troops grew lethargic. When Europe's band reciprocated with their stepped-up version of "La Marseillaise," the American doughboys looked bewildered and assumed the musicians were Senegalese or French colonials, until they played a blues tune, and then the wounded soldiers supposedly tossed away their crutches and danced, exclaiming, "They're from home! They're from home!" In the crowd on the day of the great parade, W. C. Handy watched Europe lead his band under the Triumphal Arch at Fifth and Twenty-third, filled with envy.

After the war, American workers traveling in France were often asked, "Did you hear Jim Europe's band?" Europe's regimental band had given the French a taste of American jazz, and the French wanted more. The black American writers, artists, and musicians who moved to France in the 1920s in a sense walked through a door that Jim Europe had opened for them. Writers Langston Hughes, Claude McKay, and James Baldwin; artists Palmer Hayden (himself a WWI veteran) and William H. Johnson; and musicians Josephine Baker, Benny Carter, Dexter Gordon, Arthur Briggs, and Thelonius Monk would all make their homes, for varying periods, in Paris. In August 1918, a ragtime musician named Louis A. Mitchell, who billed himself as "The World's Greatest Trap Drummer," wrote a letter to Eubie Blake, offering him a job and inviting him to join him in Paris, where Mitchell had been performing with a group of singers and dancers billing themselves as "The Seven Spades." "[Eubie,] this is the finest country in the world and if you once get over here you will never want to go back to N.Y. again, I intended to stay here the rest of my life, as you can go where you want to and have the time of your life . . . and no one to bother you. I have seen all the fellows of Jim's band and they all want to stay here after the war if possible. . . .

We only work fifteen minutes a day and thirty minutes on the day we have matinees, so you see it is like stealing money, and you are treated white wherever you go as they like spades here and these Yanks can't teach these French people any different."

The French welcomed black Americans after the war, not so much from a national commitment to egalitarianism but simply because they were *grateful*, knowing that if it weren't for the Americans, including the black Americans who'd joined the French armies, Paris in the 1920s would probably have been hosting German polka bands instead of black American jazz musicians.

After the great parade of February 17, Jim Europe wasted little time getting down to business. His band was well-known, even famous, though they had never toured nationally or put out a record. Work for New York's black musicians had dried up during the war. Now that he would be supporting his mother, his sister, his wife, his mistress, and their son, Europe's first priority was to make some money, beginning with organizing a tour for the regimental band.

On March 16, 1919, Europe's Hellfighter Band played its first American concert at Oscar Hammerstein's Manhattan Opera House on West Thirty-fourth Street.

"A streak of jagged lightning flashed across the evening sky," Sissle wrote, trying to capture the occasion. "A thunderbolt hurtled through the lightning's jagged course. A rattling of keys—the mighty clank of locks—the creaking of hinges, and the gates of heaven swung ajar. Through those majestic portals came the spectral forms of Wagner, Verdi, Handel, Chopin, and the hosts of other immortal souls, whose classical, musical compositions have helped to make this earthly abode a better place to live in. Swept along, as on the winds of a mighty storm, they hurried earthward, carrying in their midst that ghostly form of that renowned, eccentric impresario, Oscar Hammerstein. Faster and faster this ghostly party hastened on their downward course, carried along at terrific speed. The pale features of the high-hatted figure were filled with wonderment, as he was literally dragged along by the musical masters, whose faces wore only a look of consternation."

They brought the house down and drew a standing ovation from the tuxedoed and jewel-bedecked audience, an auspicious beginning to the tour, but Europe was annoyed. Herbert Wright had been clowning around during the show, erupting in a fit of uncontrolled giggles during one of his drum solos—he'd upstaged the other members of the band and it was not the sort of behavior that Jim Europe tolerated. He ran a tight ship, allowing his musicians a great amount of latitude—his cornet player, Frank Debroit, often overplayed his solos—but there was a difference between being a showman and upstaging the band.

The next gig was at another opera house, this time in Boston, and they were the first jazz band to play the classical venue. They did so well that a return engagement was booked. They rode in private Pullman cars and trained west to Springfield, Albany, Buffalo, Cleveland, Indianapolis, and Chicago, where Jim Europe looked up his old friend, Irene Castle. They had dinner in Chicago, and the two shared memories and cried over Vernon's tragic death. Europe told her he wanted to establish a memorial of some kind for his old friend and began lining up well-known singers and musicians for a benefit at Madison Square Garden to raise funds. The *Chicago Defender*, Chicago's black newspaper, wrote of Europe and his music, "The most prejudiced enemy of our Race could not sit through an evening with Europe without coming away with a changed viewpoint. For he is compelled in spite of himself to see us in a new light. It is a well known fact that the white people view us largely from the standpoint of the cook, porter and waiter, and his limited opportunities are responsible for much of the distorted opinion held regarding us. Europe and his band are worth more than a thousand speeches from so-called Race orators and up-lifters."

In Chicago, Europe added a singing group to his show, a quartet called "The Harmony Kings." They played as far west as Omaha, to sold-out houses, then turned around and moved east again. In Terre Haute, Indiana, the theater they'd booked refused to waive the local segregated-seating laws, resulting in a show on April 21 in which only two black concertgoers were in attendance. They played the Academy of Music on Broad Street in Philadelphia and between shows did a small private performance at the home of some wealthy Philadelphia society benefactors, then boarded a 10:40 P.M. train for Boston. The success of the tour had Europe contemplating a world-wide tour in the fall and maybe a new Broadway musical production.

They arrived in Boston at 7:00 A.M. on May 9 and learned they would need to change the venue for their return engagement because the Opera House had booked a Jewish black-faced singer named Al Jolson. They arranged to play at Mechanics Hall on Huntington Avenue instead. That morning, Jim Europe felt ill, probably just a cold, he said—he was usually drenched in perspiration by the end of his shows and had spent too much time in cold, drafty auditorium dressing rooms and on loading docks—but he felt ill enough that he went to find a doctor, rushing in order to make the matinee performance. It was a miserable day, rainy with a strong wind blowing in off the bay.

He rejoined the band at Mechanics Hall at 2 P.M. and found his dressing room, a large room with a library table in the middle and several chairs, reminding Noble Sissle of a conference room. Europe hurriedly opened his wardrobe trunk. Sissle asked him how he felt. Europe said the physician, a Dr. Bennie Robinson, had told him his cold could turn into pneumonia if he didn't take care of himself. The doctor had even given Europe a ride to the concert hall in his car rather than let him be exposed to the weather that day. Europe said that after the Boston engagement, he was going to take a two-week vacation. Many of the men in the band hadn't even been home since they'd returned from France.

They could use the vacation time to plan the world tour, Europe told Sissle.

The matinee went well, though the crowd (with Al Jolson in attendance) wasn't as large as expected. Jim Europe and Noble Sissle had a dinner engagement before the evening show, but Europe sent Harold Browning, one of the Harmony Kings, in his place and stayed in the dressing room to tend to his health. It had been a long, strenuous ten weeks on the road. Everybody was dragging and feeling a bit blue. Mechanics Hall had hosted some great shows in its time, but it wasn't nearly as swank as the Boston Opera House.

It was still raining by the time the evening show began at 8:30 P.M. There were a lot of empty seats, probably because of the weather, but it was disappointing. The only good news was that the band manager, a man named John Fisher, had booked a performance at 10:00 A.M. the following morning on the Boston Common for Massachusetts governor Calvin Coolidge and his staff, where Lieutenant Europe would have the honor of laying a wreath at the monument for Robert Gould Shaw, who'd led the Fifty-fourth Massachusetts Voluntary Regiment of Negro soldiers during the Civil War.

Not due on stage until the second half of the show, Sissle was in the dressing room, reading newspaper stories about the stunned German reaction to the terms of the peace treaty they would soon be forced to sign at Versailles and about the labor surplus created by all the returning soldiers, as well as other non-war-related stories, when one of the musicians from the band entered in mid-performance.

"Lieutenant Sissle," the man said, "Lieutenant Europe said to find Herbert Wright and send him back on stage. It's time for him to play the duet with Steve."

Herbert Wright had, for reasons known only to him, walked off stage once again. The finale of the first half of the show was a drum duet by the "Percussion Twins." Sissle could hear the music from the stage and knew the song was next. Sissle rushed down the hall and found Herbert Wright lying on a bench in one of the dressing rooms. He'd taken his coat off. Sissle assumed he was ill. Many of the members of the band had not been feeling so well after the long tour. Sissle asked Herbert Wright if he was sick.

"No," Wright said. "I'm not sick."

"Well, what's the matter?" Sissle asked. "Why don't you go back on the stage?"

Wright didn't answer.

"You know it's time for you and Steve to do your bit," Sissle urged.

Wright rose to a sitting position but said nothing.

"I could see," Sissle recalled, "that he was in a sulky and nasty mood."

Sissle had observed Wright's behavior for the last two years and knew him to be sullen and peculiar. Usually, Sissle could make jokes, but tonight he could tell that Herbert Wright was in an unusually foul mood and wanted to pick a fight. Sissle patted the young drummer on the shoulder and asked him what was bothering him.

"You know, Lieutenant Sissle," Wright said. "I work hard. And Steve never does anything right. And he makes mistakes, and then Lt. Europe looks back in the drummer section and frowns at me."

Sissle assured Herbert Wright that Jim considered him his number one drummer and relied on him, rather than on Steve, to pull the band through the heavy numbers and restore the time whenever the band started to veer off tempo. If Jim Europe frowned toward the drum section, Sissle told Herbert, that frown was surely meant for Steve.

"Well," Herbert Wright said, "for you, Lieutenant Sissle, I will go back on stage, but you know I work hard. And Jim has no right to frown on me."

At intermission, Jim Europe summoned his Percussion Twins to the dressing room, where Sissle had resumed reading the paper. Herbert was still carrying the drum that he played hanging from a strap around his neck. Europe closed the door because visitors often entered the dressing room at intermission. He wanted to have a word with his drummers. Europe sat down at the table. He collected his thoughts for half a minute.

"Now, Herbert," he began, perhaps only because Herbert was standing closest to him, or perhaps to single him out, "you and Steve know how sick I am. The doctor says that I should be in the hospital right now. I am trying to keep going in order to finish out this engagement, so that all of you may have your money and be able to go home or take your vacations. And you two boys, above anybody else in the band, should cause me the least worry. I have at all times tried to be a father to you. And there is nothing I wouldn't do to help both of you. And I don't want either one of you to worry me any more."

According to a report in the *Boston Globe*, Europe had called out to Herbert Wright to "put more pop in the sticks." Steve, "as a rule the more frictitious of the two," according to Sissle, promised he wouldn't cause the famous bandleader any more problems. Europe turned to the other.

"How about you, Herbert?"

But Herbert Wright was snapping.

"He seemed to be harboring some thought or some feeling other than that which was apparently brought about by Jim's attitude on this one occasion," Sissle wrote, "and he was very far from being satisfied with what he had had a chance to say. It looked as though he was trying to start an argument in order to work himself up into a frenzy that he may give vent to some pent up emotion."

"Lieutenant Europe," Wright said, "you don't treat me right. I work hard for you. Look at my hands. They're all swollen where I've been drumming, trying to hold the time. And yet Steve—he makes all kinds of mistakes. And you never say anything to him. You don't treat me right."

Before Europe could reply, there was a knock at the door. The Harmony Kings, Harold Browning, Horace Berry, Exodus Drayton, and Roland Hayes, entered. Sissle whispered into Herbert Wright's ear to forget about it, not to make a scene, just to leave. Wright was upset and couldn't forget about it. Sissle, as quietly as he could, hustled Herbert Wright out of the room, behind Jim Europe, guiding him out the door, while Jim Europe spoke to the Harmony Kings.

Suddenly, Herbert Wright burst back into the room.

He took his drum off and threw it in the corner, opposite where Jim Europe was sitting. He ripped off his uniform coat and threw that in the corner as well, cursing. The quartet from Chicago stood stunned. Herbert Wright produced a knife and clutched it in his fist.

"I'll kill anybody that takes advantage of me," Wright screamed. "Jim Europe, I'll kill you!"

Sissle rose to his feet. Herbert Wright was much smaller than Jim Europe, but with the knife in his hand, Europe took no chances and raised a chair to defend himself.

"Knock it out of his hand," somebody shouted.

Jim Europe had faced down enraged men before and knew to keep his cool, just as he'd kept his cool addressing the hotel proprietor in Spartanburg. He relaxed his body, gently set the chair down, and gave his drummer an order.

"Herbert," he said. "Get out of here."

Herbert Wright launched himself toward Jim Europe, leaping over the chair, knife in hand. Europe caught him in midair and threw him into the wall, but as he fell, Wright slashed at him with a backhanded blow, the blade of the knife catching Jim Europe in the neck. The young drummer then became suddenly docile, "quiet as a child," trembling. Sissle didn't realize at first that Jim Europe had been cut and said to Wright, "What's the matter with you? Are you crazy?"

It was a small wound, but blood spurted from it. One of the Harmony Kings found a towel and pressed it to Jim Europe's neck. A policeman summoned to the scene took Herbert Wright away. Europe ordered his men back on stage to finish the show; he turned his baton over to his assistant conductor, Felix Weir, and asked that the ambulance stretcher bearers carry him out the back door so that the audience wouldn't know what had happened.

"Sissle," he said to his friend before getting into the ambulance, "don't forget to have the band down before the State House at nine o'clock in the morning. I'm going to the hospital, and I will have my wound dressed and I will be at the Common in the morning in time to conduct the band. See that the rest of the program is gone through with. I leave everything for you to carry on."

Both Europe and Sissle had seen men survive wounds far more terrible than the one inflicted by Herbert Wright's knife. Neither of them expected this injury to be serious. After all they'd been through, it was hard to worry too much about it.

After the concert, Noble Sissle and two of the Harmony Kings went to the police station to give testimony as to what had happened. It was there that they received word that Europe had taken a turn. They jumped into a cab and rushed to City Hospital, less than a mile away.

At City Hospital, one of the oldest municipal hospitals in the country, a young orderly informed them that Lieutenant Europe was in great danger and needed a blood transfusion. It's impossible to say exactly why the doctors at City Hospital had waited until Sissle's arrival to suggest a blood transfusion, raising the suspicion that they may have waited for another colored man to show up. The technology of transfusing blood was relatively new, however, and hospitals had no way to store blood in a way that prevented clotting, requiring hospitals to use live donors. Hospitals kept lists of volunteer donors, such that if a patient needed blood, somebody would have to locate a donor with the matching blood type and bring him or her to the hospital. Doctors would also hook themselves up if donors from the list could not be located. The question of whether a doctor would give a white man's blood to a black man in need, or vice versa, might have arisen in the South, where hospitals kept separate wings for white and black patients and where the mingling of blood, through marriage or otherwise, was such an irrational cause for concern, but it was less likely to have been a factor in Boston.

Sissle waited impatiently for the orderly to return, willing to do anything to save his friend. When the orderly came back, perhaps five minutes later, there were doctors with him and, more concerning, a chaplain.

"Will it not be necessary for us to give blood?" Sissle asked.

The need had passed. Jim Europe was dead.

The band played for Governor Calvin Coolidge on Boston Common the following morning, but the wreath Coolidge had prepared, meant to be laid on the monument to Robert Gould Shaw, decorated Jim Europe's casket instead.

That night, in New York, W. C. Handy had a premonition. He awoke for an unknown reason, felt depressed, went for a walk in a misty spring rain, and rode the subways for quite some time, pondering his strange and sudden mood. Even the sound the train made seemed odd to him. It was a sound that had once seemed full of music, but he "heard only the click-click of the wheels and felt only numbness and foreboding." He had a severe case of, for lack of a better word, but perhaps there is no better word, "the blues." "When I finally emerged from the subway, it was broad day. At 135th street newsboys were excited. I stopped dead still and heard one say, 'Extra! Extra! All about the murder of Jim Europe. Extra!'"

On May 13, James Reese Europe's coffin was led through the streets of Harlem. He was the first black man to be given a public funeral in the city of New York. Thousands of people lined the streets to watch the hearse pass by. The band marched last in the funeral procession, musicians in black armbands, their instruments mute at their sides. Col. William Hayward, Maj. Hamilton Fish, and Maj. Arthur Little attended the funeral service. The French army, on short notice, sent a Lt. J. F. Gillespie of the Fifty-ninth French

Artillery to represent them. The Rev. Dr. William H. Brooks, the former chaplain for the 369th, presided at the funeral.

On May 14, 1919, James Reese Europe was buried in Arlington National Cemetery with full military honors. A memorial service was held a few weeks later in Philadelphia, again attended by Hayward and Fish, as well as by Irene Castle and Theodore Roosevelt Jr., son of the former president and a World War I veteran. A twenty-one-year-old baritone named Paul Robeson provided the music.

The *New York Times* described Europe as

a man who ranked as one of the greatest ragtime conductors, perhaps the greatest, we have had. Ragtime may be negro music, but it is American negro music, more alive than much other American music; and Europe was one of the Americans who was contributing most to its development.

The *New York Age* said,

He was not ashamed of being a Negro or being called a Negro, believing instead of worrying and arguing about what he should be called, the proper thing was to dignify the word Negro, just as he helped dignify Negro music. He was the Roosevelt of Negro musicians—a dynamic force that did things—big things. His death comes as a big loss to the musical world, but a still greater loss to the race of which he was proud to be a member.

Europe's wife, Willie Angrom, told the press, "[Herbert] Wright, I am sure, would be the last person in the world to hurt my husband if he were in his proper senses—why, Jim was the best friend Wright had."

At his arraignment, Wright claimed he'd acted in self-defense, a position not supported by the testimony of witnesses like Sissle, the Harmony Kings, or Steven Wright. Wright was held in the Charles Street jail, where physicians hired by his defense attorney examined him on two occasions and declared him "insane." Physicians hired by the state said Wright was "of such a low type of mentality that there was a question as to his entire responsibility." Herbert Wright pled guilty to manslaughter and was sentenced to ten to fifteen years.

Where had his "proper senses" gone? What unhinged him, until his moods swung from giggling fits to homicidal rages? Whence the obsessive paranoia, the sense of people taking advantage of him?

James Reese Europe's funeral was the last parade. When it was over, the mourners went home, changed out of their funeral clothes, and got on with their lives.

Epilogue

They shall go down unto Life's Borderland,
Walk unafraid within that Living Hell,
Nor heed the driving rain of shot and shell
That round them falls; but with uplifted hand
Be one with mighty hosts, an armed band
Against man's wrong to man—for such full well
They know. And from their trembling lips shall swell
A song of hope the world can understand.
All this to them shall be a glorious sign
A glimmer of that resurrected morn
When age-long faith, crowned with a grace benign,
Shall rise and from their brows cast down the thorn
Of prejudice. E'en though through blood it be,
There breaks this day their dawn of liberty.
—JOSEPH SEAMON COTTER JR.,
"SONNET TO NEGRO SOLDIERS," 1918

As a matter of historical convenience, the "Harlem Renaissance" is often generally said to have started on the day of the Great Parade, February 17, 1919. None of the accounts describing the parade, it might be noted, reported on any fliers distributed prior to that date reading, "Harlem Renaissance Starts Tomorrow—Tickets Still Available!" History seldom turns in an instant, and no one generally records the moment that the seeds of change are planted, only when they germinate or blossom. Where African American involvement in World War I is concerned, it might be argued that the "New Negro," the figure who emerged following the war, about whom much has been written, was conceived not at the Great Parade but in the "Column of Bunches," that first, sloppy, casual, and quite disorderly parade where a few dozen men gathered in front of the Lafayette Theater on a fine morning, one day in the spring of 1916, to put broomsticks to their shoulders and march for an idea. They took those first few steps together, setting off on a path in which the generations after them would follow.

The figure they left behind was the "Old Negro." The Old Negro lived in a society parallel to white America, on American soil that belonged as much to him as it ever belonged to anyone else, but apart from his cohabitants. The Old Negro believed in the possibility of change and that full citizenship in his country of birth was certainly his right, as much as it was anybody else's, but it was not a right he felt confident to demand because doing so brought so much trouble and sorrow down upon his head. The Old Negro believed in accommodation, was patient, put his faith in God, worked slowly toward a future worth living for, hated Jim Crow but stayed as far from the world of Jim Crow as possible, and pretended, when interacting with Jim Crow became unavoidable, to accommodate its awful precepts. The New Negro did not accept those precepts, didn't feel like pretending, did not agree to live in a separate, parallel society. He did not want to work slowly, was neither patient nor accommodating, and believed that God wanted the same thing he wanted—a society where African Americans lived freely and safely as equals, with dignity and self-respect.

Such ideas existed before the war, in moderation and in the extreme, just as the old ideas persisted after the war. The difference was that the war provided black Americans with a new role model, the modern colored soldier hero. The Southern humorist Irvin S. Cobb, once among the best-known, best-loved writers in America, famous enough to have served as the master of ceremonies at the very first Academy of Motion Pictures Oscar Awards ceremony, disappeared into an obscurity as deep and complete (and perhaps as deserved) as any in American letters, but before he did, he wrote one article, which may with some irony be deemed his legacy, called "Young Black Joe," that put into the American consciousness a kid named Henry Johnson, whose name flashed across the skies, then faded, but whose image stuck, as the modern colored soldier hero, who put his life on the line for his country and came home, and in the process earned for the New Negro the right to insist on fair treatment.

The name of James Reese Europe has faded almost as much as Irvin Cobb's or Henry Johnson's. It is now known only to a small population of jazz historians and musicians and late-night public radio disk jockeys, who agree that had Herbert Wright not been driven crazy by the war or whatever demons propelled him and attacked his father figure in his dressing room, "Big Jim" Europe's fame would quite likely have risen to the same level as that of Scott Joplin, Louis Armstrong, or Duke Ellington. He would be known, if not for his technical musicianship, then for his drive, ambition, and fervent belief in the possibilities of Negro music and of jazz, a belief that could only have carried him further, and higher, into film, recordings, radio, and television. At the time of his death, the newspapers across the country wrote of the passing of a famous jazz musician, but the pictures they ran were of a military officer, a lieutenant in an army uniform, standing straight and tall. Europe was, like Henry Johnson, a modern colored soldier hero, an inspiration to the New Negro.

No one feared the New Negro more than the Old White Man, the racist who had sought for so long to keep the Old Negro in his place. Soon after the war, many white Americans, threatened by the idea of black militancy or black heroes, denigrated or denied the contributions made by black soldiers. Stories of bravery were replaced by comical anecdotes about soldiers that featured all of the prewar racist stereotypes of happy/lazy/melon-lovin' Negroes dancing and singing their way across France. Southern politicians were subsequently quick to downplay the contributions of black soldiers. Sen. John Sharp Williams of Mississippi intoned, "I never expected them to do great service, and I rather pitied than blamed them when they did not. The whole thing after all was a white man's fight in which the Negro was not interested. If I had my way, I would not have had a Negro soldier in the entire army."

The Old White Man feared the New Negro because he was already fairly afraid of the Old Negro. When Alain Locke wrote in 1925's *The New Negro* of a "younger generation . . . vibrant with a new psychology," he spoke not of a new era of civil disobedience but rather of the sense of black pride that was finding its voice in art, poetry, and literature. That sense of pride struck fear in the heart of the Old White Man, who sought to suppress it, just as the MP in Brest had sought to "take it out" of any African Americans who showed signs of "feeling their oats."

The summer following the war was known as "Red Summer." It was called red for the blood that flowed from the racial violence that erupted, largely instigated by white bigots who felt threatened by black empowerment. That year, seventy-seven black men were killed by mobs, ten of them veterans. In Sylvester, Georgia, a veteran named Daniel Mack had the courage to tell a white man he'd fought in France and wasn't going to take any crap from anybody anymore; Mack was arrested, then snatched from jail and hanged. In Pine Bluff, Arkansas, when a white woman told a black veteran to get off the sidewalk, he replied that it was a free country; a mob later tied him to a tree and shot him fifty times. In Birmingham, Alabama, Sgt. Maj. Joe Green was lynched when he asked for change after paying for a streetcar ride. In Blakely, Georgia, Pvt. William Little was hanged simply because he walked around town wearing his army uniform.

Riots occurred in Longview, Texas; Knoxville, Tennessee; Omaha, Nebraska; Elaine, Arkansas; Norfolk, Virginia; and elsewhere. Anti-black riots occurred in Washington, D.C., where on July 19 and 20, white servicemen went into black neighborhoods and started beating up black citizens at random. This time, however, the black men of Washington fought back, armed themselves, and protected their neighborhoods. A black woman wrote to the journal *Current Opinion*,

> The Washington riots gave me a thrill that comes once in a lifetime. I was alone when I read between the lines of the morning paper that at last our men had stood like men, struck back, were no longer dumb, driven cattle. When I could no longer read for my streaming tears, I stood up, alone in my room, held both hands high over my head and exclaimed, "Oh, I thank God! Thank God. . . . The pent-up humiliation, grief and horror of a lifetime—half a century—was being stripped from me."

The rioting escalated and spread. In Chicago on July 27, white bathers at a Lake Michigan beach threw stones across an invisible color line and hit a black boy swimming on his side of the line, causing him to lose consciousness and drown. Local blacks demanded a policeman arrest the white stone throwers. He arrested a black man instead. After the six days of violence that followed, 15 whites were dead, 193 were injured, and 75 had been arrested. On the other side of the racial divide, 23 blacks were dead, 365 were wounded, and 154 had been arrested.

In 1921, race riots broke out again, this time in Tulsa, Oklahoma, when black World War I veterans armed themselves and marched on the county jail to prevent a white mob from lynching a black man accused of molesting a white woman on an elevator.

White rioters subsequently invaded the black neighborhood of Greenville, burning over one thousand black-owned homes. In two days of rioting, thirty-six people were killed.

Perhaps more telling is the story of what happened in Rosewood, Florida, a black community with its own school, churches, and stores, about forty miles southwest of Gainesville, in Levy County. On the morning of New Year's Day 1923, a young white woman named Fannie Taylor reported being attacked by a black stranger. For the next week, white mobs of varying sizes from surrounding white communities entered Rosewood and attacked its citizens, killing women and men suspected of being the "black stranger," even though later testimony suggested Ms. Taylor had been attacked by her white lover. At one point during the riots, a mob of vigilantes surrounded the house of a man named Aaron Carrier. During the attack on the Carrier house, two white men were killed. Ultimately, the town was burned to the ground, its occupants scattered, and no one was ever held accountable. A black newspaper, the *Chicago Defender*, published a report filed by reporter Eugene Brown, who never got any closer than Tallahassee, his news reported secondhand. The story in the paper said a World War I veteran from Chicago named Ted Cole had ridden into town, gone to the aid of the Carrier family trapped in their house, and used the skills he'd learned in the trenches in France to fight off the white mobs.

However, none of the other mainstream accounts mentioned a World War I veteran named Ted Cole. The *Chicago Defender* story was discounted as a fabrication. Eugene Brown was reporting what he'd heard from people who'd fled the scene, and there was no way to verify his story.

Was there really a Ted Cole? A modern colored soldier hero? There could have been—or someone needed to invent the legend of Ted Cole, the strong black man, not afraid, armed and willing to defend his people and his rights.

It was in regard to the racial violence following World War I that black poet Claude McKay wrote his famous lines:

If we must die let it not be like hogs
Hunted and penned in an inglorious spot,
While round us bark the mad and hungry dogs,
Making their mock at our accursed lot.
If we must die—oh, let us nobly die.

To nobly die. To stand your ground. To dig in, bear the worst of it, then fight back against a well-entrenched enemy and never give an inch . . .

It's easy to overextend the metaphor of the Great War as a way to understand the struggle for racial equality in America, the entrenched positions, the intractable battle. Yet, it's true that something ended, and something new started, when the men from Harlem and their black and white officers took up arms and sailed together to France to spend a year that changed the course of American history. The optimists were right—no one could deny them their rights, their country. The pessimists were right, too, in the sense that the powers in place were firmly in place and would not be easily defeated. What the pessimists underestimated was the fight in the men who went away and returned, as well as the pride they would inspire, without which neither battle could be won, the one in France or the one back home.

References

Alexander, Robert. *Memories of the World War, 1917–1918*. New York: Macmillan, 1931.

Allen, Frederick Lewis. *Only Yesterday: An Informal History of the 1920s*. New York: Harper and Row, 1959.

Allen, Robert L., with Pamela P. Allen. *Reluctant Reformers: Racism and Social Reform Movements in the United States*. Garden City, NY: Anchor Books, 1975.

Anderson, Jervis. *This Was Harlem: A Cultural Portrait, 1900–1950*. New York: Farrar, Straus & Giroux, 1981.

Astor, Gerald. *The Right to Fight: A History of African-Americans in the Military*. Novato, CA: Presidio Press, 1998.

Avery, Sheldon. *Up from Washington: William Pickens and the Negro Struggle for Equality*. Newark: University of Delaware Press, 1980.

Badger, Reid. *A Life in Ragtime: A Biography of James Reese Europe*. New York: Oxford University Press, 1995.

———. "The Conquests of Europe: The Remarkable Career of James Reese Europe." *Alabama Heritage* 1 (summer 1986): 34–49.

———. "James Reese Europe and the Pre-History of Jazz." *American Music* (spring 1989): 48–67.

Barbeau, Arthur E., and Henri Florette. *Unknown Soldiers: Black American Troops in World War I*. Philadelphia: Temple University Press, 1974.

Blackwell, John. "1918: They Fought Racism on Two Fronts." Capital Century. 1998. http://capitalcentury.com/1918.html.

Bourke, Joanna. "Shell Shock during World War One." BBC. March 1, 2002. www.bbc.co.uk/history/worldwars/wwone/shellshock_01.shtml.

Braim, Paul F. *The Test of Battle: The American Expeditionary Forces in the Meuse-Argonne Campaign.* 2nd ed. rev. Shippensburg, PA: White Mane Books, 1998.

Brown, Cliff. *Racial Conflict and Violence in the Labor Market: Roots in the 1919 Steel Strike.* New York: Garland Publishing, 1998.

Buckley, Gail. *American Patriots: The Story of Blacks in the Military from the Revolution to Desert Storm.* New York: Random House, 2001.

Burton, Arthur T. *Black, Buckskin and Blue.* Austin, TX: Eakin Press, 1999.

Carter, Laurence T. *Eubie Blake: Keys of Memory.* Detroit: Balamp Pub. Co., 1979.

Castle, Irene. *Castles in the Air.* New York: DaCapo Press, 1980.

———. "Jim Europe—a Reminiscence." *Opportunity* (March 1930): 91.

———. *My Husband.* New York: DaCapo Press, 1979.

Chilton, John. *A Jazz Nursery: The Story of the Jenkins' Orphanage Bands of Charleston, South Carolina.* London: Bloomsbury Bookshop, 1980.

Clarke, William F. *Over There with O'Ryan's Roughnecks.* Seattle, WA: Superior Publishing Co., 1968.

Clifford, John Gary. *The Citizen Soldiers: The Plattsburgh Training Camp Movement, 1913–1920.* Lexington: University of Kentucky Press, 1972.

Cobb, Irving. *The Glory of the Coming: What Mine Eyes Have Seen of Americans in Action in the Year of Grace and Allied Endeavor.* New York: George H. Doran Co., 1918.

Cockfield, Jamie. "Eugene Bullard, America's First Black Military Aviator, Flew for France during World War I." *Military History* 12 (February 1996): 10.

Conley, Linda. "Camp Wadsworth." *Spartanburg Herald Journal,* July 23, 2002.

Cooke, James J. *The Rainbow Division in the Great War, 1917–1919.* Westport, CT: Praeger, 1994.

Dalfiume, Richard M. *Desegregation of the U.S. Armed Forces: Fighting on Two Fronts, 1939–1953.* Columbia: University of Missouri Press, 1969.

Dalton, Robert. "They Also Fought." *Field Artillery Journal* 41 (October–November 1973): 18–23.

Diamond, Louis K. "History of Blood Banking in the United States." *JAMA* 193 (July 5, 1965): 128–32.

Dray, Philip. *At the Hands of Persons Unknown: The Lynching of Black America*. New York: Random House, 2002.

DuBois, W. E. B. "An Essay towards the History of the Black Man in the Great War." *Crisis* (June 1919): 63–87.

———. *The Oxford W. E. B. DuBois Reader*, edited by Eric J. Sundquist. New York: Oxford University Press, 1996.

Edgerton, Robert B. *Hidden Heroism: Black Soldiers in America's Wars*. Boulder, CO: Westview Press, 2001.

Ellis, Mark. *Race, War and Surveillance: African-Americans and the United States Government during World War I*. Bloomington: Indiana University Press, 2001.

Esposito, Vincent J., Brig. Gen. *(prepared for the Encyclopedia Americana). A Concise History of World War I*. New York: Frederick Praeger, 1964.

Ettinger, Albert M., and A. Churchill Ettinger. *A Doughboy with the Fighting Sixty-ninth: A Remembrance of World War I*. Shippensburg, PA: White Mane, 1992.

Fabre, Michel. *From Harlem to Paris: Black American Writers in France, 1840–1960*. Urbana: University of Illinois Press, 1993.

Fish, Hamilton. *Memoir of an American Patriot*. Epilogue by Brian Mitchell. Washington, DC: Regnery Gateway, 1991.

Fletcher, Tom. *100 Years of the Negro in Show Business: The Tom Fletcher Story*. New York: DaCapo Press, 1984.

Foley, Barbara. *Spectres of 1919: Class and Nation in the Making of the New Negro*. Urbana: University of Illinois Press, 2003.

Foner, Jack T. *Blacks and the Military in American History*. New York: Praeger, 1974.

Fussell, Paul. *The Great War and Modern Memory*. New York: Oxford University Press, 2000.

Gatski, John. "Enlisted History: Eugene J. Bullard, the First Black Combat Pilot." *Sergeants* 27 (January–February 1988): 42–43.

Gero, Anthony F., and Raymond Johnson. "369th United States Infantry, 15–16 July 1918." *Military Collector and Historian* 40 (spring 1988): 16.

Gilbert, Martin. *The First World War: A Complete History*. New York: Henry Holt, 1994.

Glenn, William W. L. "History of Blood Transfusion: A Bicentennial Look." *Surgery* 64, no. 3 (September 1968): 685–700.

Goines, Leonard, and Mikki Shepherd. "James Reese Europe and His Impact on the New York Scene." *Black Music Research Bulletin* 10 (fall 1988): 5–8.

Graf, William S. "Henry Johnson (of the 369th Colored) Was a Fighting Man (First American to Win the French Croix de Guerre)." *Soldiers* 30 (April 1975): 10–11.

Greene, Robert E. *Black Defenders of America, 1775–1973.* Chicago: Johnson Publishers, 1974.

Guttman, Jon. "Regiment's Pride (369th Infantry in WWI): Interview with Hamilton Fish." *Military History* 8 (October 1991): 34–41.

Haber, L. F. *The Poisonous Cloud: Chemical Warfare in the First World War.* New York: Oxford University Press, 1986.

Handy, W. C. *Father of the Blues,* edited by Arna Bontemps. New York: Macmillan, 1941.

Hanks, Richard K. "Hamilton Fish and American Isolationism, 1920–1944." PhD Diss., University of California, Riverside, 1971.

Harris, Bill. *The Hellfighters of Harlem: African-American Soldiers Who Fought for the Right to Fight for Their Country.* New York: Carroll and Graf, 2002.

Hartcup, Guy. *The War of Invention: Scientific Developments, 1914–18.* London: Potomac Books, 1988.

Henri, Florette, and Stillman Richard Joseph. *Bitter Victory: A History of Black Soldiers in World War I.* Garden City, NY: Doubleday, 1970.

Holway, John B. *Red Tails, Black Wings: The Men of America's Black Air Force.* Las Cruces, NM: Yucca Tree Press, 1997.

Huggins, Nathan Irvin, ed. *Voices from the Harlem Renaissance.* New York: Oxford University Press, 1995.

Jamieson, J. A., et al. *Complete History of the Colored Soldiers in the World War.* N.p.: Bennett and Churchill, 1919.

Johnson, Charles, Jr. *African-American Soldiers in the National Guard: Recruitment and Deployment during Peacetime and War.* Westport, CT: Greenwood Press, 1992.

Johnson, James Weldon. *Black Manhattan.* New York: Atheneum, 1972.

———. *The Selected Writings of James Weldon Johnson,* edited by Sondra Kathryn Wilson. 2 vols. New York: Oxford University Press, 1995.

Johnson, Raymond S. "369th U.S. Infantry Regiment (Fifteenth New York National Guard) 1918." *Military Collector and Historian* 30 (spring 1978): 31.

Katz, William L. *Eyewitness: The Negro in American History.* New York: Pitman Pub. Co., 1967.

Keene, Jennifer D. *Doughboys, the Great War, and the Remaking of America*. Baltimore: Johns Hopkins University Press, 2001.

———. "Intelligence and Morale in the Army of a Democracy: The Genesis of Military Psychology during the First World War." *Military Psychology* 6, no. 4 (1994): 235–53.

———. "Optimism at Armageddon: Voices of American Participants in the First World War." *Journal of Social History* 32 (spring 1999): 736–38.

Kennedy, David. *Over Here: The First World War and American Society*. New York: Oxford University Press, 1980.

Kenner, Charles T. *Buffalo Soldiers and Officers of the Ninth Cavalry*. Norman: University of Oklahoma Press, 1999.

Kimball, Robert, and William Bolcom. *Reminiscing with Noble Sissle and Eubie Blake*. New York: Cooper Square Press, 1973.

Lanning, Michael Lee. *The African-American Soldier*. New York: Carol Publishing Group, 1997.

Larkins, Rochelle. "James Reese Europe: A Forgotten Life." *World & I* (September 1986): 302–8.

Lawson, Anita. *Irvin S. Cobb*. Bowling Green, OH: Bowling Green State University Popular Press, 1984.

Lewis, David Levering. *W. E. B. DuBois: Biography of a Race, 1868–1919*. New York: Henry Holt, 1993.

———. *When Harlem Was in Vogue*. New York: Vintage Books, 1982.

Little, Arthur W. *From Harlem to the Rhine: The Story of New York's Colored Volunteers*. New York: Covici Friede Publishers, 1936.

Locke, Alain. "The New Negro (1925)." Introduction to *The New Negro*, edited by Alain Locke, 3–16. New York: Atheneum, 1968.

Lynk, M. V. *Negro Pictorial Review of the Great War*. N.p.: Author, 1919.

MacIntyre, W. Irwin. *The Colored Soldier*. Macon, GA: G. J. W. Burke Co., 1927.

MacLean, Nancy. *Behind the Mask of Chivalry: The Making of the Second Ku Klux Klan*. New York: Oxford University Press, 1994.

Madigan, Tim. *The Burning: Massacre, Destruction and the Tulsa Riot of 1921*. New York: St. Martin's Griffin, 2001.

Mason, Monroe, and Arthur Furr. *The American Negro Soldier with the Red Hand of France*. Boston: Cornhill Co., 1921.

May, Stephen. "World War I Veteran Horace Pippin Used Art to Purge Himself of the Horrors of the Trenches." *Military History* 14 (February 1998): 14ff.

McCormack, Jack. "'The Fighting 69th': Irish-American Troops in World War I." *Military Images* (March/April 1984): 22–28.

McKay, Claude. *Negro Metropolis*. New York: Harcourt Brace Jovanovich, 1968.

Mead, Gary. *The Doughboys: America and the First World War*. Woodstock, NY: Overlook Press, 2000.

Medical Department of the United States in the World War, The. *Medical Aspects of Gas Warfare*. Vol. 14. Washington, DC: Government Printing Office, 1926.

Mershon, Sherie, and Steven Schlossman. *Foxholes and Color Lines*. Baltimore: Johns Hopkins University Press, 1998.

Miller, Kelly. *History of the World War for Human Rights*. New York: Negro Universities Press, 1919.

Minder, Charles F. *This Man's War: The Day-by-Day Record of an American Private on the Western Front*. New York: Pevensy Press, 1931.

Moore, William. *Gas Attack!* New York: Hippocrene Books, 1987.

Nalty, Bernard C. *Strength for the Fight: A History of Black Americans in the Military*. New York: Free Press, 1998.

Niles, John J. *Singing Soldiers*. New York: Charles Scribner's Sons, 1927.

Odum, Howard W. *Wings on My Feet: Black Ulysses at the Wars*. Indianapolis: Bobbs-Merrill Co., 1929.

Osofsky, Gilbert. *Harlem: The Making of a Ghetto*. New York: Harper and Row, 1971.

Patton, Gerald W. *War and Race: The Black Officer in the American Military, 1915–1941*. Westport, CT: Greenwood Press, 1981.

Patton, John H. *History of the American Negro in the Great World War*. Chicago: G. G. Sapp, 1919.

Pearson, Charles, Jr. "History of the Troop I, 1st N.Y. Cavalry and 102d Trench Mortar Battery." *Niagara Frontier* 12 (spring 1965): 15–23.

Phillips, Laughlin, et al. *Horace Pippin, with an Essay by Romare Bearden*. Washington, DC: Phillips Collection, 1977.

Pippin, Horace. *War Memoirs, Letters and Photographs, 1920–1943*. Smithsonian Institution Archives and Manuscripts Catalog, reels 138, 4018, 4306.

Powell, Colin. *My American Journey*. New York: Random House, 1995.

Ranlett, Louis F. *Let's Go! The Story of AS No. 2448602*. Boston: Houghton Mifflin, 1927.

Raschke, Phillip E. "Harlem's Hellfighters (the All-Black 369th of WWI)." *Soldiers* 32 (August 1977): 49–52.

Renner, Craig J. "Under Arms: The Forgotten Black Soldiers of World War I." *World & I* 13 (November 1998): 206–13.

Riis, Thomas. *Just Before Jazz: Black Musical Theater in New York, 1890–1915*. Washington, DC: Smithsonian Press, 1989.

Rivers, W. H. "The Repression of War Experience." Paper presented to the Section of Psychiatry at the Royal School of Medicine on December 4, 1917. FirstWorldWar.com. February 9, 2003. www.firstworldwar.com/features/rivers1.htm.

Rodman, Selden. *Horace Pippin: A Negro Painter in America*. New York: Quadrangle Press, 1947.

Roosevelt, Theodore. *Rank and File: True Stories of the Great War*. New York, London: Charles Scribner's Sons, 1928.

Rose, Albert. *Eubie Blake*. New York: Shirmer Books, 1979.

Ross, Warner Anthony. *My Colored Battalion*. Chicago: Warner A. Ross, 1996.

Rudwick, Elliott. *Race Riot in East St. Louis, July 2, 1917*. Foreword by William Julius Wilson. Urbana: University of Illinois Press, 1982.

Samponaro, Frank N., and Paul J. Vanderwood. "War Scare on the Rio Grande: Robert Runyon's Photographs of the Border Conflict, 1913–1916." Austin: Texas State Historical Association, 1994.

Scherman, Tony. "When Europe Took Europe by Storm." *American Visions* 2 (April 1987): 29–31.

Schmidt, Paul J. "Transfusion in America in the Eighteenth and Nineteenth Centuries." *New England Journal of Medicine* 279, no. 24 (December 12, 1968): 1319–20.

Schneider, Mark Robert. *We Return Fighting: The Civil Rights Movement in the Jazz Age*. Boston: Northeastern University, 2002.

Scott, Emmett J. *The American Negro in the World War*. New York: Arno Press, 1969.

Shapiro, Herbert. *White Violence and Black Response from the Reconstruction to Montgomery*. Amherst: University of Massachusetts Press, 1988.

Sissle, Noble. *Happy in Hell*. In Schomberg Museum, New York City.

———. *Memoirs of Lt. Jim Europe* (unpublished).

Slotkin, Richard. *Lost Battalions*. New York: Henry Holt, 2005.

Smith, Jessie Carney. "Horace Pippin." In *Notable Black American Men*, edited by Jessie Carney Smith, 941–42. Detroit, MI: Gale Research, 1998.

Smith, Mary H. "The Incredible Life of Monsieur Bullard." *Ebony* 23 (December 1967): 120.

Southern, Eileen. *Music of Black Americans.* New York: W. W. Norton, 1971.

Spiers, Edward M. *Chemical Warfare.* Urbana: University of Illinois Press, 1986.

Steele, Dennis. "Hellfighters from Harlem." *Soldiers* 43 (February 1988): 6–9.

Stein, Judith. *I Tell My Heart: The Art of Horace Pippin.* New York: Pennsylvania Academy of Fine Arts, 1993.

Stovall, Tyler. *Paris Noir: African Americans in the City of Light.* Boston and New York: Houghton Mifflin, 1996.

Sweeney, Allison. *History of Black Soldiers in WWI.* Project Gutenberg. August 26, 2005. www.gutenberg.org/files/16598/16598-h/16598-h.htm.

Troncone, Anthony C. "Hamilton Fish Senior and the Politics of American Nationalism, 1912–1945." PhD Diss., Rutgers University, 1993.

Tucker, Mark. *Ellington: The Early Years.* Urbana: University of Illinois Press, 1991.

Tuttle, William M., Jr. *Race Riot: Chicago in the Red Summer of 1919.* Urbana: University of Illinois Press, 1996.

Wakin, Edward. *Black Fighting Men in U.S. History.* New York: Lothrop, Lee and Shepard, 1971.

Wascow, Arthur I. *From Race Riot to Sit-in: 1919 and the 1960s.* Garden City, NY: Anchor Books, 1960.

Weaver, John D. *The Brownsville Raid.* New York: W. W. Norton, 1970.

Welburn, Ron. "James Reese Europe and the Infancy of Jazz Criticism." *Black Music Research Journal* 7 (1987): 40.

Williams, Charles Halston. *Negro Soldiers in World War I: The Human Side.* New York: AMS Press, 1970.

———. *Sidelights on Colored Soldiers.* Boston: B. J. Brimmer Co., 1923.

WEBSITES

www.aaregistry.com/african_american_history/1993/Harrie_GibbsMarshall

www.albany.edu/cuyt/hjohnson.htm

www.arlingtoncemetery.net/henry-johnson.htm
www.army.mil/cmh-pg/websites.htm
www.chez.com/astozarmuseum
www.firstworldwar.com
www.firstworldwarstudies.org
www.gwpda.org/comment/hoover.htm
www.loc.gov
www.longwood.K12.ny.us/history/index.htm
www.negroleaguebaseball.com
www.redstone.army.mil/history/integrate/CHRON3.html
www.state.ny.us/governor/press/year02/jan8_3_02.htm
www.teacheroz/African_Americans.htm
www.theforgottenleagues.com
www.theromantic.com/patrioticlyrics/unknownsoldier.htm
www.westernfrontassociation.com
www.wfa-usa.org/new/lcmuseums.htm
www.worldwar1.com

Index

AEF. *See* American
   Expeditionary Force
   (AEF)
AFL. *See* American Federation
   of Labor (AFL)
African Americans
   as percent of population of
      Manhattan, 4–5
   popular characterization of,
      18–20
African American soldiers
   recognition by American
      army, 212–213
   rumors of German abuse
      of, 143–144
   as war heroes, 104–109,
      261–262
Afro-American (newspaper),
   160–161
Aix-les-Bains, 58, 60–61
Allies
   fall counteroffensive (1918),
      162–201
   German spring offensive
      (1918), 77–109
   summer combat (1918),
      111–155
Allingham, Henry, ix
"All of No Man's Land Is
   Ours" (song), 203

American Expeditionary Force
   (AEF), 138, 158
American Federation of Labor
   (AFL), 27
American First Army, 153–154
American Legion, 227–228
American Magazine, 105, 106
*American Negro in the World
   War, The* (Scott), 212–213
Anderson, E. D., 57
Antilynching law, federal,
   228
Appleton, Charles, 183
Armistice, 200–203
Armstrong, Louis, 261
Army. See Military
Associated Press, 107
Astaire, Fred, 224
Astor, Mrs. Vincent, 234
Atkins, Tommy, 215

Baden-Powell, Robert, 6
Baker, Josephine, 246
Baker, Newton D., 56–57,
   183
Baker, Norman, 91
Baker, Oscar, 128
Baldwin, James, 246
Ballou, Charles, 32–33, 183
Baltimore, Charles, 32, 45

support for Europe's band,
13
trouble in Spartanburg and,
37–41
voyage to France and, 51
welcome home parade and,
211, 214, 217, 218, 222,
223–224, 226, 227, 234–
235
William Jackson trial and,
143
Hearst, William Randolph, 221
Heirpont, 67
"Hell Fighters," 224
Hemingway, Ernest, x, 238
Hepburn, Katharine, 225
Hindenburg Line, 192
Hines, Earl "Father," 236
Hogan, Ernest, 10
Hooper (Sergeant Major), 101
Horne, Lena, 236
Houston race riots, 31–32
death sentences for black
soldiers, 32, 45, 171
Hudson, Ivan, 15
Hughes, Langston, 246
Hugo, Francis, 221
"Hunting the Hun" (song), 1,
14
Hyden, F. M., 21

"I Didn't Raise My Boy to Be
a Soldier" (song), 14
Intelligence tests, used by
army, 26, 148
"Iron Corps," 141

Jackson, Charles, 128
Jackson, Florence, 242
Jackson, James, 15
Jackson, James Henry, 15,
152, 242–243
Jackson, William, 15, 143, 152

Jamieson, John A., 15, 44, 72,
152, 208, 219
in combat, 177–178
poem, 70
Jazz, introduction to France,
54–55, 114, 159
Jenkins Orphanage, 13
"Joan of Arc" (song), 54
Joffre, Joseph, 141
Johnson, Edna, 107, 234, 239
Johnson, Frank, 15
Johnson, Henry, 16, 66, 128,
152, 160, 213, 214
Cobb account of combat,
104–109, 161
in combat, 93–104
post-combat military
career, 196
postwar AWOL, 216–217
postwar life, 233–234, 237–
239, 245, 261
welcome home parade and,
231–232
Johnson, Herman, 239
Johnson, Jack, 9, 63, 227
Johnson, James Weldon, 8
Johnson, John Lester, 227
Johnson, Juanita, 232
Johnson, William H., 246
Jolly Boys, 13
Jolson, Al, 249, 251
Jones, A. M., 144
Jones, David, x
Joplin, Scott, 12, 261
Joubaire, Alfred, 47–48

Kaestner, Erich, ix
Keenan, Willis H., 180, 199
Kerensky, Alexander, 27
Kernan, Francis Joseph, 63
Knickerbocker Press, 223
Knopf, Alfred, 223
Ku Klux Klan, 34